13-46

Getting Started

With

Microsoft Excel 7.0

For Windows 95

Getting Started With Microsoft Excel 7.0 For Windows 95

Babette Kronstadt

Pace Computer Learning Center
School of Computer Science and Information Systems
Pace University

Babette Kronstadt
David Sachs

Series Editors
Pace Computer Learning Center
School of Computer Science and Information Systems
Pace University

JOHN WILEY & SONS, INC.
New York / Chichester / Brisbane / Toronto / Singapore

Portions of this text were adapted from other texts in this series and from Pace University Computer Learning Center manuals.

ISBN 0-471-15871-2

Printed in the United States of America

10 9 8 7 6 5 4 3 2 1

Printed and bound by Banta Company

Preface

Getting Started with Microsoft Excel 7.0 for Windows 95 provides a step-by-step, hands-on introduction to *Microsoft Excel*. It is designed for students with basic PC and Windows skills who have little or no experience with *Microsoft Excel*. Basic skills are taught in short, focused activities which build to create actual applications.

Key Elements

Each lesson in *Getting Started with Microsoft Excel 7.0 for Windows 95* uses eight key elements to help students master specific worksheet concepts and skills and develop the ability to apply them in the future.

- **Learning objectives**, located at the beginning of each lesson, focus students on the skills to be learned.

- **Project orientation** allows the students to meet the objectives while creating a real-world application. Skills are developed as they are needed to complete projects, not to follow menus or other artificial organization.

- **Motivation** for each activity is supplied so that students learn *why* and *when* to perform an activity, rather than how to follow a series of instructions by rote.

- **Bulleted lists of step-by-step general procedures** introduce the tasks and provide a handy, quick reference.

- **Activities with step-by-step instructions** guide students as they apply the general procedures to solve the problems presented by the projects.

- **Screen displays** provide visual aids for learning and illustrate major steps.

- **Independent projects** provide opportunities to practice newly acquired skills with decreasing level of support.

- **Feature reference** at the end of the book allows students to have a single place to look for commands to carry out the activities learned in the book.

Stop and Go

The steps for completing each *Microsoft Excel* feature introduced in this book are covered in two ways. First they are described clearly in a bulleted list, which can also be used for reference. Then the steps are used in a hands-on Activity. Be sure to wait until the Activity to practice each feature on the computer.

Taking Advantage of Windows

Getting Started with Microsoft Excel 7.0 for Windows 95 provides a balanced approach to using a Windows application. The use of the mouse and buttons for carrying out commands is emphasized. However, familiarity with the menus is developed so that students can take advantage of the wider range of options available in menu commands. Shortcut keys are introduced when appropriate. The convenient **Feature Reference** at the end of the book summarizes menu commands and mouse and keyboard shortcuts for each of the features covered in the lessons. Students can use this both to review procedures or learn alternate ways of carrying out commands.

Flexible Use

Getting Started with Microsoft Excel 7.0 for Windows 95 is designed for use in an introductory computer course. As a "getting started" book, it does not attempt to cover all of the features of the software. However, the topics included in later lessons allow instructors to provide opportunities for individualized or extra credit assignments or use the book in short courses focused specifically on *Microsoft Excel*. While designed to be used in conjunction with lectures or other instructor supervision, basic concepts are explained so that students can use the book in independent learning settings. Students should be able to follow specific instructions with minimal instructor assistance.

Data Disk

Data disks are provided for distribution to the students. The projects use files from the data disk so that the focus of the lesson is on the new skills being learned in each project. Initial projects require that students develop applications from the beginning, and later projects build on those applications. Enough explanation is always included so that students understand the full application that they are building.

Acknowledgments

While the author has written the words, this book represents the work and effort of many individuals and organizations. Special thanks go to Henry Gaylord who updated three chapters of the book from the previous version for *Excel 5.0*. Sally Sobolewski's careful reading of the final manuscript and testing of all instructions were essential to ensuring the accuracy of the activities and the smooth flow of the text. Matthew Poli, Joe Knowlton, Nina Russakoff, and Nicole Ciafone provided invaluable assistance in carefully entering editing changes, catching errors, annotating the figures and handling page layout and text formatting.

I received enormous institutional support from Pace University and the School of Computer Science and Information Systems (CSIS). In particular, much personal support and personal leadership for the work has come from the Dean, Dr. Susan Merritt.

From another perspective, this book is also a product of the Pace Computer Learning Center which is a loose affiliation of approximately 15 faculty and staff who have provided more than 7,000 days of instruction to over 60,000 individuals in corporate settings throughout the United States and around the world during the past nine years. My shared experiences in the development and teaching of these non-credit workshops was an ideal preparation for writing this book. In addition, none of the books for Wiley would have been possible without the continuing support of Dr. David Sachs, the director of the Computer Learning Center.

My thanks also go to the many people at Wiley who provided needed support and assistance. The editor, Beth Lang Golub, assistant editor David Kear, editorial assistant Amy Hegarty, and production editor Lenore Belton have all been very responsive to our concerns and helpful in all of the Pace Computer Learning Center's writing projects.

Babette Kronstadt

June, 1996
White Plains, New York

Contents

2   ENHANCING A WORKSHEET   61

3   COPYING AND REARRANGING WORKSHEETS   87

4   MORE FORMULAS AND FUNCTIONS   117

5   ABSOLUTE AND RELATIVE CELL REFERENCES   137

6   CHARTS   157

Students and Instructors

Before Getting Started Please Note:

WINDOWS 95 INTRODUCTION

Getting Started with Microsoft Excel 7.0 for Windows 95 begins with the Windows 95 Basics lesson for students who are not familiar with *Windows 95* concepts and use of the mouse. Students who are familiar with Windows 95 can skip the Windows 95 Basics lesson and begin with the Introduction lesson. If instructors or students want a more in-depth introduction to *Windows 95* they may consider using the companion book, *Getting Started with Windows 95*, also published by Wiley.

A BRIEF OVERVIEW

Getting Started with Microsoft Excel 7.0 for Windows 95 provides a step-by-step, hands-on introduction to the newest version of Microsoft Excel for Windows 95. It is designed for students who have a working knowledge of the PC, but may or may not have previous experience with *Excel*. Each lesson presents carefully structured material, organized in short, focused activities which build to help the student absorb both conceptual and practical knowledge. Independent projects at the end of each lesson allow students to reinforce and expand their knowledge. Students will gain the most benefit from *Getting Started with Excel 7.0 for Windows 95* if they complete all Activities and Independent Projects.

STUDENT DATA DISKS

Most of the projects in this book require the use of a Data Disk. Instructors who have adopted this text are granted the right to distribute the files on the Data Disk to any student who has purchased a copy of the text. Instructors are free to post the files to standalone workstations or a network or provide individual copies of the disk to students. This book assumes that students who use their own disk know the name of the disk drive that they will be using it from. When using a network, students must know the name(s) of the drives and directories which will be used to open and save files.

STOP AND GO

The steps for completing each feature introduced in this book are covered twice. First they are described in a bulleted list, which can be used for reference. Then the same steps are used in a hands-on Activity. **Be sure to wait until the Activity to practice each feature on the computer.**

SETUP OF WINDOWS 95 AND EXCEL 7.0

One of the strengths of *Windows 95* is the ease with which the screens and even some of the program's responses to commands can be customized. This, however, can cause problems for students trying to learn how to use the program. This book assumes that *Windows 95* and *Excel 7.0* have been installed using the default settings, and that they have not been changed. Some hints are given about where to look if the computer responds differently from the way it would under standard settings. If your screen looks different from one or more in the book, ask your instructor or laboratory assistant to check that the defaults have not been changed.

Windows 95 Basics

Objectives

In this lesson you will learn to:

- Understand what *Windows 95* is
- Run *Windows 95*
- Identify the Desktop icons
- Use the mouse
- Open and close windows

- Identify the parts of a window
- Move and resize windows
- Maximize, Minimize, and Restore Windows
- Use menus and dialog boxes
- Shut down *Windows 95*

WHAT IS WINDOWS 95?

Windows 95 is the newest version of *Windows*, the program from Microsoft Corporation that lets you organize, run, and manage your programs and documents at the computer. Over the last few years, *Windows* has grown tremendously in importance and is now the standard operating system for IBM and other compatible brands of personal computers.

This lesson will introduce the basics of *Windows 95*, covering material that will prepare you for *Windows 95* application programs. If you are already familiar with *Windows 95* you may skip this lesson. For a complete introduction to *Windows 95*, refer to *Getting Started with Windows 95*, John Wiley & Sons, 1996.

BEGINNING WINDOWS VOCABULARY

Window	A four-sided frame within which a program, document, or message to the user is enclosed. Almost everything you do in the *Windows* environment will take place inside a window.
Icon	A small picture used to represent a program or document.
Desktop	The background screen of *Windows 95,* which holds all icons and windows.
Mouse	A small hand-held device used for giving commands to the computer.
Operating system	A type of software program that every computer must have. It works behind the scenes to direct the flow of data in the computer and makes it possible for you to organize and manage your documents.

Table Basics - 1

Windows 95 features will be covered in two ways—in **bulleted lists** and in **numbered activities**. **Read** the bulleted instructions carefully. Then, **carry out** the **numbered** instructions in the Activity. Remember **not** to carry out the bulleted items on your computer. The icon in the margin will remind you to wait for the Activities before carrying out instructions.

1

RUNNING WINDOWS 95

Every computer must have an operating system, and *Windows 95* is now the operating system for your computer. To run *Windows 95*, all you need to do is turn on your computer!

Instructions for all Activities:

- Read and follow each numbered instruction.
- Read italicized text. It provides additional information you will need to know.
- Read **PROBLEM SOLVERS** only if you cannot proceed.

Activity Basics.1: Running Windows 95

1. Turn on your personal computer.

   The boot-up procedure may take longer than you expect. Make sure there is no disk in the floppy drive. Some systems display a Welcome screen before the Desktop appears.

   If you are using Windows 95 on a network, you may be asked to sign on. You must type your User ID and password. If you need help, ask your instructor or lab assistant.

2. You will see the Desktop, the opening screen of *Windows 95*. Your monitor screen should look similar to Figure BAS - 1.

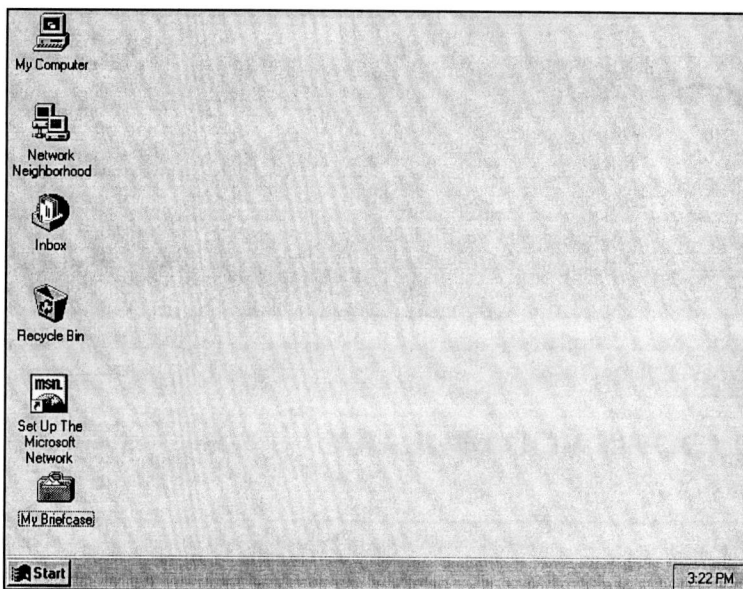

Figure BAS - 1

✓ **PROBLEM SOLVER:** *If the Windows 95 Desktop does not appear, your computer may have been set to run a different program or a different operating system when you boot up. Ask you instructor or lab assistant for help.*

3. Leave the computer on for the next activity.

WHAT IS ON THE DESKTOP?

The Desktop (Figure BAS - 1) is displayed when you run *Windows 95*. The icons on the Desktop may vary slightly, depending on how your computer was set up (see Table BAS - 2).

	My Computer	My Computer contains the contents of the drives on your computer.
	Inbox	The Inbox holds the electronic mail messages you have sent and received using Microsoft Exchange.
	Network Neighborhood	This icon appears if your computer is connected to a network. It contains all the computers and shared resources, such as printers, that are part of the network.
	Recycle Bin	The Recycle Bin is used to hold files you are planning to delete. The files are held in the Recycle Bin until you delete them or restore them.
	Microsoft Network	Microsoft Network is a new online service offered to all *Windows 95* users. It provides connectivity to the Internet and many other features.
	My Briefcase	My Briefcase helps you keep important files up-to-date when you work on them on the road and at your home or office. It is installed if you choose the Portable option or the Custom option during the *Windows 95* setup.
	Start Button	The **Start** button is your gateway to the programs, documents, settings, and all other features on your computer. It is located on the Taskbar.
	Taskbar	The Taskbar extends from the **Start** button across the bottom of the screen to the clock. It displays the name of all open windows in *Windows 95*.

Table BAS - 2

USING THE MOUSE

You need to learn to use the mouse before you begin to explore *Windows 95*. If you already use the mouse comfortably, you may skip to the next section, *Parts of a Window*.

To Use the Mouse:

Point	Touch the point of the arrow to a spot on the screen.
	Pointing highlights menu choices and positions your mouse pointer for the next action. It is important to touch the object you are pointing to. It is best to get near the center of the object rather than the edge.
Click	Lightly press and immediately release the *left* mouse button. Occasionally, the right mouse button will be specified.
	Clicking is used to highlight or select an object so that the next action taken will affect it. Clicking also opens and closes menus, chooses menu items, and closes or resizse windows.
Drag	Point to an object on-screen, press the left mouse button and hold it down while sliding the mouse. The object you are pointing to will move on-screen along with the mouse arrow.
	Dragging performs different tasks such as moving objects or text, resizing windows, and highlighting text in documents.
Double-click	Click and release the mouse button twice in rapid succession. Click quickly and lightly. Do not move the mouse as you click.
	Double-clicking is used to open windows and run programs.

Table BAS - 3

To Hold and Move the Mouse:

- Put the palm of your hand on the mouse. Your fingers should rest lightly on the mouse buttons.

- Slide the mouse around the mouse pad or flat surface next to your computer. The mouse must be guided by the palm of your hand, *not* by your fingers.

Activity Basics.2: Using the Mouse

In this activity you will practice using the mouse.

1. Turn on your computer, if it is not already on.

2. At the Desktop, place the palm of your right hand on the mouse and move it slowly on the mouse pad or flat surface. Watch the movement of the mouse pointer onscreen.

    The index finger of your right hand should rest easily on the left mouse button.

    If you are left-handed, move the mouse to the left side of the computer and hold it with your left hand.

3. Point to the icon labeled **My Computer**. Do not click the mouse button.

    Remember to touch the arrow point to the icon (see Figure BAS - 2).

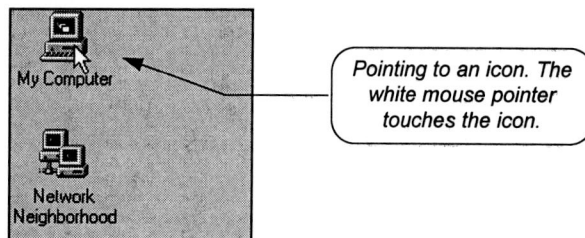

Pointing to an icon. The white mouse pointer touches the icon.

Figure BAS - 2

4. Point to the **Start** button in the lower left corner of your screen.

    ✓ **PROBLEM SOLVER:** *If the **Start** button is not visible, point to the bottom of the screen, and the button will appear.*

5. Point to the **Recycle Bin** icon.

6. Keeping your mouse pointer on the **Recycle Bin,** click the left mouse button. Keep your hand steady as you click.

    Both the icon and its label will change color. The icon is now selected. You will learn more about selected objects later.

    ✓ **PROBLEM SOLVER:** *If the mouse does not work, or works incorrectly, its settings may have been changed. Ask your instructor for assistance.*

7. Click on a blank part of the Desktop to unselect the **Recycle Bin** icon.

8. Click on the **My Computer** icon to select it.

9. Click on a blank part of the Desktop to unselect the icon.

10. Point to the **Start** button again.

11. When you see the mouse pointer on the **Start** button, click.

    *The **Start** menu will open (see Figure BAS - 3).*

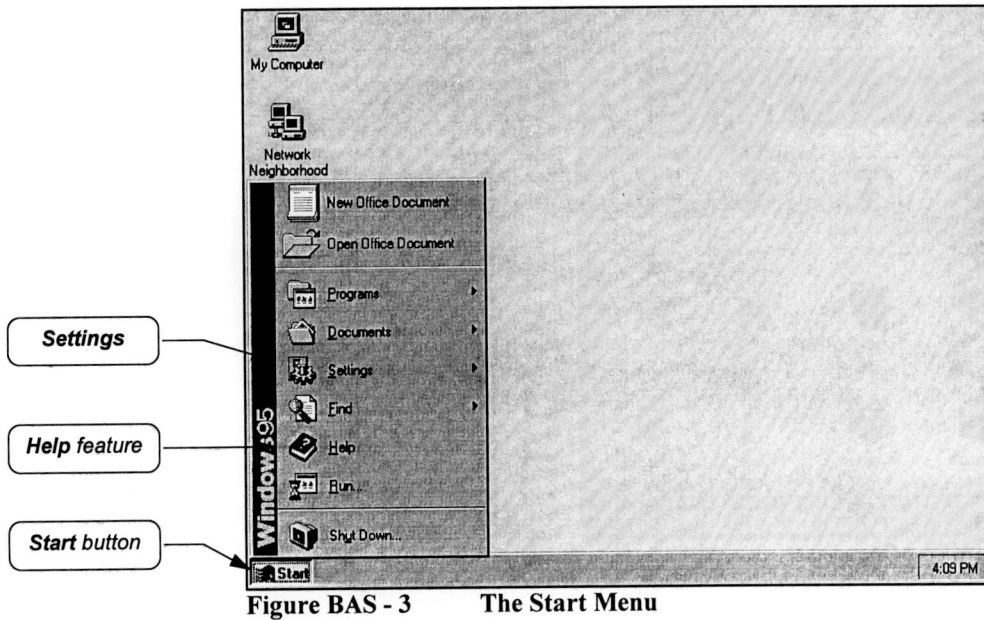

Figure BAS - 3   **The Start Menu**

12. Now point to **Settings** (Figure BAS - 3). Notice the triangle pointing to the right.

   The triangle indicates that Settings contains another group of choices. As you point to Settings, a smaller list containing three items opens (Figure BAS - 4).

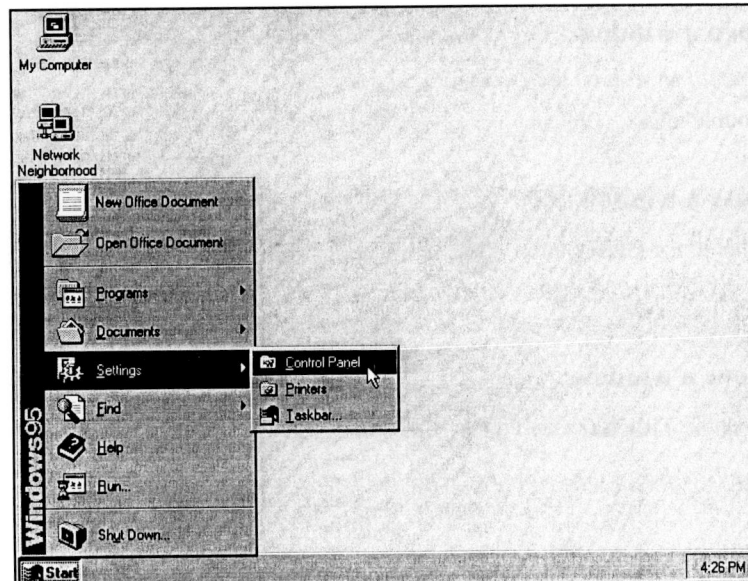

Figure BAS - 4

13. Point to the **Start** button and click again to close the **Start** menu.

14. Leave your computer on for the next activity.

PARTS OF A WINDOW

Figure BAS - 5 shows the elements of a typical *Windows 95* window.

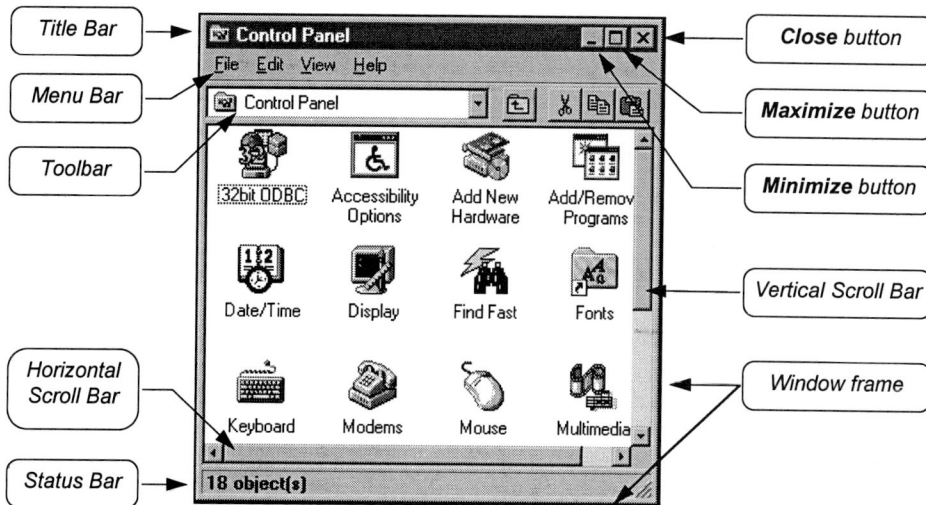

Figure BAS - 5

OPENING, CLOSING, MOVING, AND SIZING WINDOWS

To work easily in *Windows 95*, you will need to be able to be able to open and close windows, as well as move them around the Desktop and change their size.

To open a window:

*   Point to an icon on the Desktop or in a window.
*   Double-click.

To close a window:

*   Point to the **Close** button ▓ in the upper right corner of the window.
*   Click.

To move a window:

*   Drag the **Title Bar** (see Figure BAS - 5) of the window to the new location.

    The Title Bar is the colored band at the top of a window that contains its name.

To size a window:

*   Point to a side or corner of the window frame.

    When the mouse pointer touches the window frame, it is displayed as a double-headed arrow. Do not proceed until you see the double-headed arrow.

*   Drag the window frame to resize the window.

    Dragging one of the four sides will move only that side, while dragging one of the corners will change two sides of the window at once.

MAXIMIZING, MINIMIZING, AND RESTORING WINDOWS

There are two preset sizes for windows— **Maximized** and **Minimized**— that can be chosen by clicking buttons that appear on every window. Another button, **Restore**, will return a window to its previous size.

A *maximized* window fills the entire screen. This setting gives you the best view of a window's contents, but blocks all other windows.

When a window is *minimized*, its name appears on the Taskbar but its contents cannot be seen. When a window is *restored*, it returns from maximized or minimized to its previous size.

To maximize a window:

- Click on the **Maximize** button ▢ , which is the middle button at the right end of the Title Bar.

To restore a window:

- If a window has been maximized, it will not contain a **Maximize** button, but will contain a **Restore** button ⊡ instead. Clicking **Restore** will return a window to its previous size.

To minimize a window:

- Click on the **Minimize** button ▬ to the left of the **Maximize/Restore** button.

Activity Basics.3: Working with Windows on the Desktop

In the next two activities, you will open, close, resize, move, maximize, minimize and restore windows.

1. Turn on your computer, if it is not already on.

2. At the Desktop, double-click on the icon called **My Computer**.

   *The **My Computer** window will open. Figure BAS - 6 shows the **My Computer** window with large icons displayed. If your screen does not match the figure, at the Menu Bar click on the word **View** and then, on the drop-down menu, click on **Large Icons**.*

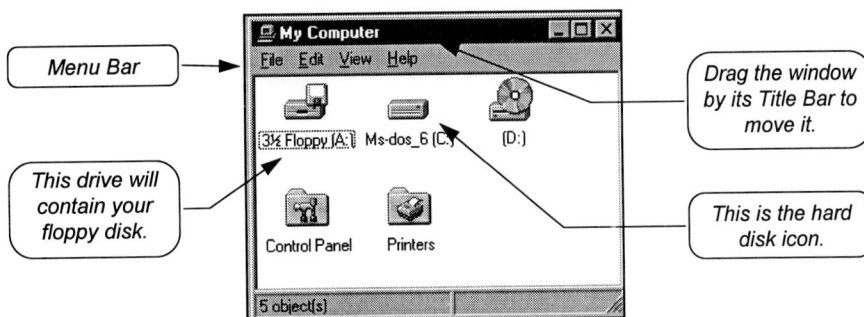

Menu Bar →

Drag the window by its Title Bar to move it.

This drive will contain your floppy disk.

This is the hard disk icon.

Figure BAS - 6

*If the **My Computer** window fills the entire screen, click the **Restore** button near the upper right corner of the window to make it smaller.*

3. Click and drag the window by its Title Bar (Figure BAS - 6) to a different place onscreen.

As you start to drag, the outline of the window will appear. Position the outline where you want the window moved and release the mouse button.

4. Touch any one of the four sides of the window with the mouse pointer.

   The mouse pointer will appear as a double-headed arrow.

5. Change the size of the window by dragging the frame.

6. Touch one of the four *corners* of the window with the mouse pointer and drag to change the window's size.

   When the double-headed arrow is positioned diagonally, you will move two sides of the window simultaneously.

7. In the **My Computer** window, double-click on the icon for the hard disk (**C**).

   *A second window will open that lists the contents of the hard drive. This window may be bigger or smaller than the **My Computer** window.*

   PROBLEM SOLVER: *If this new window covers the entire screen, follow the instructions in italics at the end of Step 2 to Restore the window.*

   PROBLEM SOLVER: *If there is no icon for the hard drive, it may have been deliberately hidden when Windows 95 was set up in your lab. Double-click on another icon instead and continue with Step 8.*

8. Move the two windows next to each other so that they do not overlap (see Figure BAS - 7). You may need to make one smaller.

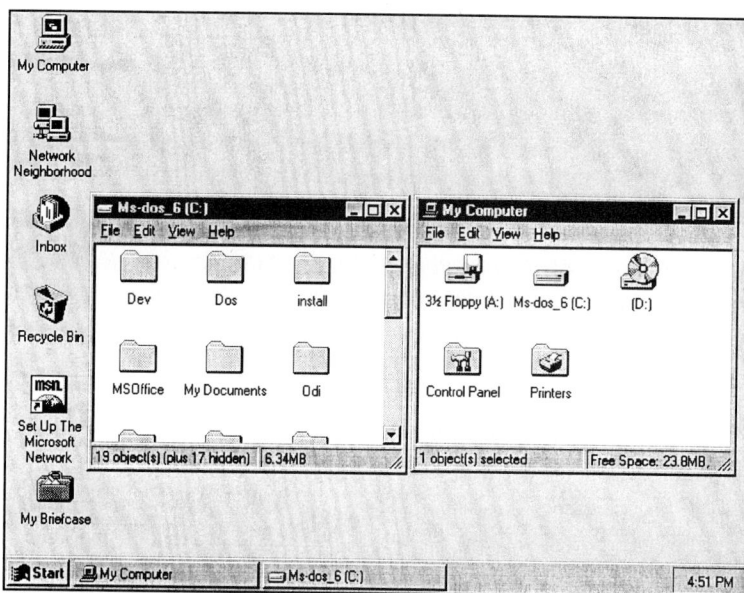

Figure BAS - 7

It will take at least several maneuvers to accomplish this. Take your time.

PROBLEM SOLVER: *If one window covers the other, move the one in front aside by dragging its Title Bar.*

9. Click the **Close** button (the **X** in the upper right corner) of the **My Computer** window.

10. Close the hard drive window.

    The Desktop should have no windows open at this point.

11. Leave the computer running for the next activity.

Activity Basics.4: Using Maximize, Minimize, and Restore

1. Turn on your computer, if it is not already on.

2. At the Desktop, double-click on the **Recycle Bin** icon (see Figure BAS - 8). Be careful not to move the mouse while you are double-clicking.

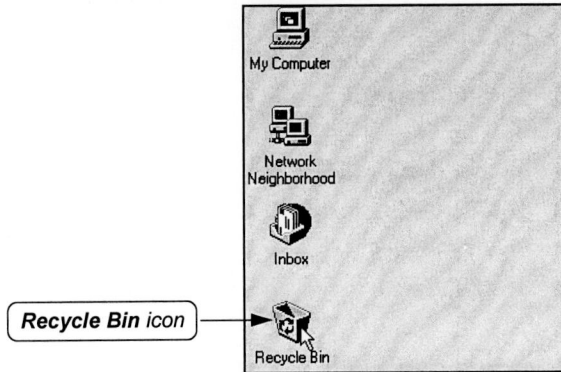

Figure BAS - 8

The Recycle Bin window opens.

3. Click the **Maximize** button on the Recycle Bin window, if it is showing. If not, continue with Step 4.

4. Click the **Restore** button. Remember that the **Maximize** and **Restore** buttons occupy the same location.

   Now the Recycle Bin window returns to its previous size.

5. Click the **Minimize** button.

   *The **Recycle Bin** window is minimized. All that is visible is its name on the Taskbar at the bottom of the screen. This lets you know that the Recycle Bin has not been closed.*

6. On the Taskbar, click on **Recycle Bin** to restore the window.

7. **Close** the Recycle Bin.

8. Double-click on the **My Computer** icon to open it.

9. In the **My Computer** window, double-click on the icon for the **Control Panel**.

   PROBLEM SOLVER: *If the **Control Panel** icon is not visible, increase the size of the **My Computer** window.*

10. **Maximize** the **Control Panel** window if it is not already maximized.

    Notice that both open windows are listed on the Taskbar.

11. Close the **Control Panel** window.

12. Close the **My Computer** window.

13. Close any other windows that are open.

    PROBLEM SOLVER: *If the **Close** button is not visible on any of these windows, drag the Title Bar to the left until you can see the **X**.*

14. Leave the computer running for the next activity.

RUNNING A PROGRAM FROM THE START MENU

The *Windows 95* Start Menu holds listings for all the programs you can run. You reach the Start Menu by clicking the **Start** button at the left edge of the Taskbar. The Start Menu displays both programs and program groups. Program groups may be identified by a triangle pointing to the right next to its name. Pointing to a program group name opens a list of all programs in that group. If you point to the wrong program group, slide your mouse pointer back to the left and the group will close. Do not click until you are pointing to the name of the program you want to run. Then, click to run the program.

To run a program:

- Click on the **Start** button;

- Point to **Programs**;

- Point to the program you want to run, or to a program group;

- When you are pointing to the name of the program you want to run, click the left mouse button.

Activity Basics.5: Running a Program

1. Point to the **Start** button and click to open the **Start** menu.

2. Point to **Programs**. Do not click.

3. Examine the list which opens. Notice that program groups are listed at the top.

4. Point to the **Accessories** program group. Examine the list of Accessory programs.

5. Slide the mouse pointer back to **Programs**. Notice how the Accessory list closes.

6. On the second panel, point to the listing for *Microsoft Word*. If this program is not listed, choose another program.

7. Click to run the program.

8. When the program has opened, click its **Close** button to close the program.

MENUS AND DIALOG BOXES

In addition to working with icons, buttons, and windows, you will be using menus and dialog boxes to give commands to your computer.

A *menu* is a list of commands. When you click on a menu name on a Menu Bar (pictured in Figure BAS - 6), a list of related commands drops down onto your screen (hence the term *drop-down menu*). You then click on the command of your choice. When a window contains a Menu Bar, you will find it directly below the Title Bar. Some menu commands have keyboard shortcuts associated with them, and these shortcuts are noted on the menus.

When you examine menu commands you will notice three possibilities. First, the menu command may appear in a light gray color. This means the command is not currently available.

Second, the command may be followed by three dots (an ellipsis). This means the computer needs more data before it can execute the command. A *dialog box,* a small window containing areas where you can provide information, will open automatically. The dialog box may contain areas in which to type, lists to select from, boxes to check, and buttons to click.

Third, if the command is neither gray nor followed by an ellipsis, it will be carried out as soon as you choose it.

To use a menu:

- Point to the menu name (e.g., **File**) on the Menu Bar and click to open (see Figure BAS - 9).

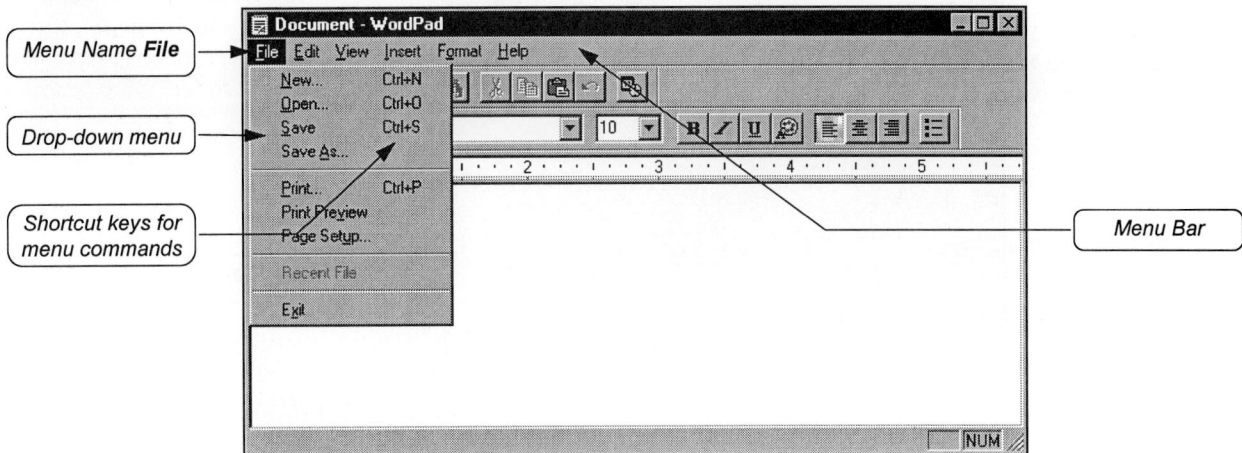

Figure BAS - 9

- To choose a command from the menu, point to the word on the menu and click.

  ALTERNATE MOUSE METHOD: *Keep the mouse button down when you click on the menu name and drag down the menu, releasing the button at the command you want.*

- To close a menu without choosing a command, click again on the menu name on the Menu Bar.

Using Menus with the Keyboard

Although you may be comfortable with the mouse by now, you should also learn the keystrokes for using menus. In situations where both hands are on the keyboard, you may prefer to open a menu without having to reach for the mouse.

To use a menu with the keyboard:

- To activate the Menu Bar, press the **ALT** key (found on either side of the **SPACEBAR**).
- Tap the underlined letter of the menu name of your choice (e.g., the **F** on the **File** menu).

  The menu will open, meaning that a list of commands will drop down onto your screen.

- To choose a command, tap the underlined letter of the command.
- To close a menu, press the **ESC** key (in the upper left corner of the keyboard). This closes the menu that is open, but keeps the Menu Bar activated in case you want to use a different menu.
- To deactivate the Menu Bar, press the **ALT** key.

To use a dialog box:

- When a dialog box opens, use the following procedures to change the settings to meet your needs (see Figure BAS - 10).

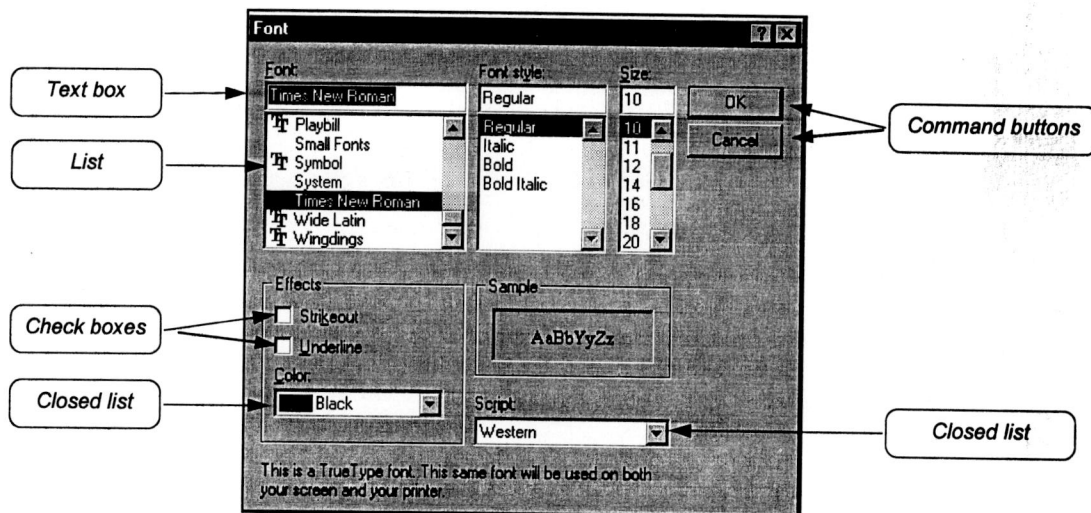

Figure BAS - 10

- o   Type in the **text boxes**.

- o   Select items from **open lists** by clicking on the item of your choice.

- o   If a list is **closed**, click on the [▼] to open the list. If less than the entire list is visible, you may click the down and up triangles next to the list to see more choices. This is called *scrolling* the list.

- o   If there is a set of **check boxes** (square), click on the appropriate one(s). You may select as many as you wish, or none at all. If a box is checked, click on it again to uncheck it.

- o   If there is a set of **buttons** (round), click on the appropriate one. Because only one may be selected at a time, clicking on one removes the previous selection (not displayed).

- o   Some dialog boxes have more than one panel. Click on the appropriate **index tab** to reach the screen of your choice (not displayed).

- •   You may use the mouse or the **TAB** key to move from one section of the box to another.

- •   When the dialog box has been filled as desired, click **OK** to carry out the instructions or **Cancel** to remove the dialog box. The **OK** and **Cancel** buttons are called *command buttons*.

    KEYBOARD ALTERNATIVE: *Instead of clicking on **OK**, press the **ENTER** key. Instead of clicking on **Cancel**, press the **ESC** key, in the upper left corner of your keyboard.*

- •   Some dialog boxes contain a **Help** icon [?], located to the left of the **Close** button. Clicking on the **Help** icon and then on the element of the dialog box you are interested in displays a description of the element and how to use it.

Activity Basics.6: Using Menus and Dialog Boxes

In this activity you will work with menus and dialog boxes.

1.   Turn on your computer, if it is not already on.

2.   At the Desktop, double-click on the **My Computer** icon. Is the Toolbar showing?

    The Toolbar, a row of buttons positioned below the Menu Bar may or may not appear.

3.   **Maximize** the window, if necessary, by clicking on its **Maximize** button.

4.   At the Menu Bar, click on the word **View**. Is there a check next to **Toolbar**?

If so, the Toolbar is displayed. If not, the Toolbar is not displayed. The display of the Toolbar is turned on and off by clicking on the Toolbar command on the View menu.

5. If there is no check, click on **Toolbar**. If there is a check, click on **View** to close the menu.

    The Toolbar will be displayed (see Figure BAS - 5). A Toolbar is a row of buttons that appears directly below the Menu Bar. Each button is associated with a command.

6. Click on the **View** menu again and see if there is a check in front of the **Status Bar** command.

7. If there is no check, click on **Status Bar**. If there is a check, click on **View** to close the menu.

    The Status Bar will be displayed at the bottom of the window, directly above the Taskbar. It displays additional information about the contents of the window.

8. Click on **View** again and examine the next four menu items: **Large Icons**, **Small Icons**, **List**, and **Details**.

    These choices refer to how the contents of the window are displayed.

9. Click on **Large Icons**.

    Notice the appearance of the window with large icons displayed.

10. Click on **View** and click on **Small Icons**.

    Notice the difference between large and small icons.

11. Click on **View** and click on **List**.

    List arranges the icons in a vertical list.

12. Click on **View** and click on **Details**.

    The Details command adds information about the icons.

13. Now that you have examined all the choices, return to **Large Icons**.

14. At the Menu Bar, click on **HELP**.

15. Click on **About Windows 95**.

16. Read the screen and click on **OK**.

17. Click on **View** again and click on **Options**.

18. Click on the **File Types** index tab.

19. To scroll the list, click on the down triangle to the right of the list of file types. Examine the list as you scroll.

20. Click on the **View** index tab and notice the two check boxes. Do they contain checks?

21. Click on each box at least twice and watch the checks appear and disappear. Leave the boxes the way you found them.

22. Click on **Cancel** to close the **Options** dialog box without carrying out any changes you made.

23. Close the **My Computer** window.

24. Click on the **Start** button. Click on the **Shut Down...** command.

    The ellipsis tells you that a dialog box will open.

25. Do **not** click on **Yes** or you will shut down your computer. Instead, click on the **Help** command button.

26. Follow the directions in the **Help** box to learn about the **Shut Down Windows** box.

27. Close the **Windows Help** box when you are finished.

28. Leave your computer running for the final activity.

CLOSING WINDOWS 95

Don't shut your computer down merely by turning it off! When you exit improperly from *Windows 95*, files that should be deleted when you exit the program are not, and, instead, stay permanently on your system. Sooner or later this will cause a problem.

To exit from Windows 95:

- Click on the **Start** button [Start].
- Click on the **Shut Down** command.
- When the **Shut Down Windows** dialog box appears, click on the **Yes** button.
- Turn off your computer when you see the message that says you may do so.

Activity Basics.7: Closing Windows 95

1. Close any windows that are open on the Desktop.
2. Click on the **Start** button.
3. Click on **Shut Down** and **Yes** in the **Shut Down Windows** dialog box (see Figure BAS - 11).

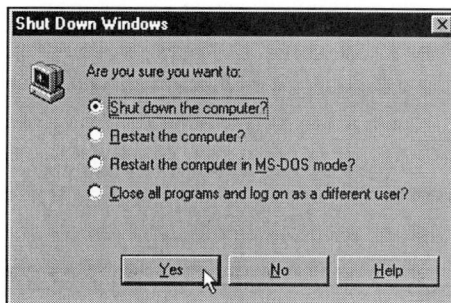

Figure BAS - 11

The fourth option will not be present unless you are working on a network.

4. Turn off your computer when you are permitted to do so.

SUMMARY

This introduction has covered the essential terms and procedures needed to open programs and perform basic tasks in *Windows 95*.

KEY TERMS

Cancel button	Icon	Operating System
Check boxes	Inbox	Point
Click	List	Program Group
Closed List	Maximize	Recycle Bin
Command buttons	Menu	Restore
Control Panel	Microsoft Network	Start button
Desktop	Minimize	Start menu
Dialog box	Mouse	Taskbar
Double-click	My Briefcase	Text box
Drag	My Computer	Toolbar
Drop-down list	Network Neighborhood	Window
Hard drive	Open list	

Introduction to *Excel* 7.0 for *Windows 95*

Objectives

In this lesson you will learn:

- What a worksheet is used for
- How to start *Excel*
- The parts of the *Excel* screen that are common to *Windows* programs
- The parts of the *Excel* screen specific to *Excel*
- Terminology used in worksheets

- How to display the Formula Bar, Status Bar, Toolbars, and ToolTips
- How to select a cell
- How to use Help
- How to exit from *Excel*
- The typographical conventions used in this book

PURPOSE OF THE INTRODUCTION

In each of the other lessons in this book you will develop a specific project. This introduction is designed to teach you the basic concepts, terminology, and techniques that you will need to use *Excel* successfully to complete the projects that follow. It will introduce the parts of the *Excel* window that are not common to all *Windows* applications and will introduce basic spreadsheet concepts. It assumes that you know all of the concepts covered in the *Windows 95* Basics section of this book.

The last section in this chapter describes the typographical conventions used in this book. In this chapter, more explicit instructions will be given. Most commands that you are to follow are given using the mouse, unless a keyboard combination is particularly easy. However, the task list in Appendix A includes shortcut keys for most tasks that you will do in this book.

WHAT IS *MICROSOFT EXCEL 7.0 FOR WINDOWS 95*?

Excel is an electronic spreadsheet or worksheet. Release 7.0 is the version of *Excel* designed to be run with the *Windows 95* operating system. Earlier releases of *Excel* will work with *Windows 95*, but release 7.0 will not work with *Windows 3.11*.

Worksheets are essential tools used by all businesses and can be used in your life as a student as well. A worksheet is an organized way to keep track of numerical data. It is used when you need to perform calculations to analyze the data. Oftentimes the data in a worksheet change frequently. One of the strengths of a worksheet is that after you create formulas to perform the calculations, they are automatically updated, or recalculated, whenever you update the data.

More importantly, the worksheet can answer questions about the data. What was the company's profit in the last quarter? Did actual revenues and expenses meet budget expectations? What was the total payroll for the week? What is the effect of different interest rates on the amount of money that can be borrowed?

Because worksheets recalculate automatically, they can also be used to make projections into the future. These projections are often called *what-if* analyses. *What* will be the effect on profits *if* the company can hold expenses for materials to 15%? *What* will be the effect on my grade *if* I get a 95 on the next exam?

15

Excel also lets you easily create *charts* that graphically represent your data. These charts let you quickly see changes and trends in the data. In addition, they, too, update whenever the data the charts are based on change.

Finally, since data in worksheets are often organized in a *list* (labeled rows containing similar sets of data), *Excel* can also be used to perform typical *database* tasks such as sorting data or filtering data to display just those sets that meet certain criteria. Database tasks will not be covered in the lessons in this book, but sorting is introduced in Independent Project 3.4.

GETTING STARTED

Since *Excel 7.0* runs under *Windows 95*, the appearance of the *Excel* window, and the methods of starting *Excel*, selecting commands from menus, completing dialog boxes, and performing basic file commands like opening, closing, and saving files are the same as those used for any other *Windows 95* application package.

STARTING *EXCEL*

Excel features will be covered in two ways—in **bulleted lists** and in **numbered activities**. **Read** the **bulleted** instructions carefully. Then, **carry out** the **numbered** instructions in the Activity. Remember **not** to carry out the bulleted items on your computer. The icon in the margin will remind you to wait for the Activities before carrying out instructions.

To start *Excel*:

- Turn on your computer. Enter any passwords or other information necessary to use your computer system.

- Click on the **Start** button on the Taskbar.

- Point to **Programs.** When the program list appears, click on **Microsoft Excel.**

Activity I.1: Starting Excel

1. Turn on your computer. Enter any passwords or other information necessary to use your computer system.

2. Click on the **Start** button.

   PROBLEM SOLVER: *If the **Start** button is not visible, click in the bottom left corner of the screen.*

3. Point to **Programs.** When the program listing appears, point to **Microsoft Excel** (Figure I - 1).

   PROBLEM SOLVER: *If Microsoft Excel does not appear on the list of programs, look for Microsoft Office. Once Microsoft Office is highlighted, another list containing Microsoft Excel should appear. Point to Microsoft Excel. If you cannot find a listing for Microsoft Office or Microsoft Excel, ask your instructor or lab assistant for the name of the program listing that opens Excel.*

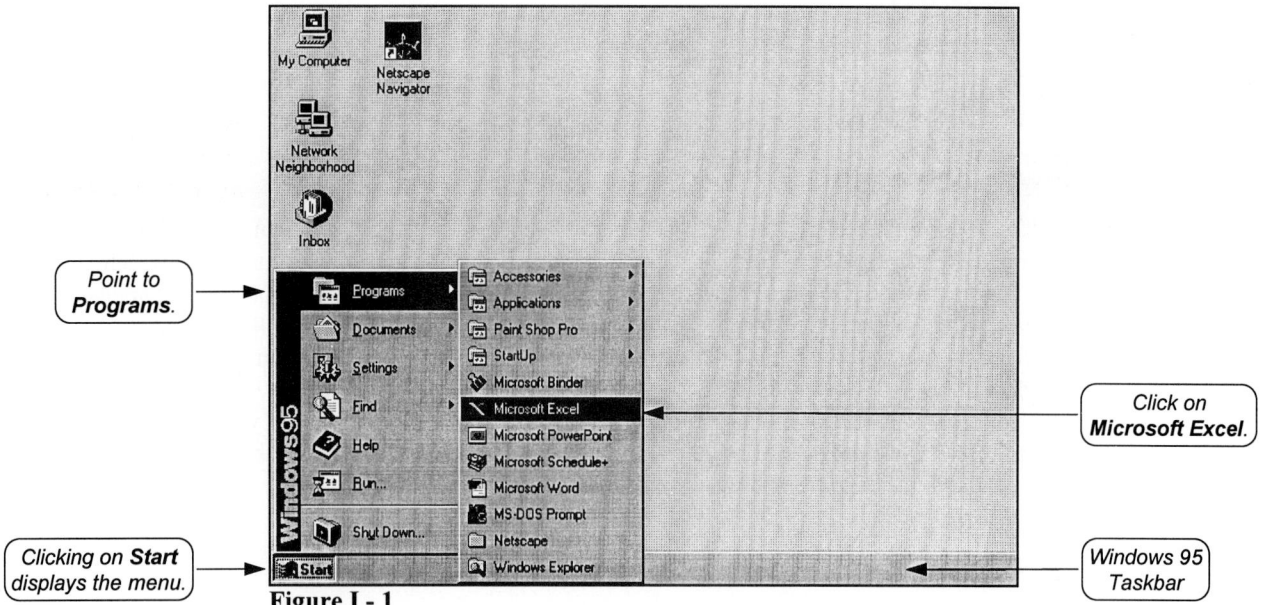

Figure I - 1

Clicking on Start displays the menu.

Point to Programs.

Click on Microsoft Excel.

Windows 95 Taskbar

4. Once **Microsoft Excel** is highlighted, click the mouse button.

   The Taskbar is used to switch between open applications or to start programs. Since we will not be using the Taskbar in this book, it has been omitted from all of the figures.

   The Microsoft Excel window should be displayed (Figure I - 2).

   Your screen probably displays the Windows 95 Taskbar below the Excel Status Bar.

   PROBLEM SOLVER: *If a Help window entitled Microsoft Excel for Windows 95, and listing new features of Excel 95 appears, close it by clicking on the Close button* ✕ *on the right side of the Title Bar.*

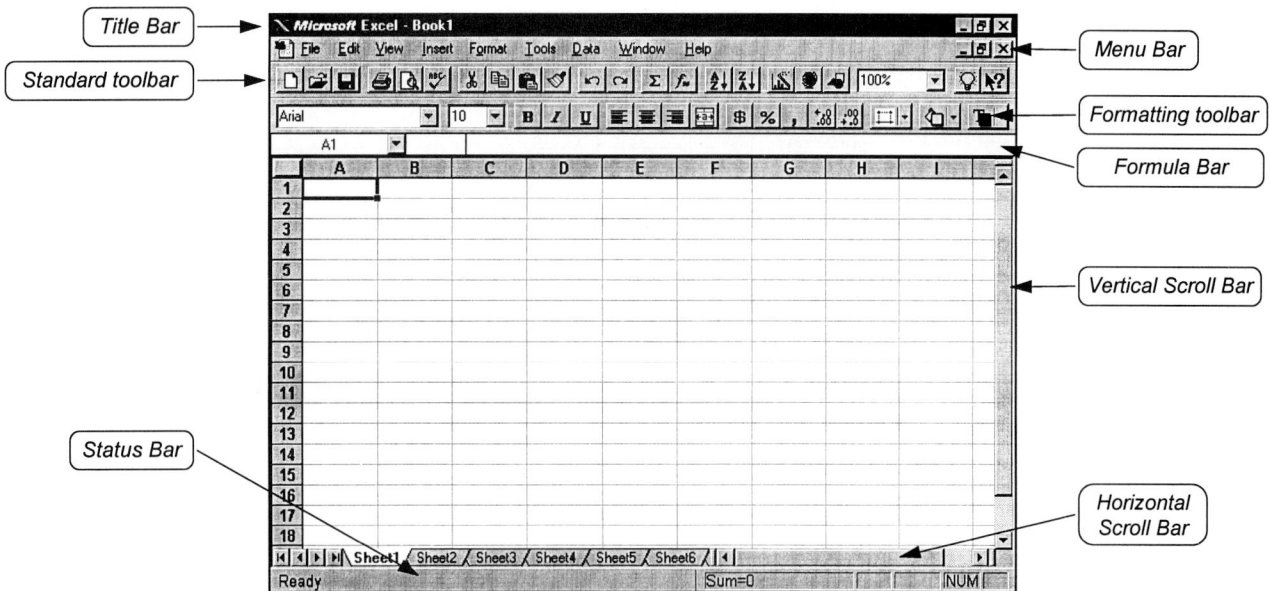

Figure I - 2

Title Bar

Standard toolbar

Status Bar

Menu Bar

Formatting toolbar

Formula Bar

Vertical Scroll Bar

Horizontal Scroll Bar

THE *EXCEL* SCREEN

Most of the *Excel* screen is made up of components that are familiar to you from other *Windows 95* applications. Other elements may be less familiar because they are specific to working with worksheets or with *Excel.*

Typical Windows Components

Figure I - 2 labels the parts of the *Excel* window that should be familiar to you from using *Windows 95* or from other *Windows 95* applications. It also includes the Formula Bar, which you will learn more about in the next section. Figure I - 2 shows the screen components that appear when *Excel* is first installed according to a standard setup. As is true with all *Windows* applications, your screen may look somewhat different than Figure I - 2 if someone has changed the default settings. In the next activity, we will review a few commands that will help make sure that your screen is set up similarly to ours. As you work through this book, if your screen differs from those in the book even after you have tried the techniques described in the next activity, check with your instructor or lab assistant.

Activity I.2: Setting Up the Excel Window

In this activity you will check that some features of the *Excel* window are set up to match those used in the instructions and figures in this book. You may refer back to this activity later in the book if you forget how to resize the windows or change the parts of the screen that are visible.

1.   Look at the right side of the Title Bar. If the second button from the right is the **Maximize** button, ▢ click on it. If it is the **Restore** button, ⯗ go on to step 2.

2.   If **Book 1** appears on a separate Title Bar (Figure I - 3), click on its **Maximize** button. If the Title Bar on the top of the screen is entitled *Microsoft Excel - Book1*, the workbook is already maximized, and you can go to step 3.

     It is generally better to work with the Excel and workbook windows maximized so that you can display the maximum work area.

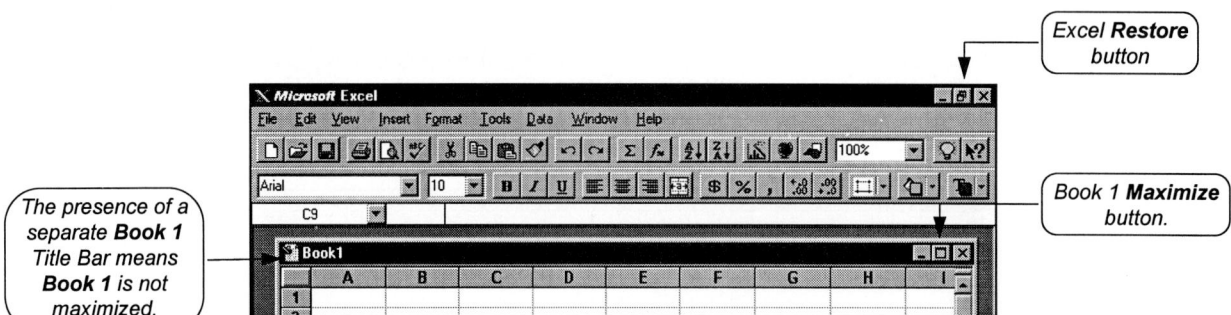

Figure I - 3

3.   Click on the word **View** on the Menu Bar. Are there checks next to both **Formula Bar** and **Status Bar**? If there are, click on **View** again to close the menu, and go on to step 4. If one of them is not preceded by a check, click on the name of the one that is not checked. If both are not checked, click on one name, click on **View** again and click on the other one.

4.   The Standard and Formatting toolbars should be displayed (see Figure I - 2). If both are displayed, go on to the next section. If one or both is not displayed, click on the **View** menu and choose **Toolbars**. If either **Standard** or **Formatting** is not preceded by a check, click on it. When a check precedes both, click on **OK**.

PROBLEM SOLVER: *If the Title Bar, Status Bar, Windows 95 Task Bar and other screen parts are not visible on the screen, and the **Full Screen** command on the **View** menu is preceded by a check, the quickest way to display the missing screen parts is to click on **Full Screen** to unselect it.*

Workbooks and Worksheets

In *Excel* each new file is called a *workbook*. When a new file is created, its default title is **Book1**, **Book2,** etc. A workbook is a container that holds one or more sheets. Each sheet can be a separate worksheet, a chart, or instructions used to automate working with *Excel*.

A *worksheet* is the main type of sheet used in *Excel* to store data, perform calculations on data, and otherwise manipulate the data. Most of the terms used to describe parts of the worksheet are described in this section.

Figure I - 4 shows a worksheet with its main components labeled. Many of these terms may not be familiar to you unless you have used another worksheet package. Look at your screen and Figure I - 4 while you read the following description of terms:

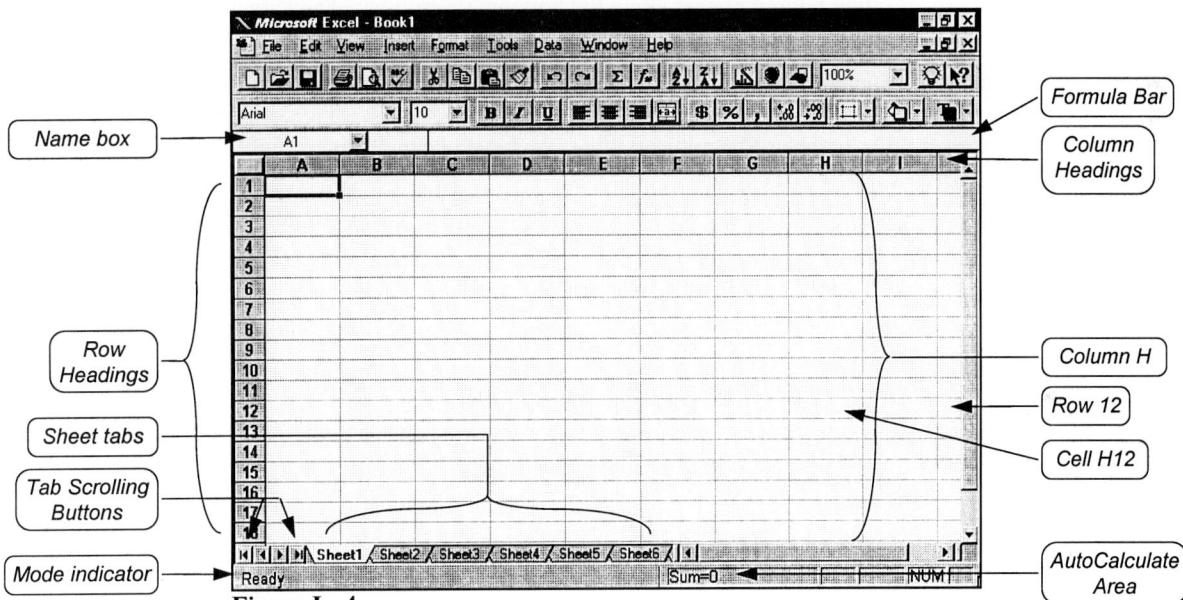

Figure I - 4

PROBLEM SOLVER: *If the Status Bar, Menu Bar, or Tool Bars are not displayed on your screen, review Activity I.1 to make sure that you displayed them. If the sheet tabs, scroll bars, or gridlines are not visible, or if the column names are numbers instead of letters, ask your lab instructor for help in redisplaying these items.*

- *Columns* run vertically down the length of the worksheet; a single worksheet contains 256 columns.

- The *column heading* is the shaded row at the top of the worksheet which contains the names for each of the columns. Columns are named by letters (**A** through **Z**, followed by **AA** through **AZ**, **BA** through **BZ**, etc., ending with **IA** through **IV**).

- *Rows* run horizontally across the width of the worksheet. A single worksheet contains 16,384 rows.

- The *row heading* is the shaded column to the left of the worksheet, which contains the names of the rows. Rows are named by numbers, beginning with **1** and ending with **16, 384**.

- *Cells* are the individual locations on the worksheet. A cell is the intersection of a column and a row, so its name is the column name followed by the row name with **no** spaces (e.g. **A1**, **B62**, **BI203**). There are more than 4,000,000 cells on each worksheet. The name of the cell may also be called the *cell address* or the *cell reference*.

- The part of the worksheet that contains the cells is sometimes called a *grid*. The *gridlines* are the horizontal and vertical lines that separate columns and rows. They may be removed from the worksheet, but their presence makes it easier to identify cells.

- The *active cell* is the cell in which you are working. It will receive any data you enter and will be acted upon by any commands you choose. It is surrounded by a dark border.

- The *Formula Bar* is a bar above the worksheet window that is used to enter or edit the contents of the worksheet. The *name box* on the left side of the Formula Bar usually tells you the location of the active cell. The rest of the Formula Bar shows you the cell contents.

- *Sheet Tabs* are used to switch among the different sheets in a workbook. A new workbook may have as many as 256 sheets, but typically only 16 sheets are available when a new workbook is opened.

- The *Tab Scrolling buttons* appear along the horizontal scroll bar. They are used to move to the first, previous, next, and last sheet in the workbook.

- The *Mode Indicator* appears on the Status Bar. It provides information on the task that you are currently performing. For example, **Ready** indicates that *Excel* is waiting for you to perform a task. **Enter** or **Edit** indicates that you have begun to enter or edit data and must finish that task before doing something else.

- The *AutoCalculate* area on the Status Bar automatically performs a calculation on the selected cell or range (i.e., sums, averages, counts or finds the minimum or maximum).

THE MOUSE POINTER

As you move the mouse, a mouse pointer moves across the screen. The shape of the pointer changes depending on the part of the screen to which it is pointing. For example, the mouse pointer is an ▯ when you are pointing to items on the Menu Bar, Toolbar, or Status Bar, but changes to a ▯ when it is pointing to cells on the worksheet grid so that you can select the cell(s).

More importantly, the shape of the mouse pointer may also change to indicate what activity will be performed if you press the mouse button. For example, if you point to certain parts of an already selected cell, the pointer will change from a ▯ to an ▯ or a **+**. When this happens clicking the mouse button will copy or move the cell contents rather than select the cell. As you follow the activity instructions in this book, look for descriptions of the shape of the mouse pointer and make sure the mouse pointer on your screen is the correct shape before you click!

THE ACTIVE CELL—SELECTING A CELL

Before you can enter data into a cell or perform a command on the contents of the cell, you must select that cell (i.e., make it the *active cell*). The active cell is indicated by the heavy border surrounding it. The name of the active cell can also be seen in the **name box** on the left side of the Formula Bar.

To select a cell that is already visible on the worksheet:

- Move your mouse pointer ▯ to the cell and click with the left mouse button, *or*

- Press the **ARROW** keys (← ↑ → ↓) until the heavy border indicating the active cell surrounds the cell of your choice.

Activity I.3: Selecting a Single Cell

1. Point to the cell at the intersection of column **B** and row **3** (cell **B3),** and click with the left mouse button.

   *The dark highlight surrounds B3, and B3 appears in the **name box** on the Formula Bar (Figure I - 5).*

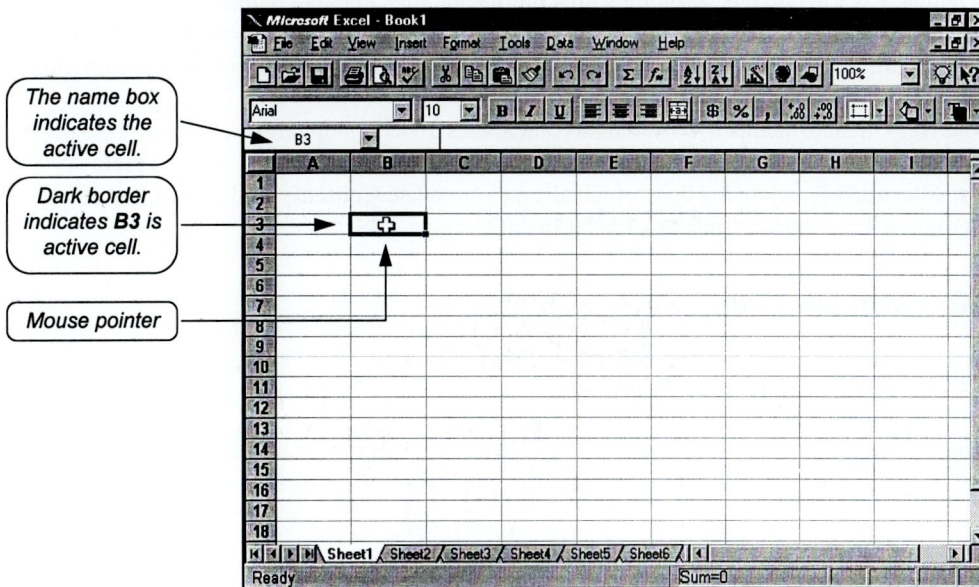

The name box indicates the active cell.

Dark border indicates B3 is active cell.

Mouse pointer

Figure I - 5

2. Press the **DOWN ARROW** key twice and the **RIGHT ARROW** key once.

   *C5 is selected as indicated by the dark border surrounding it and the C5 in the **name box**.*

USING TOOLBAR BUTTONS

Toolbar buttons can be used to perform many of the commands that the menus perform. While using the toolbars is quicker than using the menus, sometimes your choices are limited or you receive less information about the effects of your command.

ToolTips help you identify the function of each toolbar button. When you point to a toolbar button, the name of the button appears in a colored box next to the button and a description of the button appears on the Status Bar.

To use a toolbar button:

- Move the mouse pointer to the toolbar button and click the left mouse button.

To find out what a specific toolbar button does:

- Move the mouse pointer until it is pointing to the toolbar button.
- Read the name of the button in the **ToolTips** box that appears next to the mouse pointer. Read a description of the button on the Status Bar.

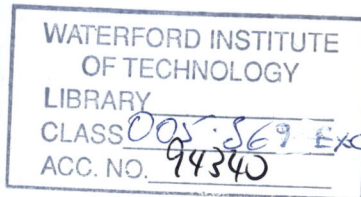

To find out more about what a specific toolbar button does:

- Click on the **Help** button ▶? and then click on the toolbar button about which you want a more detailed description. *Excel* calls this description a *ScreenTip*.

GETTING ON-LINE HELP

ToolTips and ScreenTips are two examples of the help *Excel* provides. Many of the dialog boxes also contain **Help** buttons, which *Excel* also calls **Question Mark** buttons because of their icon ?. These **Question Mark** buttons are located on the Title Bar of the dialog box next to the **Close** button. Clicking on the **Question Mark** button and then clicking on part of the dialog box displays help about that part of the dialog box. Another source of help is the **TipWizard** button 💡 on the Standard toolbar. It displays or hides the **TipWizard** toolbar, which contains tips on more efficient ways to use *Excel*.

The **Help** menu contains two commands that access general help on *Excel* topics: **Microsoft Excel Help Topics** and the **Answer Wizard**. Choosing either command displays the **Help Topics: Microsoft Excel** dialog box, which allows you to use **Contents, Index, Find,** or the **AnswerWizard** to search for information on specific topics.

Activity I.4: Using Help

In this activity you will practice using Help. If you already know how to use *Windows 95* Help, do this activity anyway to learn more about *Excel*.

1. Point to any of the toolbar buttons. Read the name of the button in the box that appears below the mouse pointer. Read the description of the button on the Status Bar.

✓ **PROBLEM SOLVER:** *If ToolTips do not appear, move the mouse so that it is pointing to a different part of the button. If ToolTips still are not displayed, that option may be turned off. To check, click on the **View** menu and then on **Toolbars**. The **Show ToolTips** box on the bottom of the **Toolbars** dialog box should be checked. If it is not, click on it to check it, and then click on **OK**.*

2. Click on the **Help** button on the Standard toolbar.

3. Point to the same toolbar button you used in step 1 and click. Read the ScreenTip that appears. Click on the **Help** button or a blank part of the screen to remove the display.

4. Click on **Help** on the Menu Bar, and then click on **Microsoft Excel Help Topics**.

    *The **Help Topics** dialog box has four tabs. We will use two of them in this activity.*

5. Click on the **Contents** tab.

    A listing of help topics, each preceded by a closed book, appears.

6. Click on **Working with Workbooks and Worksheets** and then click on the **Open** button.

    *The Working with Workbooks and Worksheets topic expands. Its icon changes from a closed book to an open book. Several of the items under it are also preceded by closed books, indicating that if you click on them and then on **Open**, more topics will be revealed. The first topic, **Workbooks and worksheets,** is preceded by an icon indicating that it is a help document (Figure I - 6).*

7. Click on **Workbooks and worksheets** and then click on the **Display** button at the bottom of the window.

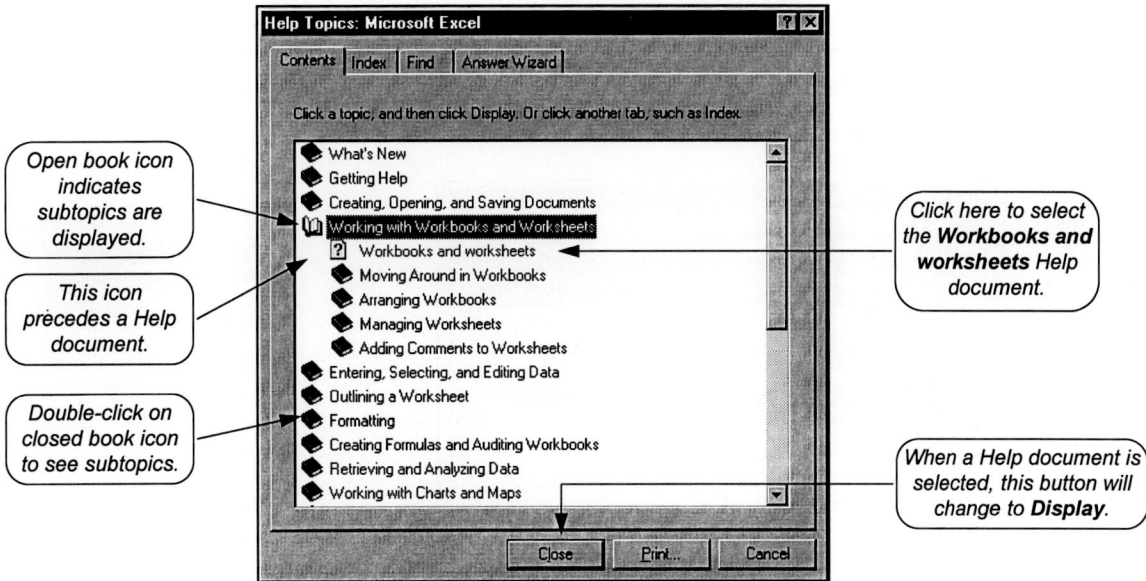

Open book icon indicates subtopics are displayed.

This icon precedes a Help document.

Double-click on closed book icon to see subtopics.

Click here to select the Workbooks and worksheets Help document.

When a Help document is selected, this button will change to Display.

Figure I - 6

8. Read the information on workbooks and worksheets. This reviews some of the concepts discussed earlier in this chapter.

    Some of the words appear in green and are underlined. You can obtain definitions of these words by clicking on them (see Figure I - 7).

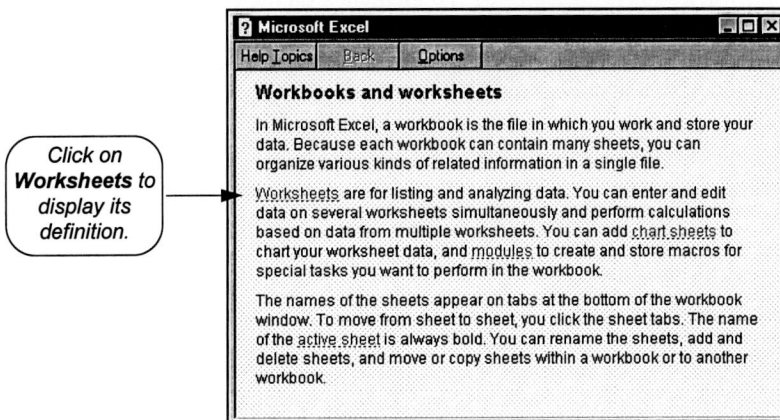

Click on Worksheets to display its definition.

Figure I - 7

9. Point to the green and underlined word **Worksheets**. When the mouse pointer changes to a hand 🖑 click and read the definition. Click again to remove the definition.

10. Use the same procedure to read the definitions of the other defined words.

11. Click on the **Help Topics** button to return to the **Contents** screen.

12. Click on the **Index** tab.

    The Index provides another way of getting help.

13. The cursor should be in the text box at the top of the screen. Type: **workbooks**

The list in the second box will scroll until the part of the index relating to workbooks is displayed (Figure I - 8). Don't worry if the help topics listed on your screen differ slightly from those in Figure I - 8. Some Excel installations have a few more Help screens than others.

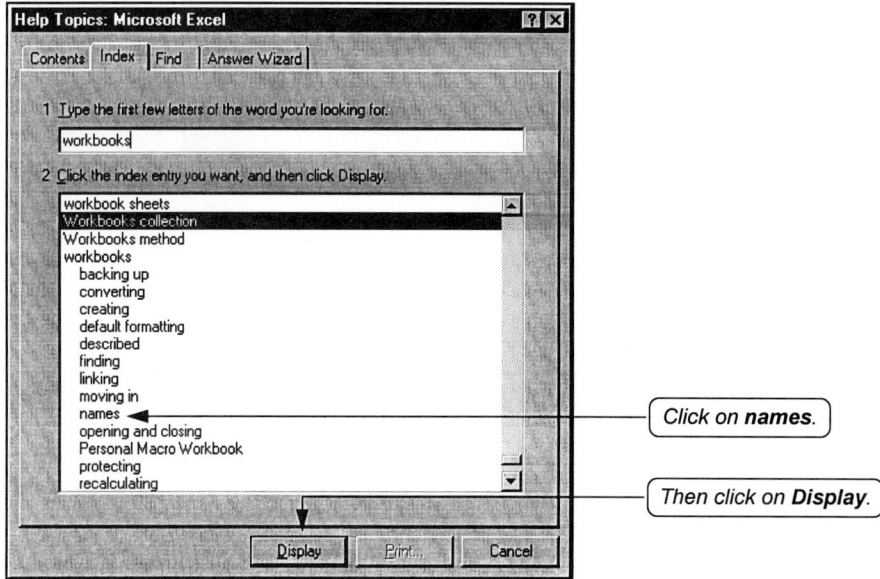

Figure I - 8

14. Click on **names** under **workbooks** (Figure I - 8) and then click on the **Display** button.

15. Read the rules for naming workbooks (documents). You will be using them in Lesson 1.

16. Click on the **Close** button to exit help.

EXITING FROM *EXCEL*

While you are working, *Excel* creates temporary files to help it with its work. Therefore, it is always important to exit correctly from a program, rather than to turn off the computer while in the middle of the program.

To exit from *Excel*:

- Click on the **Close** button ☒ on the Title Bar.

- If you have made any changes to the workbook and have not saved your work, an *Alert box* containing three choices, **Yes, No,** and **Cancel,** will appear. To save changes to the file, click on **Yes.** To exit without saving changes to the file, click on **No.** To continue working in *Excel*, choose **Cancel**.

- If you are finished using the computer, click on the **Start** button and then click on **Shut Down**. Respond **Yes** to the dialog box. Turn off the computer when told to do so.

Activity I.5: Exiting from Excel

1. Click on the **Close** button on the Title Bar.

2. If an Alert box asking **Save changes in 'Book1?'** appears, click on **No** to exit the program *without* saving the workbook.

3. If you are finished using the computer, click on the **Start** button and then click on **Shut Down**. Respond **Yes** to the dialog box. Turn off the computer when told to do so.

SUMMARY

In this introduction you have seen the parts of the *Excel* screen that are common to all *Windows* applications and those that are specific to *Excel* or to worksheet software. You have seen how to use **View** to display certain parts of the screen and how to use **Help** to find out about the toolbar buttons and to learn more about workbooks.

The Independent Project at the end of this Introduction lets you use the **Help** button to learn more about the toolbar buttons and the parts of the screen unique to worksheets.

CONVENTIONS FOLLOWED IN THIS BOOK

Table I - 1 shows the way instructions are abbreviated in this book.

Task	Words used in this book	Explanation
Using the mouse	"click on" or "click the mouse button"	Move the mouse pointer to the item to be selected (cell, toolbar button, menu name, command name, etc.) and click the **left** mouse button.
Using the **right** mouse button	"click the right mouse button"	Every time the **right** mouse button is to be used instead of the left mouse button, the instructions will specifically include the word **right**.
Selecting a cell	"select *cell name*" where *cell name* is the name of a cell (e.g., select **A21**)	Move the mouse pointer to the cell and click the left mouse button, or press the **ARROW** keys until the thick frame surrounds the desired cell.
Choosing a command from the Menu Bar	"Choose **MENU NAME/Command Name, SubMenu Command**, or **Dialog Box tab**" (For example, "Choose **FORMAT/Cells, Font**")	• Point to the **menu name** with the mouse and click the left mouse button. • In the menu that is displayed, point to the **Command Name** and click the left mouse button. • If a SubMenu is displayed, point to the **SubMenu Command** and click the left mouse button. • If a tabbed dialog box is displayed, point to the desired tab and click the left mouse button or press the **CTRL** key and keep it depressed while pressing the **TAB** key until the tab that you want is on top.
Using two keys together	Press **ALT+letter** (for example, press **ALT+I**)	• Press the **ALT** key (or the **CTRL, SHIFT,** etc., key) and, while keeping it depressed, type the letter.

Table I - 1

KEY TERMS

Active cell	Gridlines	Sheet tab
AnswerWizard	Help button	Status Bar
Cell	Index	Tab scrolling buttons
Cell address	Insertion point	TipWizard
Cell reference	Maximize button	Title Bar
Column	Menu Bar	Toolbar
Column heading	Name box	Toolbar button
Contents	Question Mark button	ToolTips
Find	Row	What-if analysis
Formula Bar	Row heading	Workbook
Grid	ScreenTips	Worksheet

INDEPENDENT PROJECT

Independent Project I.1: Learning More About Toolbar Buttons and Parts of the Excel Screen

In this project, you will use the **Help** button to learn more about Toolbar buttons and to review the parts of the worksheet and workbook discussed in this introduction.

1. Open *Excel.*

2. Click on the **Help** button.

    Your mouse pointer should now include a question mark in addition to an arrow ▧? .

3. Find the **New Workbook** button, by pointing to the toolbar buttons until ToolTips indicates that you have found it. (It should be the leftmost button on the Standard toolbar.) Click the mouse button to read a description of the button.

4. Click on the **Help** button again and then click on another one of the Standard or Formatting toolbar buttons.

5. Repeat step 4 until you have learned more about at least seven of the buttons. *Remember* you must click on the **Help** button before clicking on *each* new Toolbar button. If the mouse pointer does not contain a question mark, you will carry out the command associated with the toolbar button rather than just read about it!

6. Click on the **Help** button again. Then click on the *column heading.* (**HINT:** If you forget where the column heading is refer to Figure I - 4.)

7. Click on the **Help** button before clicking on each part of the screen to learn more about the *row headings, formula bar, name box, sheet tabs,* and *tab scrolling bars.*

8. Click on the **TipWizard** button. If the **TipWizard** toolbar was not previously displayed, it will now be displayed. If it is not displayed, click again to display it. Read the Tip of the Day or any other tips that appear. Click on the **TipWizard** button again.

Lesson
1 Creating a Simple Worksheet

Objectives

In this lesson you will learn how to:

- Distinguish between text and value entries
- Enter text and values
- Correct errors
- Change column widths
- Enter formulas

- Edit a worksheet
- Undo commands
- Save, close, and open a workbook
- Print a worksheet
- Display formulas on the worksheet

PROJECT DESCRIPTION

In this lesson you will create your first project. ECAP Consulting, Inc. is a small consulting company that hires employees on an hourly basis and bills clients based on the number of hours worked by the employee. In this project you will create a worksheet to calculate the total salary and the total amount billed by each employee for one week, and to calculate the profit and percent profit generated in the week.

To create this worksheet, you will perform most of the basic tasks involved in creating any worksheet — entering data, entering text that explains the data, performing calculations on the data, saving the worksheet, and printing it. By the end of this lesson, your worksheet will look like Figure 1 - 1. In Lesson 2, you will improve the appearance of the worksheet by changing the alignment of some of the data, formatting the numerical data with commas, dollar signs, and percent signs, and using lines and text enhancements to make different parts of the worksheet stand out.

Before you create this or any other worksheet in *Excel*, you must plan the worksheet.

PLANNING A WORKSHEET

Before you enter anything into the worksheet, you must first decide what the general objectives of the worksheet are and how you will design the worksheet to meet its objectives. The general steps in planning a worksheet and how they are applied to our first project follow:

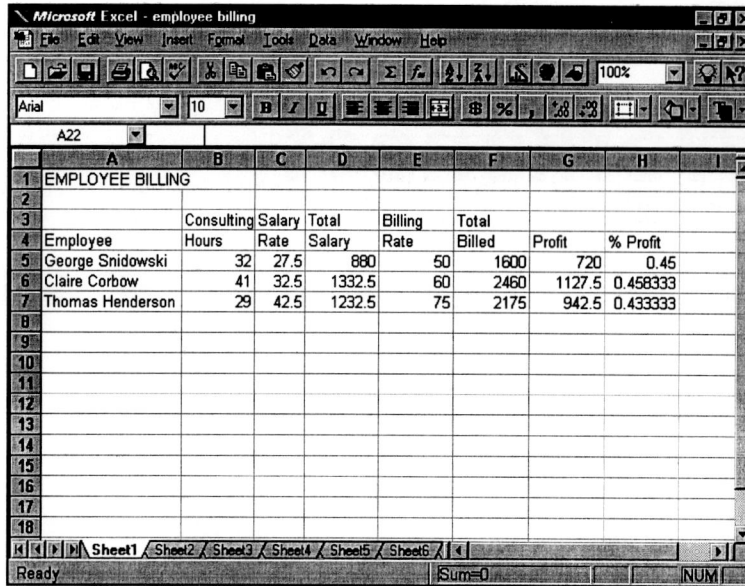

Figure 1 - 1

To plan a worksheet:

- Define the general objectives of the worksheet.

   ECAP Consulting needs to determine the total salary and the total amount billed by each consultant, and the gross profits resulting from these billings.

- Define the specific results you want the worksheet to provide.

   The worksheet must provide: (a) the salary due each consultant;(b) the amount billed by each consultant; (c) the gross profit generated by each consultant; and (d) the percent profit generated by each consultant.

- Specify and obtain the data needed to obtain the results.

   The required data are: (a) names of each of the consultants; (b) hours worked by each consultant; (c) salary rate for each consultant; and (d) billing rate for each consultant.

- Specify the calculations to be performed on the data:

RESULT	*CALCULATION*
Total salary for each consultant	*Number of consulting hours times salary rate*
Total billed by each consultant	*Number of consulting hours times billing rate*
Profit generated by each consultant	*Total billed minus total salary*
Percent profit generated by each consultant	*Profit divided by total billed*

- Organize the worksheet on paper. Determine which data will go in each column and row. Choose a title for the worksheet and for each column and row. Indicate where the calculations will be entered.

Worksheet Title							
Employee	Consulting Hours	Salary Rate	Total Salary	Billing Rate	Total Billed	Profit	% Profit
Data (Names)	Data (# hours)	Data (Salary)	Calculation	Data (Billing $)	Calculation	Calculation	Calculation
↓	↓	↓	↓	↓	↓	↓	↓
↓	↓	↓	↓	↓	↓	↓	↓

ENTERING TEXT AND VALUES

The first steps in creating a worksheet are to enter labels (or titles) that describe the contents of the worksheet, data (which may be either text or numbers), and formulas that perform calculations on the data. All of these cell entries can be classified as either *text* or *values*.

Text

A text entry can generally be thought of as any entry made up of letters, letters and other characters, or of a combination of numbers and nonnumeric characters. Therefore, all of the following entries are treated as text:

    Name   R&D   AD440X   52+32   555-1212 42nd 55 66 77

Text is used to identify the data that you will be putting into the worksheet. Text can appear anywhere on the worksheet, but it is often used across the top of the worksheet as column labels or down the left side of the worksheet as row labels. You will use text in both ways in this lesson. If you accidentally include a text entry in a calculation, it has the value of zero.

When you type text it is automatically *left aligned*. This means that the text starts at the left edge of the cell. You will learn how to change this alignment, should you choose to do so, in Lesson 2.

Values

A value is an entry that is a *number* or a *formula*. Values can be used in all mathematical calculations such as addition, subtraction, multiplication, and division. To enter a value, you typically type the value without any formatting symbols (dollar signs, percents, commas, etc.). Then you use one of *Excel*'s formatting commands to enter these symbols automatically. When entered, values are automatically *right aligned* in the cell. An entry is considered to be a number if it contains only numeric digits and any of the following characters used as described below:

.	to indicate a decimal point
,	to separate the number into thousands; if you type a comma in the wrong place, it makes the entry a label
+	to indicate that a number is positive
-	to indicate that a number is negative
( )	to indicate that a number (not a calculation) is negative
/	to indicate a fraction
$	to display a number as currency
E e	to display a number in exponential format
%	to indicate that a number is a percent

Numbers (e.g., 54, -364) are sometimes also called *constants* because they cannot change unless they are edited or retyped.

Formulas are used to calculate. We will discuss them in a few pages when you are ready to use them.

Entering Text

Now you're ready to start creating your worksheet.

> **REMEMBER:** Read the bulleted list that follows, but do not actually perform the steps until you reach *Activity 1.1*.

To enter text or values:

- Select the cell to contain the data by clicking in the cell or using the **ARROW** keys to move the highlight to the cell.

- Type the data. If you notice any errors while you are typing, press the **BACKSPACE** key until the error is removed and finish typing.

- Press the **ENTER** key or click on the **enter box** to enter the data. Alternatively, you may press an **ARROW** key or click on another cell to both enter the data and move the highlight.

Activity 1.1: Entering Text

First, you will enter text for the title of the worksheet, EMPLOYEE BILLING, and for the labels of each of the columns. Some of your column labels, such as Consulting Hours, are very long. To keep your columns as narrow as possible when you have two-word column labels, you will type the first word in one cell and the second in the cell directly below it. See Figure 1 - 6 for an illustration of what you are about to do. After you enter the column labels, you will enter the row labels, which are the names of the employees.

1. Start *Excel*. Follow the instructions in the Introduction to *Excel* lesson, if necessary.

   A blank worksheet will be displayed. Cell A1 will be enclosed in a dark border. This border indicates that A1 is the selected cell and that any data you type will be entered in that cell.

2. If the Microsoft **Excel** or **Book 1** windows are not maximized, maximize them. See Activity I.2 in the Introduction to *Excel* for instructions.

3. With the cursor still in **A1**, press the **CAPS LOCK** key and type: **EMPLOYEE BILLING**.

   As soon as you begin to type, three buttons – the cancel box ☒*, the enter box* ☑*, and the Function Wizard button* 🔧 *– appear on the screen. A blinking vertical line, called the insertion point appears in A1 to show you where the next typed character will appear. As you type, the text is visible in A1 and in the Formula Bar (Figure 1 - 2). The mode indicator on the Status Bar changes from Ready to Enter.*

4. Press **CAPS LOCK** again to turn off capitalization.

5. Press the **ENTER** key or click on the **enter box** in the Formula Bar.

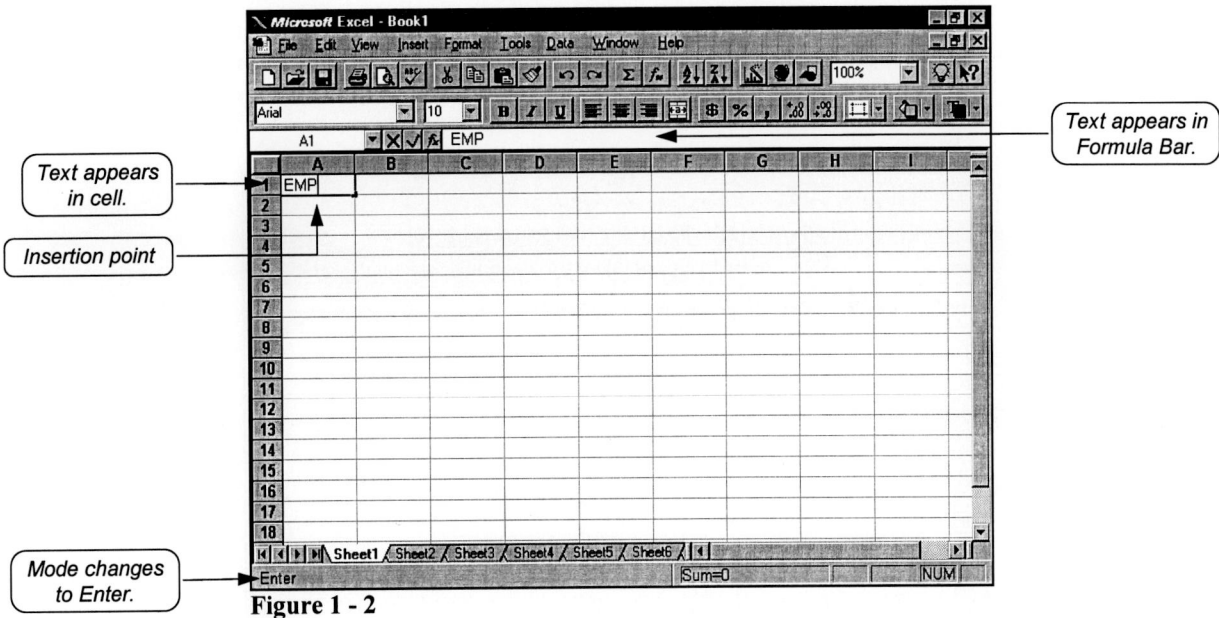

Text appears in cell.

Insertion point

Text appears in Formula Bar.

Mode changes to Enter.

Figure 1 - 2

*If the default settings have not been changed, clicking the **enter box** will leave the highlight in cell **A1,** whereas pressing the **ENTER** key will move the highlight down one cell to **A2**. The movement of the highlight after pressing the **ENTER** key is controlled by the **TOOLS/Options,Edit** dialog box. If **Move Selection after Enter** is checked, the highlight moves in the direction indicated in the **Direction** list box; otherwise it remains in the cell. **Employee Billing** is too wide to fit in cell **A1**. Since its adjacent cell, **B1,** is empty, it overflows into that cell (Figure 1 - 3).*

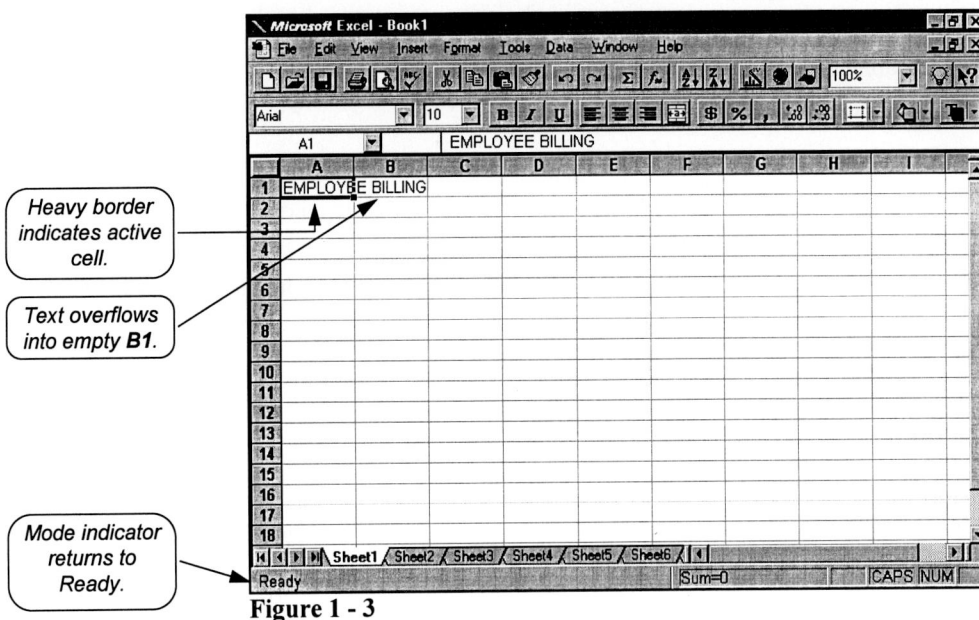

Heavy border indicates active cell.

Text overflows into empty B1.

Mode indicator returns to Ready.

Figure 1 - 3

6. Click on cell **A4** to select it.

7. Type: **Employee** and click on the **enter box** or press the **ENTER** key.

*Since Employee is text, it is left aligned in the cell. In Figure 1 - 4, the highlight remains in A4. The highlight on your screen will be in cell A5 if the **Move Selection after Enter** option is in effect, the direction selected is down, and you pressed the **ENTER** key.*

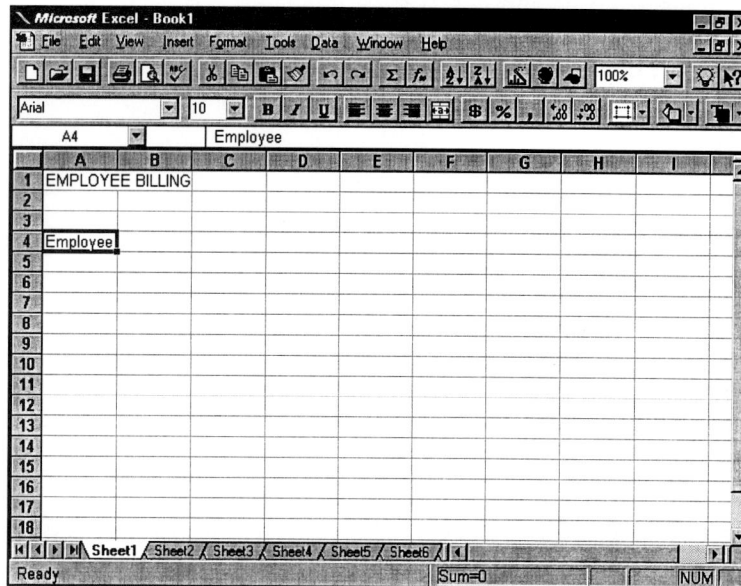

Figure 1 - 4

8. Click on **B3** to select it.

9. Type: **Consulting**

10. Press the **DOWN ARROW**.

    *The highlight will move to cell **B4**. Pressing any **ARROW** key enters the data and moves the highlight one cell in the direction of the arrow key.*

11. In **B4** type: **Hours**

12. Click on **C3**.

    ***Hours** is entered in **B4** and the highlight moves to C3. Clicking on a new cell enters the data in the original cell and selects the new cell.*

13. In cell **C3** type: **Salary** and in **C4** type **Rate** using the method of your choice to enter the data and move from cell to cell.

14. In cell **D3** enter: **Total** and in **D4** enter: **Salary**

15. In cell **E3** enter: **Billing** and in **E4** enter: **Rate**

16. In cell **F3** enter: **Total** and in **F4** enter: **Billed**

17. In **G4** enter: **Profit**

18. In **H4** enter: **% Profit**

    Your worksheet should resemble Figure 1 - 5. If you have made typing errors, don't worry. You'll learn how to correct them in the next section.

PROBLEM SOLVER: *If you have entered data into a cell that should be blank, click on that cell and press the **DELETE** key to erase the data. If a cell contains the wrong information, click on the cell containing incorrect information, retype the entire cell contents and press the **ENTER** key or click on the **enter box**.*

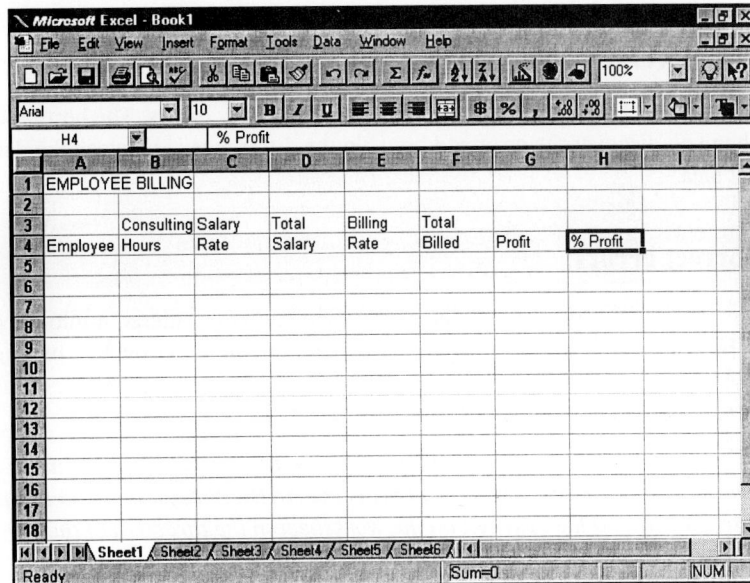

Figure 1 - 5

19. Move the highlight to cell **A5** and in cells **A5, A6, A7,** and **A8,** type the employee names listed below. After typing each one, press the **DOWN ARROW.** (Alternately, you may press **ENTER** if the active cell automatically moves down when you press **ENTER.**)

> **George Snidow**
>
> **Claire Carbow**
>
> **Thomas Hender**
>
> **Naomi Gold**

*The employee names overflow into column **B**. You will correct this problem shortly. Your worksheet should resemble Figure 1 - 6.*

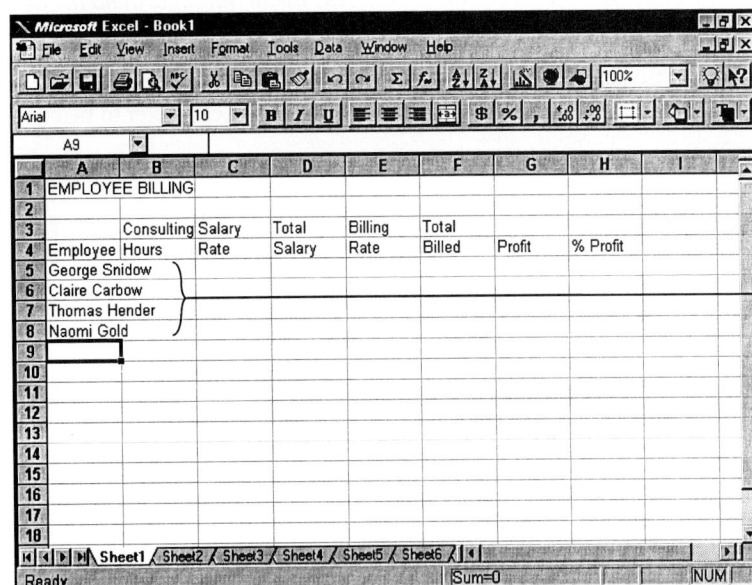

Figure 1 - 6

CORRECTING ERRORS

There are several different ways of correcting data entry errors. The best procedure to use depends on when you discover the error and how big the difference is between the data you typed and the correct data.

To correct errors:

- To correct an error that you discover *before* you have entered it into the cell (by pressing an **ARROW** key or the **ENTER** key or by clicking on the **enter box** or a new cell), press the **BACKSPACE** key until you erase the incorrect data. Type the rest of the cell contents and press the **ENTER** key or click on the **enter box**.

  *When you are entering data, you may not use the **ARROW** keys to move the cursor back to an incorrect character. When you press the **ARROW** keys, the data is entered into the current cell and the next cell on the worksheet in the direction of the arrow becomes the active cell.*

- To correct a major error that you notice *after* you have entered the data, select the cell in which you have made the typing mistake. Type the correct cell contents and then press the **ENTER** key or click on the **enter box**.

- To correct an error involving only a few characters, or to add to the cell contents, edit the cell contents using the directions for editing cells.

When only a small part of the cell contents is wrong, it is easier to *edit* the entry rather than erase or retype it. In *Excel for Windows 95*, you may edit directly in the cell or in the Formula Bar.

To edit cells:

- Double-click the cell containing the data you want to edit.

  *Excel will enter Edit mode. There are three changes to the screen: the word **Edit** replaces **Ready** in the far-left side of the Status Bar, the highlight around the cell changes from a double border to a single border, and the insertion point appears in the cell.*

- Click immediately to the left of the character to be changed or use the **RIGHT** or **LEFT** **ARROW** keys to move the cursor to the left of the character to be changed.

- To delete characters, press the **DELETE** key once for each character to be deleted. To insert characters, type them. To change characters, press the **INSERT** key. The insertion point will increase in size so that it is the width of the next character. Type the new characters.

- When editing is completed, press the **ENTER** key or click the **enter box**.

ALTERNATE METHOD: *To edit data in the Formula Bar, first click in the cell to be edited and then click in the Formula Bar immediately to the left of the characters to be changed, inserted, or deleted. Edit the data as described above.*

KEYBOARD ALTERNATIVE: *Press **F2** to begin editing. The insertion point will appear in the cell at the end of the data. Move it before the character(s) to be changed and edit the data as described above.*

AutoCorrect

Excel 7.0 has introduced the AutoCorrect feature. AutoCorrect automatically corrects entries that have the following types of errors:

- Text that begins with two capital letters;

- Days that begin with lowercase letters;

- Mistyped words that are listed in the dialog box associated with the **TOOLS/AutoCorrect** command. For example, if you type "hte", *Excel* will automatically replace it with "the" as soon as you press the **SPACE BAR** or the **ENTER** key.

Activity 1.2: Correcting Errors

There are three errors in the data you entered. George's last name is Snidowski instead of Snidow, Claire's last name is Corbow, not Carbow and Thomas's last name is Henderson.

1. Double-click anywhere in cell **A5**.

   *Your screen should resemble Figure 1 - 7, although the insertion point will appear in **A5** at the point you clicked rather than between the **G** and the **e** as shown in Figure 1 - 7.*

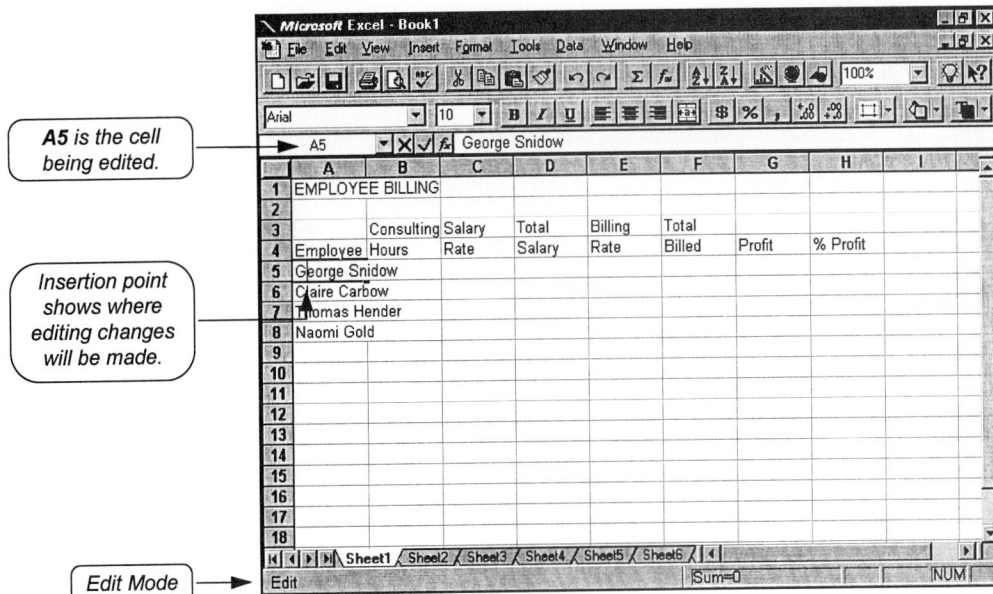

Figure 1 - 7

PROBLEM SOLVER: *Does the **name box** in the Formula Bar (left-side) indicate that the active cell is **A5**? Since George Snidow's name overflows into **B5**, if the mouse is pointing to the end of the name when you double-click, you will be editing cell **B5**, an empty cell. To solve this problem, press the **ENTER** key, move the mouse so that it is pointing to cell **A5**, and double-click.*

2. Click to the right of the **w** in **Snidow**.

   The insertion point will be positioned to the right of Snidow as in Figure 1 - 8.

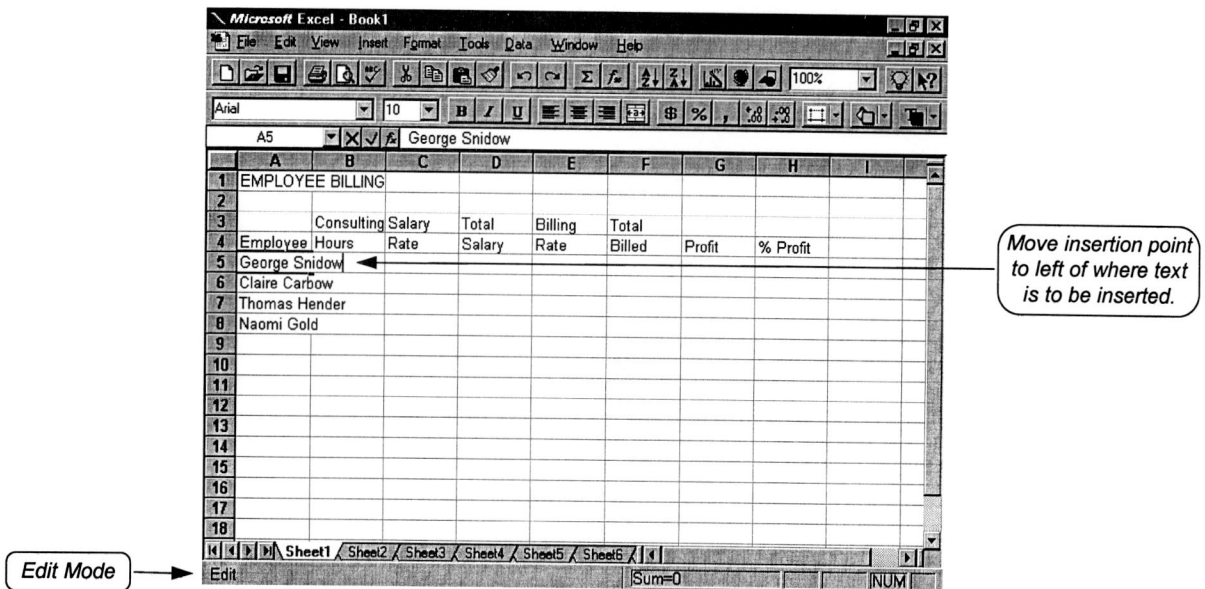

Figure 1 - 8

3. Type: **ski** and press the **ENTER** key or click on the **enter box**.

4. To change Carbow, double-click in cell **A6**.

5. Click immediately to the left of the **a** in **Carbow**.

6. Press the **INSERT** key.

*The letter **a** in Carbow in cell **A6** should be highlighted (Figure 1 - 9).*

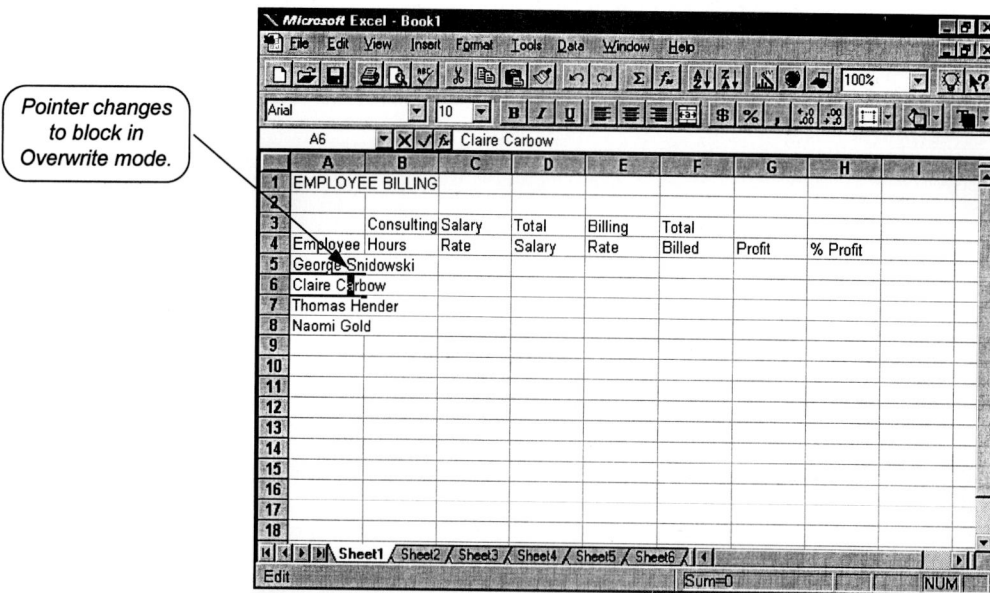

Figure 1 - 9

7. Type: **o** and press the **ENTER** key or click on the **enter box**.

8. Use the procedures in steps 1-3 to change Thomas Hender's name to **Thomas Henderson.**

   KEYBOARD ALTERNATIVE: *When you are in Edit Mode, pressing **END** moves the insertion point to the end of the cell, and pressing **HOME** moves it to the beginning of the cell.*

Clearing Cell Contents

Sometimes you want to erase the entire contents of a cell. The easiest way to do this is to use the **DELETE** key.

To clear the contents of a cell:

- Click on the cell.
- Press the **DELETE** key.

Activity 1.3: Clearing the Contents of a Cell

After entering the employee names in the worksheet, you learn that Naomi Gold no longer works for the company.

1. Click on cell **A8**.
2. Press the **DELETE** key.

   Cell A8 should now be empty.

Undoing Actions

Excel lets you undo many commands if you realize your mistake immediately after making it.

To undo an action:

- Open the **Edit** menu.

   *The top command on the **Edit** menu will either indicate the action that you can do (i.e., **Undo Clear**) or will indicate that you **Can't Undo**.*

- Choose **Undo (action)**.

   ALTERNATE METHOD: *Press the **Undo** button* ↶ *instead of selecting **EDIT/Undo**.*

Immediately after **EDIT/Undo** or the **Undo** button has been selected, *Excel* changes the **Undo** menu item to **Redo.** That way, if **EDIT/Undo** did not correct your problem, you may "undo" the undo!

To reverse EDIT/Undo:

- Open the **Edit** menu.

   *If you have used **EDIT/Undo** and that action can still be reversed, the top menu choice will be **Redo (action)***

- Choose **Redo (action)**.

Activity 1.4: Undoing the Last Command

You decide that you don't want to delete Naomi Gold's name after all.

1. Click **Edit** on the Menu Bar to open the **Edit** Menu.

   *The first menu choice is **Undo Clear**.*

2. Click **Undo Clear**.

Naomi Gold should reappear in cell *A8*.

3.   To clear Naomi Gold's name again, choose **EDIT/Redo [u] Clear**.

ENTERING VALUES

You enter values in the same way that you enter text. However, *Excel* aligns values on the right side of the cell instead of the left side. In addition, when you type values, you have some additional choices to make in how you enter them. For example, should you type dollar signs or the commas that separate thousands? *Excel* gives you the option to type *formatting characters* such as dollar signs and commas when you enter the data, or to wait and add all of these characters at once. When you enter data in this lesson, only type the numeric digits and the decimal point. In Lesson 2 you will learn how to add the formatting characters.

Activity 1.5: Entering Values

You will enter the values for the **Consulting Hours**, **Salary Rate**, and **Billing Rate** columns.

1.   Select cell **B5** and type: **32**

   As soon as you start typing, the part of George Snidowski's name that had overflowed into that cell disappears. Don't worry, it is still in Excel's memory. After you finish entering values, you will increase the width of column A so that all of the data are visible.

2.   Press the **DOWN ARROW**.

3.   In cell **B6,** type: **41** and press the **DOWN ARROW**.

4.   In cell **B7**, type: **129** and press the **ENTER** key.

   Your screen should resemble Figure 1 - 10.

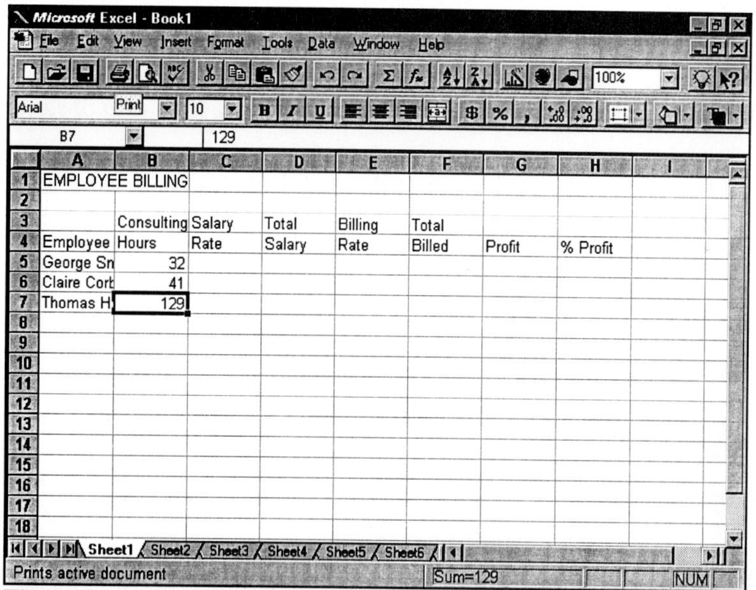

Figure 1 - 10

5.   Select cell **C5**, and enter: **27.50**

   *As Figure 1 - 11 indicates, Excel enters 27.50 as **27.5**. In Excel's default format, digits that do not change the value of the number are omitted. After you format the cell in the next lesson, the zero will be displayed.*

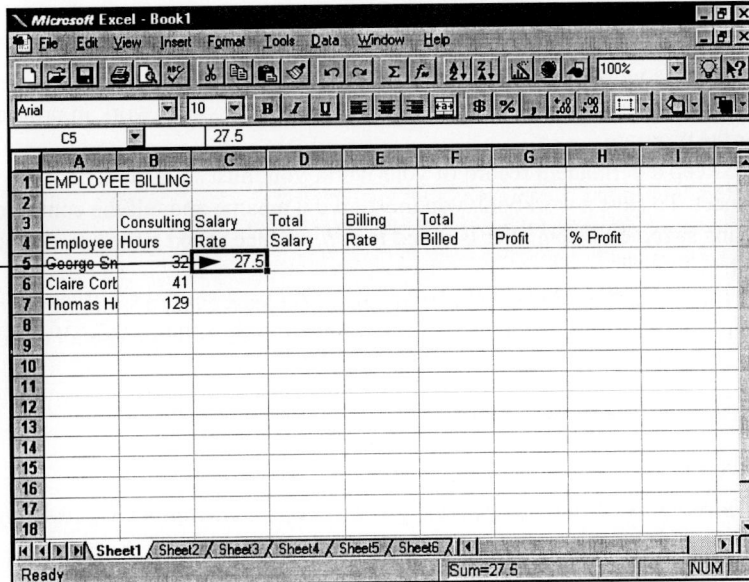

27.50 is displayed as **27.5** in General (default) number format.

Figure 1 - 11

6. In cell **C6**, enter: **32.50**

7. In cell **C7**, enter: **42.50**

8. Select cell **E5**, and in cells **E5, E6,** and **E7**, enter the billing rates for each employee listed below:

George Snidowski	**50**
Claire Corbow	**60**
Thomas Henderson	**75**

9. Compare your worksheet with Figure 1 - 12. If any of the values on your screen are different, use one of the error-correcting procedures you learned to correct the entries.

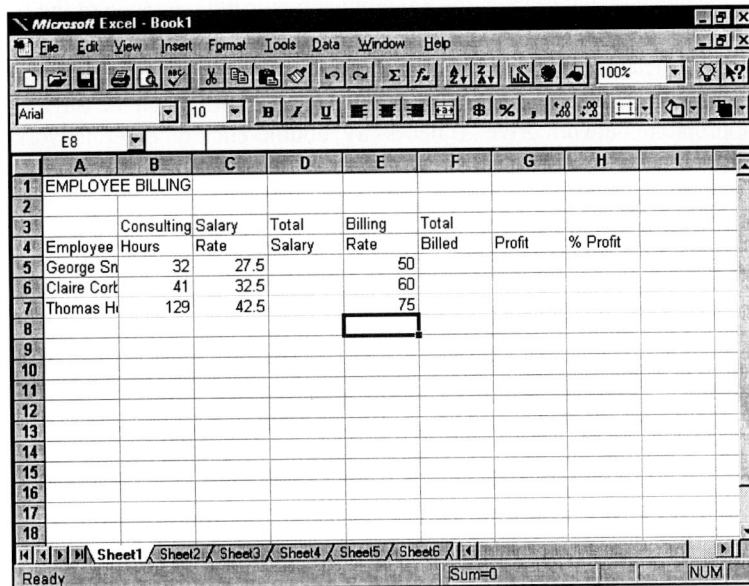

Figure 1 - 12

SAVING A WORKBOOK

While you are working on a worksheet, your data is held in the *RAM* or *Random Access Memory* of your computer. RAM is the computer work area that stores work in progress until you close the file or the program.

To keep a permanent record of your work, you must *save* the workbook containing the worksheet. To save a workbook you must give it a name and tell the computer where to store it. Anything saved on a computer is saved in a *file*. Once saved a file can be accessed any time you need it.

It is important to save your work regularly (at least every 15 minutes), so that if you should make a serious mistake, or if the power should fail, you will not lose all of your work.

To save a workbook as a file:

• Choose **FILE/Save As.**

   *The **Save As** dialog box appears. The text in the **File name** text box is highlighted.*

• Type a name for your file. Your file name must follow the rules shown in Table 1 - 1.

RULES FOR NAMING A FILE

• Like all other applications written specifically for *Windows 95*, *Excel 7.0* allows long file names. The complete file name, including drive letter, server name, and folder path, which tell where the file is located, can contain up to 218 characters.

• It may NOT include any of the following symbols:

   ; : * [ ] | / \ < > ? "

• File names <u>may</u> include spaces.

Table 1 - 1

• If the name that appears in the **Save in** list box is not the name of the folder to which you should save your files, click on the triangle to the right of the box and then click on the correct location. If you are saving your files on a floppy disk, you will probably select **3 1/2 Floppy [A:]**. If you are saving your file on a network, open the **Save in** list box and select the appropriate network drive. If necessary, double-click on other network or folder names as they appear in the box in the middle of the screen until the correct location is indicated in the **Save in** list box.

• Click on **Save** or press **ENTER.**

• The **Properties** dialog box may be displayed. Enter any information that you want and then click on **OK** or press **ENTER.**

Activity 1.6: Saving Your Workbook

1. If you are saving your files on a floppy disk, put it in the disk drive.

2. Click on **File** on the Menu Bar.

3. Click on **Save As**.

   *You have selected the **FILE/Save As** command and the **Save As** dialog box is displayed. The default file name, **Book1,** is highlighted in the **File name** box (Figure 1 - 13).*

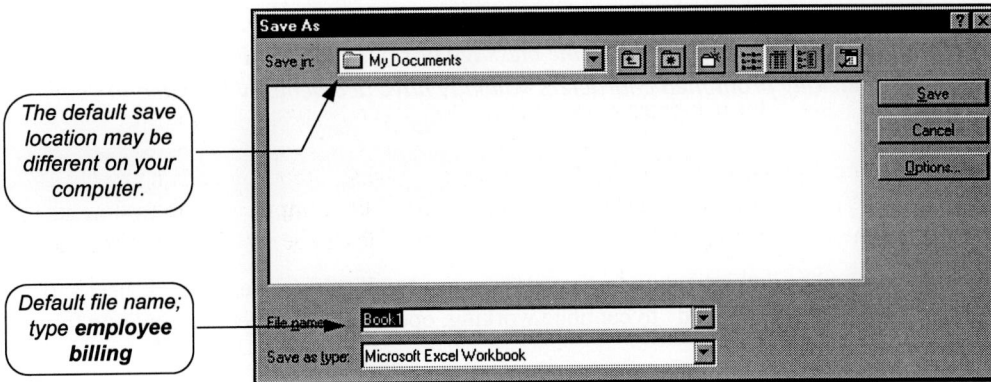

The default save location may be different on your computer.

Default file name; type **employee billing**

Figure 1 - 13

4. Type: **employee billing**

   As soon as you begin to type, **employee billing** *should replace* **Book1** *in the* **File name** *text box.*

   ☑ **PROBLEM SOLVER:** *If any letters remain from the old title,* **Book1**, *use the* **BACKSPACE** *or* **DELETE** *keys to remove them.*

   It is possible that the default file name will be Book1.xls, instead of Book1. This means that your computer has been set up to show the MS-DOS file extensions used in previous versions of Excel. The presence of the .xls extension will not affect your work. It can only be removed by changing one of the view options in My Computer or Windows Explorer.

5. Look at contents of the **Save in** text box at the top of the **Save As** dialog box. The text box may include an icon of a file folder and the name of the folder (e.g. **My Documents**; Figure 1 - 13) or the icon of a drive (e.g., **3 1/2 Floppy (A:)**) .

6. If you are saving your files on a floppy disk, click on the ▼ next to the **Save in** text box and choose **3 1/2 Floppy (A:)** or the appropriate name for your floppy disk drive.

   The list of files already on your exercise disk will appear in the large box in the middle of the screen.

   If you are saving files on a network drive and the network is listed in the **Save in** box, a list of folders on the network will be displayed in the large box in the middle of the screen. Double-click on the name of the folder to which you wish to save your file. Since folders may be arranged hierarchically, it may be necessary to double-click on several folders until the one that should contain your file is listed. Ask your instructor for the name of the file folder to which you should save all files and the path of folders you must take to reach your folder.

   If you are saving on a network and the name of your network location does not initially appear in the **Save in** box, click on the ▼ next to the **Save in** box and choose **Network Neighborhood.** Then continue with the directions in the preceding paragraph.

7. Click on **Save** to save the file.

8. The **employee billing Properties** dialog box may be displayed. If it is displayed, press **ENTER** or click on **OK** to leave the screen without changing it.

   Look at the Status Bar. The message **Saving employee billing** *and a graphic showing the amount of the file that has been saved will appear. After the file has been saved, the Title Bar name will change to* **Microsoft Excel - employee billing***.*

PROBLEM SOLVER: *If Excel produces a warning box with the message,* **File name is not valid**, *click on the* **OK** *button in the message box. Click in the* **File name** *box and retype or delete any prohibited characters you may have accidentally included in your file name.*

TAKING A BREAK

You can stop any project in this book before you have completed it. Just save the worksheet and exit from *Excel*. When you are ready to continue working, open the worksheet and continue from where you stopped.

To open a previously saved workbook:

- Choose **FILE/Open** or click on the **Open** button on the Standard toolbar.

   The **Open** *dialog box will appear on the screen.*

- The location in which *Excel* expects to find your file appears in the **Look in** box. If your file has been saved to a different location, click on the at the right of the list box and click on the appropriate icon. If necessary, double-click on icons in the large box in the center of the screen until the drive or folder containing your files has been selected.

- The file names are listed in alphabetical order in the large box in the center of the dialog box. Click on the name of the file you want to open.

PROBLEM SOLVER: *If you cannot see all of the file names, click on the List button at the top of the dialog box so that maximum number of files will be displayed. If a scroll bar appears on the bottom edge of the screen, click the ▸ to scroll the file name listing.*

- Click on **Open** or press **ENTER**.

Activity 1.7: Exiting from Excel

1. Choose **FILE/Exit** or click on the **Close** button.

PROBLEM SOLVER: *If you have made any changes to* **employee billing** *since you last saved it, or if you have any other open, unsaved worksheets, Excel will display an Alert box. Click on* **Yes** *to save the worksheet, or click on* **No** *if you do not want to save the worksheet. If you don't know whether or not you want to save the worksheet, click on* **Cancel**, *take a look at the worksheet, and then save it if you want to.*

Activity 1.8: Returning to Excel and Your Workbook

1. If you just completed Activity 1.7, the Desktop will be displayed.

2. Click on the **Start** button.

3. Highlight **Programs** and then click on the **Microsoft Excel** icon.

4. Choose **FILE/Open**.

   The **Open** *dialog box will be displayed (Figure 1 - 14). The drive or folder listed in the* **Look in** *box may be different on your computer. If the drive or folder contains files or folders they will be displayed in the middle of the dialog box.*

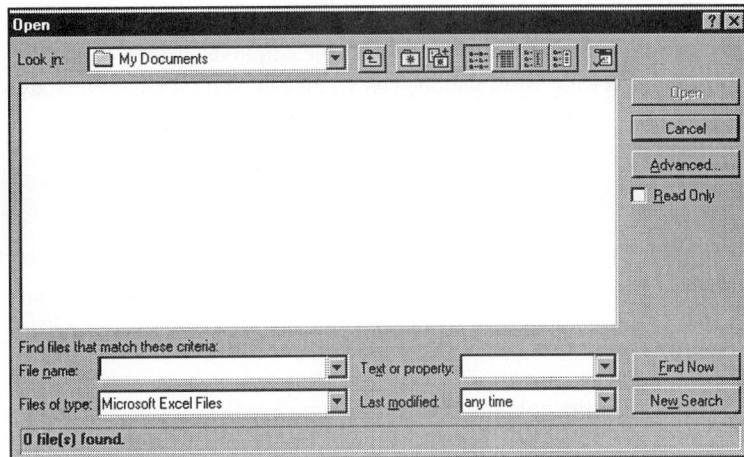

Figure 1 - 14

5. Look at the location listed in the **Look in** text box (Figure 1 - 14). If the location listed is not the folder, drive, or network containing your file, click the ▼ to the right of the **Look in** drop-down list box.

6. Click the icon representing the drive containing your data disk, probably **a:** or **b:**, or on the network drive you are using or on **Network Neighborhood** if the network drive isn't listed.

   If your files have been saved on a network, you may need to double-click on one or more icons in the middle of the screen before locating the folder containing your files. Follow the same path that you used to save your file in Activity 1.6.

7. Look at the list of files in the middle of the screen. If **employee billing** is visible, click on it. If it is not visible, click on the triangles on the scroll bar until the name is visible, and then choose it.

   *Figure 1 - 15 shows the completed dialog box if your disk is in the **a:** drive.*

8. Click on **Open** to open the file.

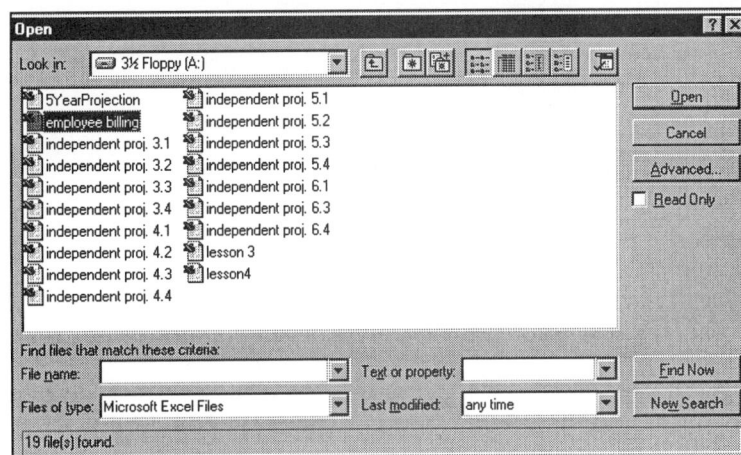

Figure 1 - 15

CHANGING COLUMN WIDTH

Excel sets a default width for all the columns in a new worksheet. The default column width in *Excel* is 8.43 spaces. All the employee names are too wide to fit in column **A**. Once you entered text into the adjacent cells in column **B**, their names were truncated — however, the data are still in the cell; you just can't see them. To view the employee names, you must increase the column width. There are several ways that the cell width can be increased. They are summarized in this section.

AutoFit

Excel can automatically calculate the optimum width for a column, based on the widest entry in that column.

To use AutoFit:

- To select the entire column, click the column heading or select one cell in the column, and then press **CTRL+SPACEBAR**.

- Choose **FORMAT/Column, AutoFit Selection** from the menus, or double-click the right border of the column heading.

Activity 1.9: Using AutoFit to Change Column Width

Let's change the width of column **C**.

1. Point to the **C** in the column headings. Make sure the pointer is a ⊕ and click.

   The entire column is selected (Figure 1 - 16).

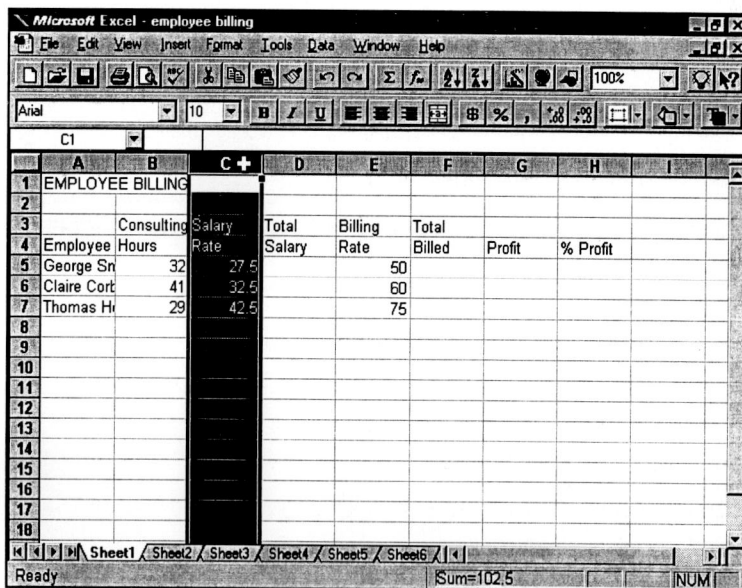

Figure 1 - 16

2. Choose the **FORMAT/Column** command by first clicking on **Format** in the Menu Bar and then highlighting **Column**.

   *Since **Column** is followed by a ▶, a submenu is displayed (Figure 1 - 17).*

3. Choose **AutoFit Selection** by clicking on it in the **Column** submenu.

   *The column width automatically decreases so that it is slightly wider than **Salary**, which is the widest entry in the column.*

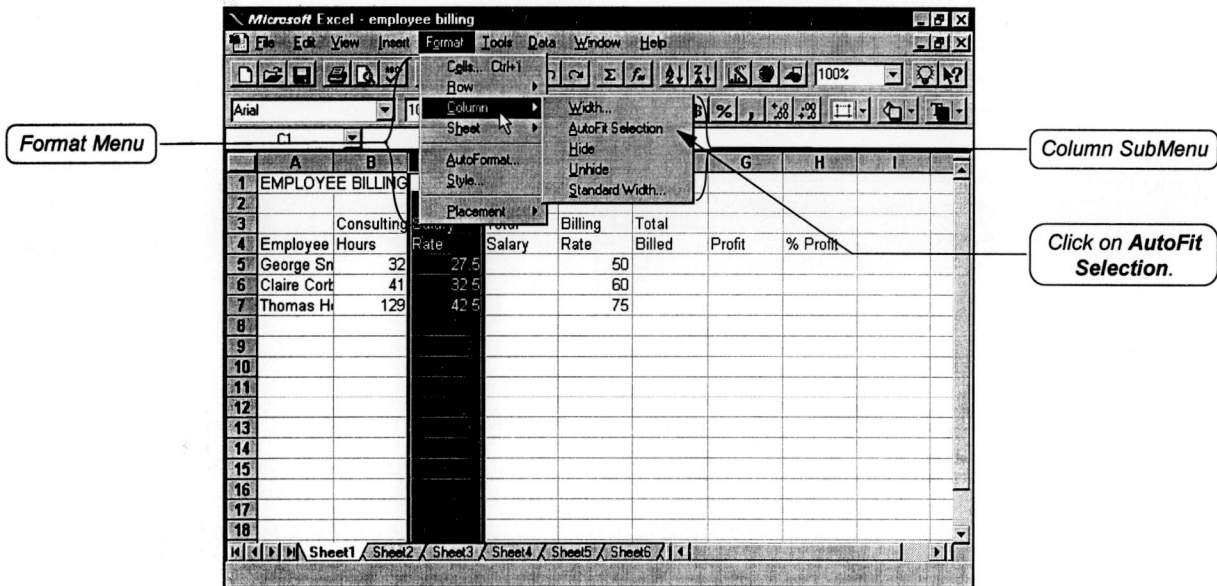

Figure 1 - 17

Changing the Column Width Manually

Sometimes you want a column to have a different width than AutoFit selects. In your worksheet you cannot use AutoFit to change the width of column **A** because the worksheet title is the widest entry in column **A**, while you only want the column to be as wide as the widest employee name.

To change the column width using the menus:

- Select the column by clicking on the column name in the column heading bar or by selecting one cell in a column and then pressing **CTRL+SPACEBAR**.

- Choose **FORMAT/Column,Width** from the menus.

- Type the desired column width in the **Column Width** text box and press the **ENTER** key or click on **OK**.

To change the column width by dragging:

- Point to the line to the right of the column whose width should be changed.

- When the mouse pointer changes to a ┿ click and drag until the column width appears correct.

- If the column width is narrower or wider than you wish, repeat the last step until it is the desired width.

Activity 1.10: Changing the Column Width Manually

1. Place the mouse pointer in the column **A** header and click.

   Column A is selected.

2. Choose **FORMAT/Column,AutoFit Selection**

   The width of column A increases to accommodate EMPLOYEE BILLING, which is the widest entry in the column. However, you only want the column to be wide enough to fit the widest employee name.

3. With column **A** still highlighted, choose the **FORMAT/Column** command.

4. Click on **Width** in the **Column** submenu.

*The **Column Width** dialog box is displayed and the **Column Width** text box is highlighted (Figure 1 - 18). It displays the current width of column A.*

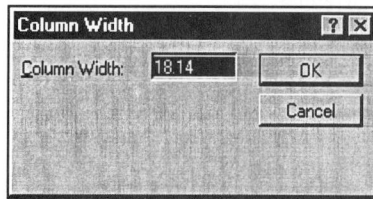

Figure 1 - 18

5. Type: **10** and click on **OK** or press the **ENTER** key.

*The column is still not wide enough to display the full employee names. Since most people use proportional fonts, it is hard to guess how wide to make a cell. (With proportional fonts the width of each character varies, so that a "skinny" letter like **l** is narrower than a letter like **W**.)*

6. Position the mouse pointer in the column heading on the line between column **A** and column **B**.

7. When the shape of the mouse pointer changes to a ✛ click and drag the mouse to the right until you think the cell is wide enough for all the data. If you make the column too wide or too narrow, repeat until you can just see the complete employee names (Figure 1 - 19).

Figure 1 - 19

ENTERING FORMULAS

Formulas do the work that worksheets were designed to do — they provide the information to answer your questions. For example, you want to know George's total salary. Therefore, in cell **D5** you will to enter a formula that will multiply the number of consulting hours he worked by his salary rate.

Formulas contain several components. The first component in any formula is an equal sign (=) that tells *Excel* to treat the data in the cell as a formula rather than as text. The formula may contain numbers and/or cell addresses and mathematical operators such as plus or minus signs. When the number that you want to use in a formula is on the worksheet, you always use the cell address rather than the value in the formula. That way, if the value changes, the formula will automatically recalculate and the results will still be accurate.

It is possible to enter a formula by typing its contents into the cell. However, it is preferable to type part of the formula and then *point* to the other information that you wish to include. Specifically, you will type the mathematical symbols (= and +), but *each time* a cell address should be added to the formula, you will use the mouse (or the arrow keys) to point to the cell rather than type the cell name. Pointing is better than typing because you can see exactly what data are being used in the formula, and you are less likely to make an error in entering the cell address.

To enter a formula using pointing:

- Select the cell to contain the formula.

- Type an equal sign (=).

- Click on the first cell containing data that should be part of the formula.

- Type a mathematical operator. The symbols for the mathematical operators are + for addition, - for subtraction, * for multiplication, / for division, and ^ for exponentiation.

- Repeat the last two steps until the formula is complete. Do NOT type a mathematical operator after the last cell entry.

- Press the **ENTER** key or click on the **enter box**.

Activity 1.11: Creating Formulas

You will enter formulas to calculate the total salary, total billed, profit, and percent profit for each employee.

1. Select cell **D5**.

2. Type: =

3. Select cell **B5** by clicking on it or pressing the **LEFT ARROW** key twice.

   *Cell **B5** is enclosed in a moving border, and the formula =**B5** appears in the Formula Bar and in cell **D5** (Figure 1 - 20). The word **Point** also appears on the Status Bar because you are pointing to the cells to be included in the formula.*

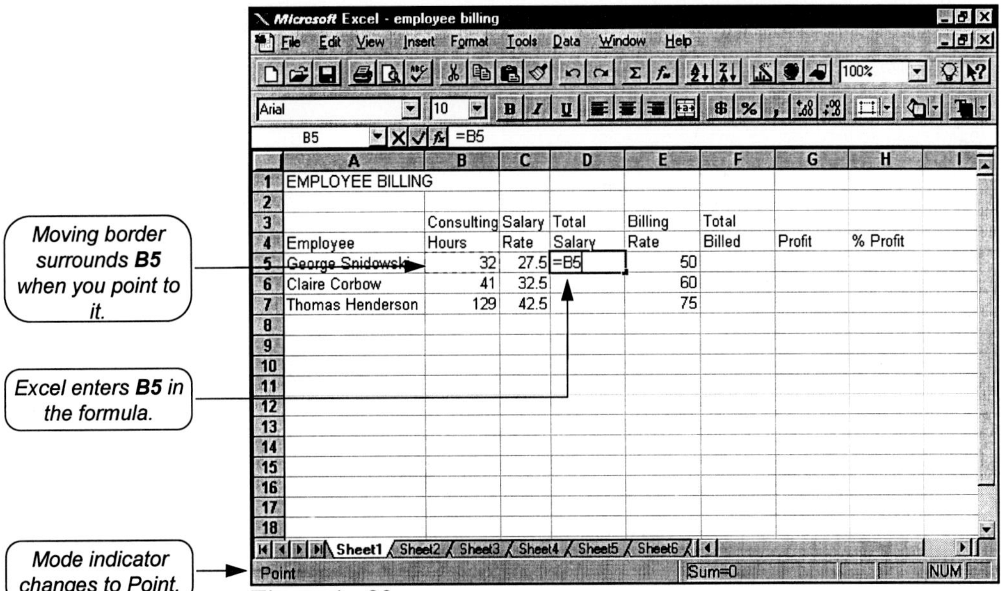

Moving border surrounds **B5** when you point to it.

Excel enters **B5** in the formula.

Mode indicator changes to Point.

Figure 1 - 20

4. Type the multiplication operator, the asterisk (*).

   *The * indicates that you are multiplying the contents of cell B5 by the next part of the formula. As soon as you type the asterisk, the moving border line is removed from cell B5.*

5. Click on cell **C5**.

   *The contents of cell D5 should now be =B5*C5. The formula is complete (Figure 1 - 21).*

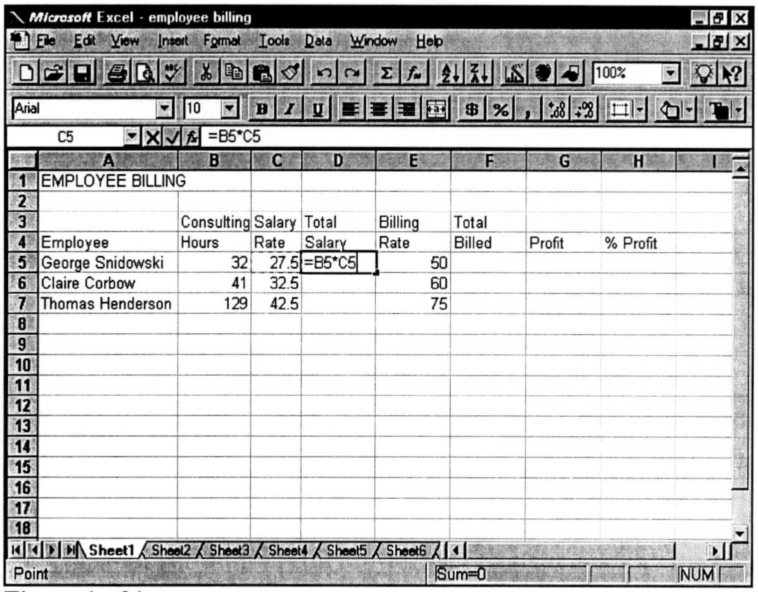

Figure 1 - 21

6. Press the **ENTER** key or click on the **enter box**.

   *When cell D5 is selected, the formula =B5*C5 remains visible in the Formula Bar, but the value of that formula, 880, is inserted in the cell.*

   PROBLEM SOLVER: *If you have made an error in the syntax of the formula, Excel will display an error message. Read the message and click on OK. Excel will automatically switch to Edit mode. Compare your entry with that shown in Figure 1 - 21 and make any necessary corrections.*

7. Click on **D6**.

8. Type: =

9. Click on **B6**.

10. Type: *

11. Click on **C6**.

12. If the formula in **D6** is **=B6*C6**, press the **ENTER** key or click on the **enter box**. If it is not, press **ESC** and repeat steps 7–12.

13. The formula for cell **D7** is exactly the same as the one in cell **D6**, except that the rows are different. Therefore, you should repeat steps 7-12 using the cells in row 7 instead of row 6.

    Your worksheet should resemble Figure 1 - 22.

14. Click on cell **F5**.

15. Use pointing to enter the formula **=B5*E5** and press the **ENTER** key.

*The value **1600** should appear in cell **F5**. If not, reenter the formula. If the formula is correct, but your answer is still incorrect, check that the values in **B5** and **E5** match those shown in Figure 1 - 22.*

16. Use pointing to enter similar formulas in cells **F6** and **F7**.

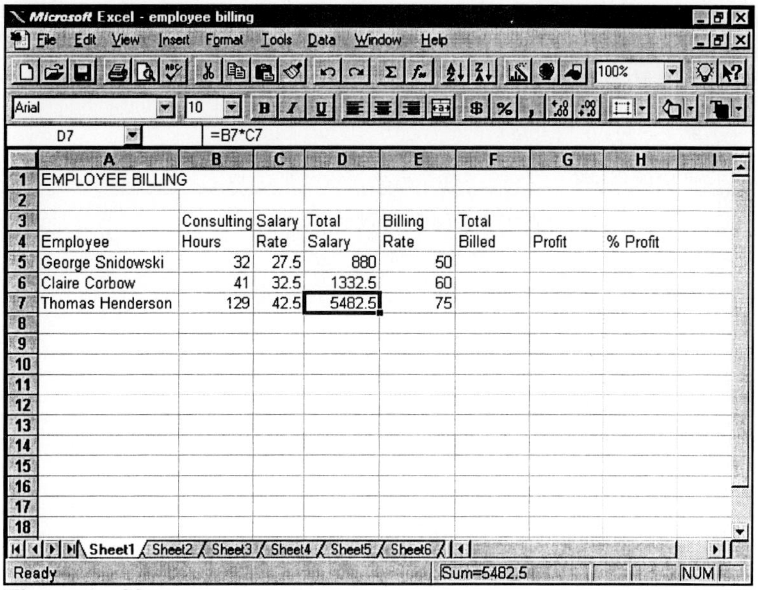

Figure 1 - 22

17. In cell **G5**, use pointing to enter the formula to calculate the profit. This formula equals the total billed for George minus his total salary.

Your worksheet should resemble Figure 1 - 23.

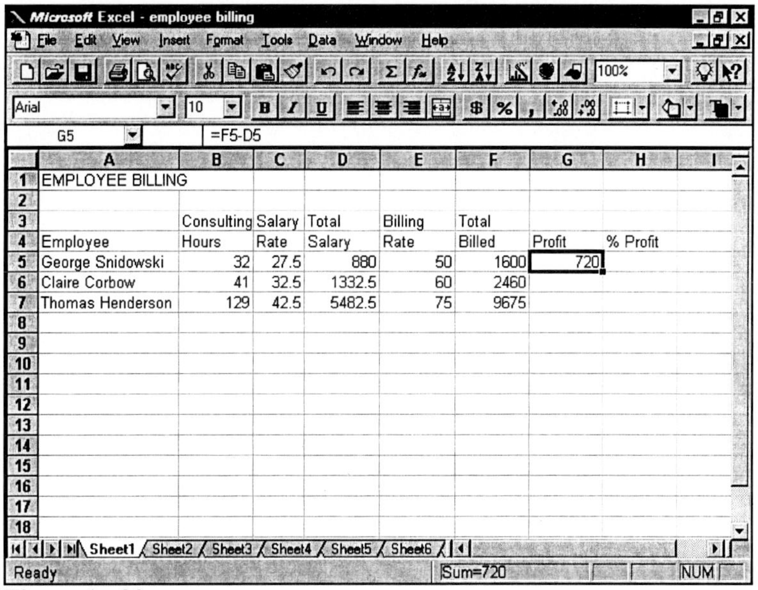

Figure 1 - 23

18. Use pointing to enter similar formulas in cells **G6** and **G7**.

19. In cell **H5**, use pointing to enter the formula to calculate the % Profit. The % Profit equals the profit divided by the total billed.
20. Use pointing to enter similar formulas in cells **H6** and **H7**.

    Your worksheet should resemble Figure 1 - 24.

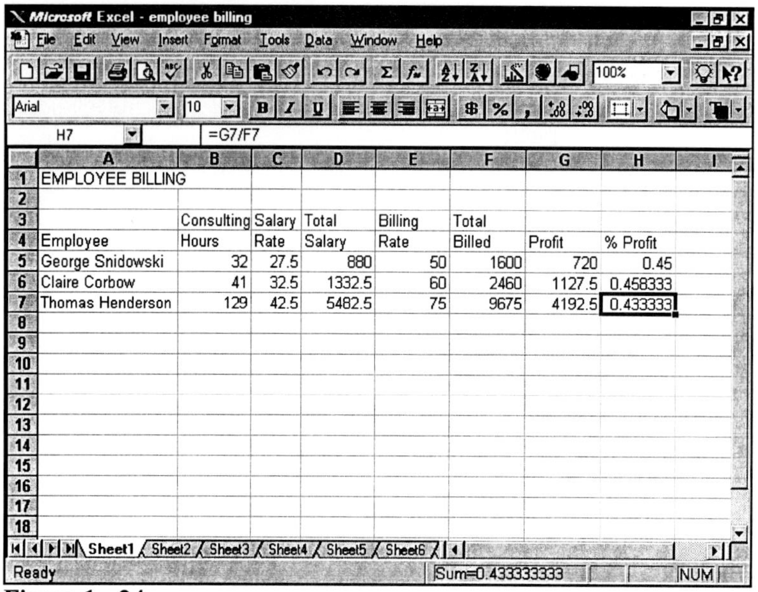

	A	B	C	D	E	F	G	H
1	EMPLOYEE BILLING							
2								
3		Consulting	Salary	Total	Billing	Total		
4	Employee	Hours	Rate	Salary	Rate	Billed	Profit	% Profit
5	George Snidowski	32	27.5	880	50	1600	720	0.45
6	Claire Corbow	41	32.5	1332.5	60	2460	1127.5	0.458333
7	Thomas Henderson	129	42.5	5482.5	75	9675	4192.5	0.433333

Figure 1 - 24

Activity 1.12: Letting Formulas Recalculate

One of the benefits of using formulas is that whenever any of the data in cells contained in the formula change, the value of the formula automatically changes. In looking over your worksheet, you realize that Thomas Henderson worked 29 hours not 129. You will correct this error now.

1. Position the mouse pointer on cell **B7** and double-click.

   *You should be in Edit Mode. (**HINT**: **Edit** should be indicated on the left-side of the Status Bar.)*

2. Click immediately to the left of the **1** and press the **DELETE** key.
3. Press the **ENTER** key.
4. Compare your screen with Figure 1 - 24, which shows the worksheet before you changed Thomas Henderson's hours. Which values changed?
5. Click on each cell with a changed value and look at the Formula Bar. The formula in each of the cells should contain the address of the cell you changed, **B7**, or of a cell such as **F7**, which itself contains a formula referencing **B7**. (Figure 1 - 25 shows one of the changed cells.)

SAVING A FILE WITH THE SAME NAME

Every time you make changes to a file, you must save the file again or the changes will be lost when you close the worksheet or exit from *Excel*. When you save the file using the same name, the current version of the worksheet replaces the previously saved version.

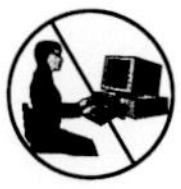

To save a file again with the same file name:

- Choose **FILE/Save** or click the **Save** toolbar button.

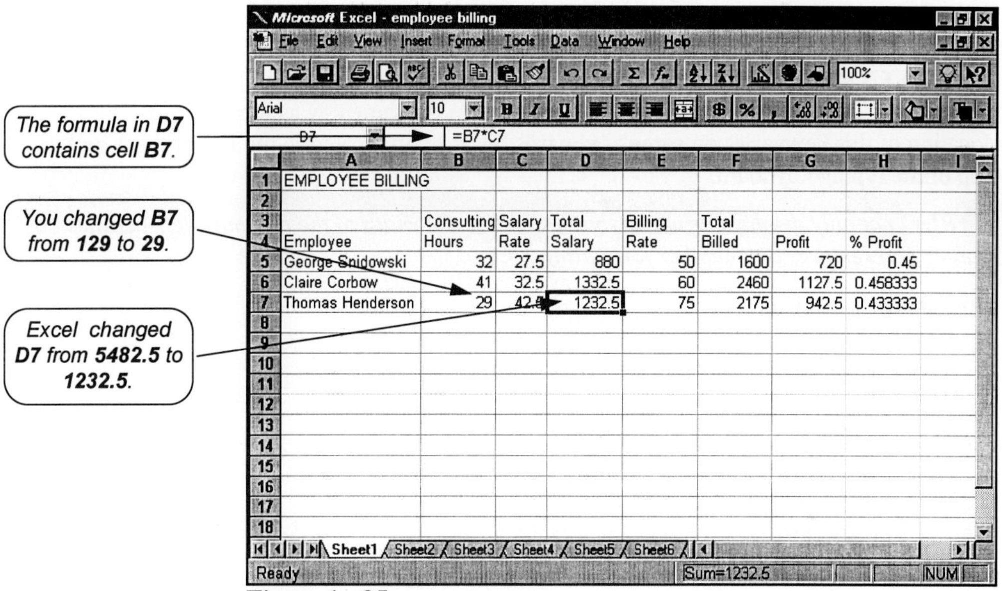

The formula in **D7** contains cell **B7**.

You changed **B7** from **129** to **29**.

Excel changed **D7** from **5482.5** to **1232.5**.

Figure 1 - 25

Activity 1.13: Saving a File Again with the Same Name

This time when you save the file, you will use the toolbar instead of the menus.

1. Click on the **Save** toolbar button.

   Saving employee billing and a bar showing the progress of the save will appear on the Status Bar while the file is being saved. Depending on which disk you are saving to, and the speed of your computer, the message may appear only briefly.

PRINTING A WORKSHEET

Typically, you want to print worksheets so that you can share the information with others. Your worksheet is complete, although its appearance is not as attractive as you would like. Let's print it now and then you will enhance its appearance in Lesson 2. You will print using the default settings. In Lesson 2 you will learn how to change the appearance of the printout.

To print a worksheet using the default settings:

- Make sure that the printer is turned on.
- Choose **FILE/Print** or click on the **Print** button 🖨. 
- Click on **OK**.

Occasionally you want to have a printed copy of the formulas contained in the cells instead of the values. In the business world you can use this copy to document your worksheet, so that you and everyone else can see what formulas you used to obtain your results. If there are errors in the worksheet, a printout containing formulas can help find them. In school instructors often want a printout with formulas displayed to see what formulas were used in constructing the worksheet.

To print formulas instead of cell contents:

- Press the **CTRL** key and while keeping it depressed, press the ` (the single left quotation mark, *not* the apostrophe). The ` is usually found on the same key as the tilde (~). The location of this key varies on some keyboards but is often located to the left of the **1** on the top of the typing keyboard.

  CTRL+` not only displays formulas, but it doubles the width of the columns, left-justifies all values and removes any number formatting.

- Print the document.

- Press **CTRL+`** again to return to normal display.

Activity 1.14: Printing a Worksheet

1. Make sure that the printer is turned on.

2. Choose **FILE/Print**.

   *The **Print** dialog box will appear (Figure 1 - 26.).*

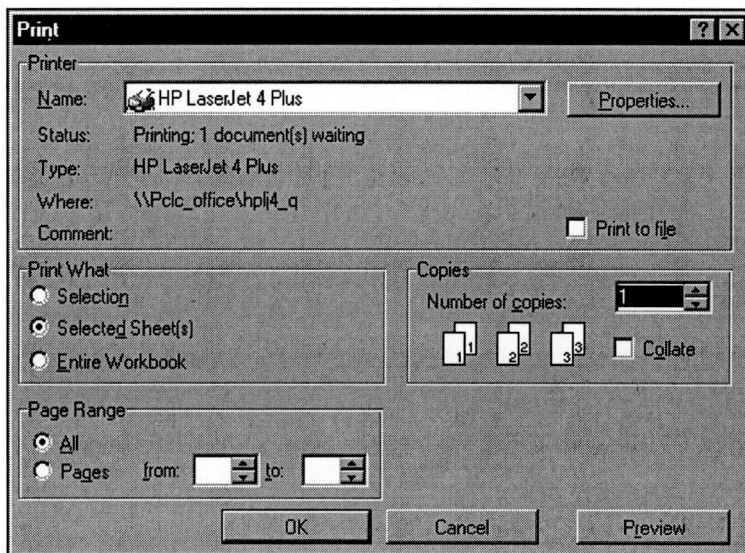

Figure 1 - 26

3. Look at the name of the printer listed. If it is not the one that you are using, click the ▼ at the end of the box containing the name of the printer. Click on the name of the printer that you are using. If this does not work, ask your lab instructor for help.

4. In the **Print** dialog box, click on **OK** to print the worksheet.

5. Press **CTRL+`** (left single quote) to display formulas in all cells (Figure 1 - 27).

6. Print the worksheet again.

   The worksheet will be printed on two pages instead of one.

7. Press **CTRL+`** again to display values in all cells.

8. Choose **FILE/Close**. If asked **Save changes in 'employee billing'?** choose **YES. FILE/Exit** *Excel* or go on to Independent Project 1.1.

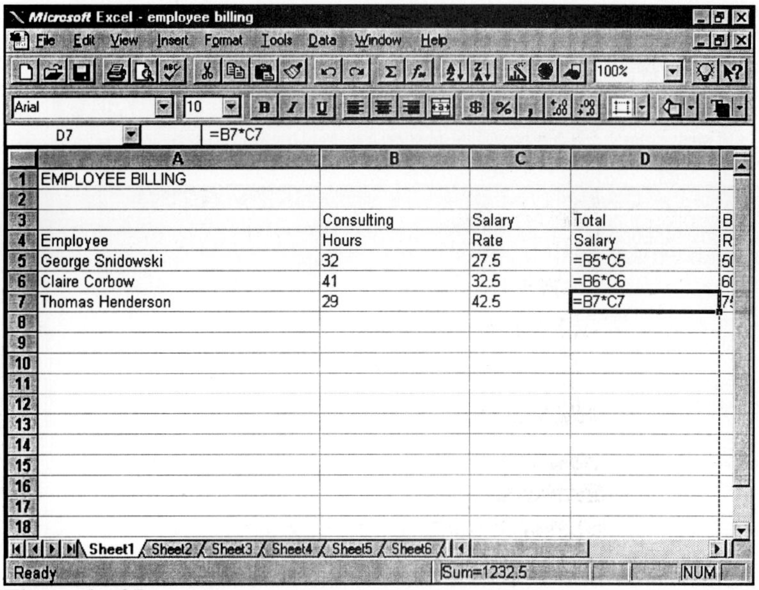

Figure 1 - 27

SUMMARY

In this lesson, you completed the basic tasks of entering text, values, and formulas, editing cell contents, changing column widths, and saving, opening, and printing a worksheet. In Lesson 2 you will learn how to make the worksheet more attractive. In Lesson 3 you will learn some more advanced editing skills and how to use *Excel*'s various copying strategies to save you time.

KEY TERMS

Cancel box	Enter Mode	Point
Cell overflow	Formulas	Ready Mode
Closing	Insertion point	Right aligned
Constants	Labels	Saving
Edit Mode	Left aligned	Text entry
Enter box	Opening	Values

INDEPENDENT PROJECTS

The four independent projects allow you to practice the basic skills involved in creating worksheets: entering text, values, and formulas; changing data; and printing and saving the worksheet. The first two projects specifically indicate all the tasks that you need to complete the project. Independent Project 1.3 leaves some of the worksheet design up to you. In Independent Project 1.4 you must plan the worksheet before creating it.

Independent Project 1.1: Comparing Budgets for Two Years

You have been asked to create a worksheet that compares the 1995/1996 and 1996/1997 budgets for one of the departments at your school. The worksheet will contain the budgeted amounts for four categories of expense: faculty, staff, hardware/software, and research. For each category you will calculate the amount of increase in the 1996/1997 budget and the percent of the increase. The first draft of your worksheet should resemble Figure 1 - 28.

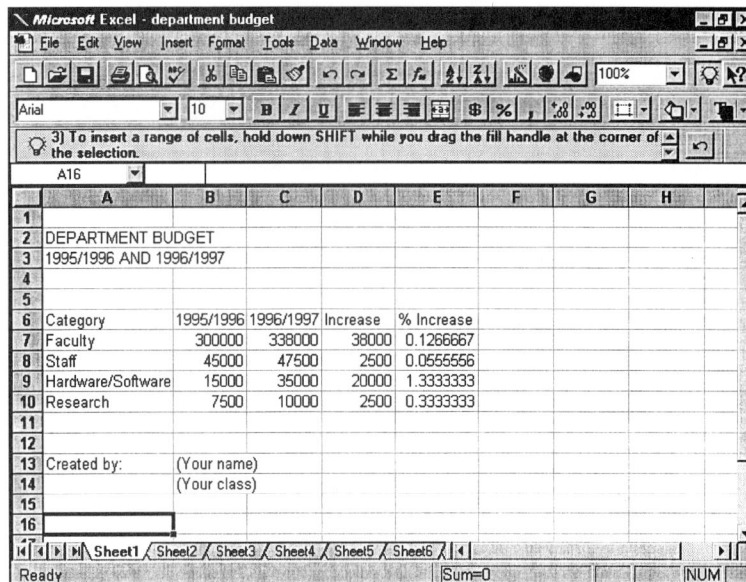

Figure 1 - 28

When you finish this project, your worksheet will be complete, but not attractive. You will enhance its appearance at the end of Lesson 2.

Use Figure 1 - 28 and the following instructions to help you complete the project:

1. Start *Excel*. Maximize *Excel* and **book1** if they are not already maximized. If you start this project immediately after finishing the lesson, close all open files. If no workbook is open, choose **FILE/New** or click on the **New Workbook** tool.

2. Enter the worksheet title in column **A** of rows **2** and **3**.

3. Enter the column labels in row **6.**

4. Enter the budget categories (**Faculty, Staff,** etc.) in cells **A7** through **A10.**

5. Increase the width of column **A** manually so that all the expense category labels are visible. The worksheet title, DEPARTMENT BUDGET should still overflow into column **B.**

6. If **% Increase** or any of the other column labels are too wide to fit in their columns, use **AutoFit Selection** to make the column(s) wider.

7. Enter the values for columns **B** and **C** (shown in bold in Table 1 - 2).

Category	1995/1996	1996/1997
Faculty	**300000**	**338000**
Staff	**45000**	**47500**
Hardware/Software	**15000**	**35000**
Research	**7500**	**10000**

Table 1 - 2

8. Enter a formula in cell **D7** to calculate the increase in the faculty budget. The increase is equal to the **1996/1997** faculty budget minus the **1995/1996** faculty budget.

9. Make sure that the result in **D7** is the same as in Figure 1 - 28. Enter similar formulas in the rest of column **D** to calculate the increase for the other budget categories.

10. Next, enter a formula in **E7** that reflects the percent of increase. This is equal to the **Increase** divided by the **1995/1996** budget amount.

11. When you are sure that the formula in **E7** is correct, enter similar formulas in the rest of the column.

12. In cell **A13**, enter: **Created by:**

13. Enter your name in cell **B13**. Don't worry if it overflows into column **C**.

14. Enter your class or any other identifying information requested by your instructor in **B14**.

15. Compare your worksheet to Figure 1 - 28 and make any editing changes necessary.

16. Save the worksheet using the file name: **department budget**
Be sure that you save the file to your Data Disk or to the network drive to which you have been instructed to save files.

17. Print the worksheet.

18. Display formulas.

19. Print the worksheet again.

20. Redisplay values.

21. The department has just received two grants for 1996/1997. The Hardware/Software budget can increase by 5000 and the Research budget by 5000. Change the **1996/1997 Hardware/Software** budget to **40000** and the **1996/1997 Research** budget to **15000**.

22. Print your worksheet again displaying the new values.

23. Use **FILE/Save As** to save your file using the name: **department budget, rev. 1**

24. Exit *Excel* or continue with the next project.

Independent Project 1.2: Calculating the Current Caseload

You work for a social services agency. You have been asked to create a worksheet that calculates the July caseload for each case worker. You are given the case workers' names and each case worker's June caseload, the number of new July cases and the number of cases discharged in July. You are to calculate the final July caseload and the difference from the June caseload. The first draft of your worksheet should resemble Figure 1 - 29.

When you finish this project, your worksheet will be complete, but not attractive. You will enhance its appearance at the end of Lesson 2.

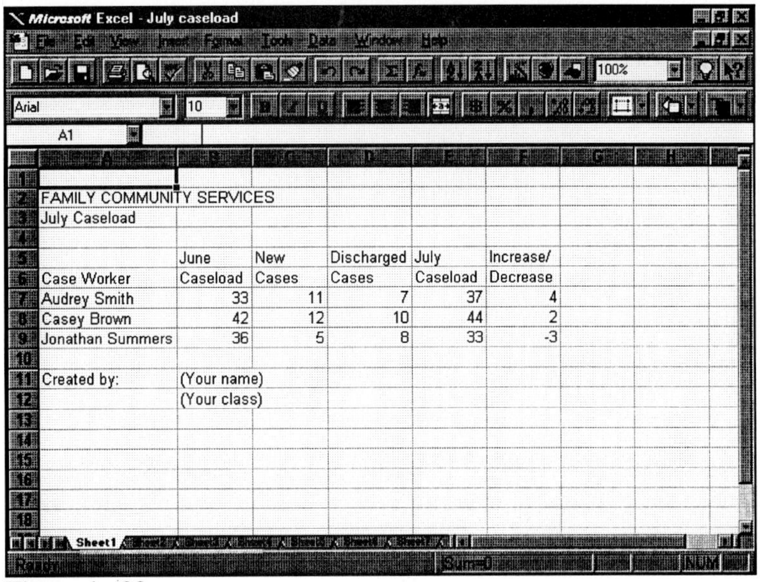

Figure 1 - 29

Use Figure 1 - 29 and the following instructions to help you create the project:

1. If you have just completed Independent Project 1.1, close it and choose **FILE/New** or the **New Workbook** tool to create a new worksheet.

2. Enter the worksheet title in cells **A2** and **A3**.

3. Enter the column labels in rows **5** and **6**.

4. Enter the case workers' names in cells **A7** through **A9**.

5. Increase column widths as necessary so that all of the labels are fully contained in their cells. The first line of the worksheet title, FAMILY COMMUNITY SERVICES, should still overflow into column **B**.

6. Enter the values for the **June Caseload**, **New Cases,** and **Discharged Cases** as shown in Table 1 - 3.

Case Worker	June Caseload	New Cases	Discharged Cases
Audrey Smith	33	11	7
Casey Brown	42	12	10
Jonathan Summers	36	5	8

Table 1 - 3

7. In cells **E7** through **E9** enter the formulas to calculate the **July Caseload**. The **July Caseload** is the **June Caseload** plus the **New Cases** minus the **Discharged Cases**.

8. In cells **F7** through **F9** enter formulas to calculate the **Increase/Decrease**, which is equal to the **July Caseload** minus the **June Caseload**.

9. Put the information identifying who prepared this worksheet on the bottom of the worksheet as shown in Figure 1 - 29.

10. Save the worksheet using the name: **July caseload**

11. Print the worksheet.

12. Display formulas.

13. Print the worksheet again with displayed formulas.

14. Redisplay values instead of formulas.

15. You are given updated information on July caseloads. **Audrey Smith** had **1 more New Case** than initially reported and **Jonathan Summers** had **2 fewer Discharged Cases**. Change the data to reflect the new information.

16. Use **FILE/Save As** to save your worksheet using the name: **July caseload, rev. 1**

17. Print the worksheet displaying the new values.

18. Close the file.

Independent Project 1.3: Calculating Hockey Game Revenue

You are responsible for calculating the net revenue from ticket and food sales at the school hockey game. Table 1 - 4 shows the data that you have collected. Table 1 - 5 shows the calculations that need to be made.

Attendance:			
	Full Price	Students	
Number Sold	178	234	
Fee	5.25	3.75	
Food:			
	Hot Dogs	Hamburgers	Sodas
Number Sold	355	248	557
Unit Cost	.50	.75	.35
Sales Price	1.00	1.50	.75

Table 1 - 4

RESULT	*CALCULATION*
Total Number of Tickets Sold	Number of full-price tickets plus number of student tickets sold
Total Revenue for Full Price Tickets	Number of full-price tickets times fee
Total Revenue for Student Tickets	Number of student tickets times fee
Total Revenue from Ticket Sales	Revenue from full-price tickets plus revenue from student tickets
Profit per Item (food)	The difference between the sales price and the unit cost
Profit for Total Sales (food)	The profit per item times the number of items sold
Total Food Profit	The sum of the profit for total sales of each of the food items
Total Hockey Game Profit	The total revenue from ticket sales plus the total food profit
Do **NOT** calculate (a) the sum of the Full-Price and Student Fees; (b) the totals of the Number, Unit Cost, Sales Price or Profit Per Item of each of the foods sold.	

Table 1 - 5

Your worksheet may resemble Figure 1 - 30 or it may be organized differently as long as it displays all of the data.

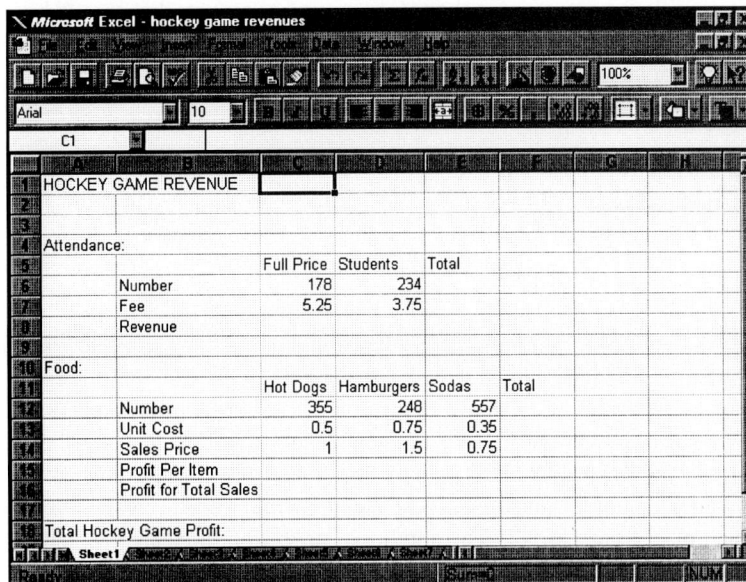

Figure 1 - 30

When you finish this project, your worksheet will be complete, but not attractive. You will enhance its appearance at the end of Lesson 2.

Use the following instructions to help your create your worksheet:

1. Plan your worksheet on a piece of paper. You may use Figure 1 - 30 as a guide for placing the values and text or you may create a design of your own.

2. Enter a worksheet title in cell **A1.**

3. Enter subtitles identifying the two parts of the worksheet (attendance and food) and column and row labels. Place them as they appear in your design; they do not need to be placed as they are in Figure 1 - 30.

4. Change column widths as necessary.

5. Enter the values shown in Table 1 - 4.

6. Enter formulas to perform the calculations indicated in Table 1 - 5.

7. Enter your name and any other required identifying information a few rows below the last row used in the worksheet.

8. Save your worksheet using the name: **hockey game revenues**

9. Print your worksheet displaying values.

10. Print your worksheet displaying formulas.

11. Replace the existing data with the following new data:

Number of Full-Price Tickets Sold:	**182**
Number of Student Tickets Sold:	**236**
Number of Sodas Sold:	**580**
Unit Cost of Soda:	**.32**

12. Save your revised worksheet as: **hockey game revenues, rev. 1**

13. Print your worksheet displaying the new values. Close the worksheet.

Independent Project 1.4: Planning a Budget

You are responsible for determining the **total amount of money** that should be budgeted for the purchase of sporting equipment for a girls' hockey program that will be added to the community athletic program. You need to purchase:

*   shirts (1 per person, as they will serve as the team uniform)

*   hockey sticks (1 per person plus a few extra)

*   balls (only one is used for a game, but you will want a few extras)

*   nets (2)

*   corner flags (4)

Unlike the previous projects, in this project you will perform all the steps in planning the worksheet. Then you will create the worksheet using test data. Use your own figures for the **number of each item** purchased and for the **costs of each item**. Don't worry about the accuracy of the numbers that you include. Save your worksheet using the name: **sports equipment**

The hockey program must be self-supporting. Therefore, you also need to include a calculation which determines how much each team member must pay to cover the costs of all of the equipment purchased. (**HINT**: The number of people on the team is equal to the number of shirts purchased.)

The completed project should include:

1. A statement of the general objectives of the worksheet. (See the section on **PLANNING A WORKSHEET** in the beginning of this lesson.)

2. A statement of the specific results you want the worksheet to provide;

3. A statement of the data needed to obtain the results;

4. A statement of the calculations to be performed on the data ;

5. A handwritten design of what the worksheet will look like;

6. A printout of the worksheet showing values;

7. A printout of the worksheet showing formulas;

Lesson 2

Enhancing a Worksheet

Objectives

In this lesson you will learn how to:

- Select a range of cells
- Change the format of value entries
- Change the alignment of labels
- Change fonts and font sizes

- Add bold, italics, and underlining
- Add borders to cells
- Enhance printouts by changing the page setup
- Check spelling

PROJECT DESCRIPTION

In Lesson 1 you created a simple worksheet, **employee billing**. The information it contains is correct, but it is hard to read and not very attractive. For example, the numbers in each column have a different number of decimal places, don't have commas separating thousands, and lack the formatting symbols that indicate if the numbers are dollars or percents. Similarly, the labels are not aligned over the numbers in the same column, the title isn't centered, and there is no variety in the font. In this lesson you will enhance **employee billing**, so that it is more attractive and more clearly conveys the information it contains. When you are finished, your worksheet will resemble Figure 2 - 1.

EMPLOYEE BILLING

Employee	Consulting Hours	Salary Rate	Total Salary	Billing Rate	Total Billed	Profit	% Profit
George Snidowski	32	$27.50	$880.00	$50	$1,600.00	$720.00	45.0%
Claire Corbow	41	$32.50	$1,332.50	$60	$2,460.00	$1,127.50	45.8%
Thomas Henderson	29	$42.50	$1,232.50	$75	$2,175.00	$942.50	43.3%

Figure 2 - 1

RANGES

Most of the changes that you want to make affect groups of cells. Therefore, instead of changing the format of each cell individually, you will apply most changes to a *range* of cells. In a worksheet a *range* refers to a rectangular block of cells that has been selected to be operated on as a whole (Figure 2 - 2). The range is selected first, and then the operation affecting the entire range is specified. The range remains selected until another cell or range is selected. Therefore, you may apply more than one command to a range without selecting it again.

There are many ways to select a range. The two most basic techniques are described below.

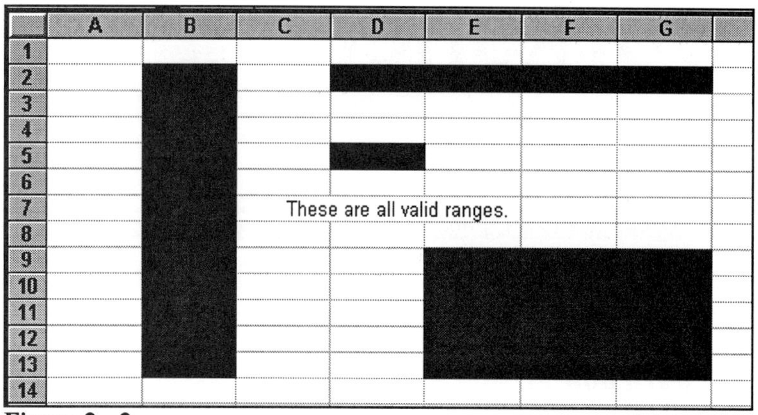

Figure 2 - 2

REMEMBER Read the bulleted list that follows, but do not actually perform the steps until you reach *Activity 1.1.*

To select a range of cells:

- To use the mouse, point to the cell at one corner of the range, click and drag the mouse until the highlight extends to the diagonally opposite corner of the range, *or*

- To use the keyboard, select the first cell of the range, hold down the **SHIFT** key and, keeping **SHIFT** depressed, use the **ARROW** keys to extend the highlight.

*Ranges are named by the upper left and bottom right cells in the range, separated by a colon (:). For example, the range that starts in **A3** and ends in **G7** is **A3:G7**.*

CAUTION: *The mouse pointer **must** be a ✛ when you begin highlighting cells to select a range. If the mouse pointer is an ↖ , you are pointing to the cell frame and will **move** the cell contents. If the mouse pointer is a ➕, you are pointing at the fill handle and will **copy** the cell contents.*

SELECTING MULTIPLE COLUMNS

In Lesson 1 you changed the width of individual columns. If you want to make the same change to more than one column, you must select the range of columns first.

To select more than one adjacent column:

- Point to the first column heading. Make sure the mouse pointer is a ✛ . Click and drag the mouse until all columns are highlighted. Release the mouse button.

FORMATTING CELLS

Making formatting changes is such a frequent activity that in the default setup the Formatting toolbar (Figure 2 - 3) is displayed in addition to the Standard toolbar. All the formatting changes that you wish to make can be made using this toolbar. They also can be made by selecting **FORMAT/Cells** from the menu. You will use both of these approaches in this lesson.

Figure 2 - 3

Activity 2.1: Becoming Familiar with the Formatting Toolbar

1. Start *Excel*. Maximize the *Excel* window if it is not already maximized.

2. If the Formatting toolbar (Figure 2 - 3) is NOT displayed, use **VIEW/Toolbars** to display it. (See Activity I.2 in the Introduction.)

    The Formatting toolbar is normally displayed near the top of the worksheet. However, it may be displayed at the bottom or sides of the worksheet (or as a block anywhere on the worksheet).

3. With the mouse, point to each of the buttons on the Formatting toolbar and read the name that appears below the toolbar and the description that appears on the Status Bar.

Most of the formatting changes that you want to make can be applied to both values and text. Before you look at those, however, you will look at changes that can only be applied to values.

Formatting Numbers

When numbers are typed into a cell, they appear exactly as entered, except that any zeroes that do not change the value of the number are dropped. This is the *general number format*. You want to format the numbers on the worksheet so that they contain a specified number of decimal places, commas to separate thousands, and dollar or percent signs, if appropriate. Three of the most common number formats can be accessed from the Formatting toolbar. Each one displays the currently defined style for the selected format. If the style definitions have not been changed in your copy of *Excel*, the styles are:

*   Currency style — commas to separate thousands, two decimal places, and a dollar sign ($); the dollar sign is on the *left side of the cell*

*   Percent style — multiplies the number in the cell by 100, and displays a percent sign and no decimal places

*   Comma style — displays commas to separate thousands and two decimal places

In all of the formats, the value that appears on the worksheet is rounded to the specified number of decimal places. However, the actual value is kept by *Excel* and used in all calculations. This can make your worksheet appear to be incorrect when it is really correct. For example if *2.4, 3.4,* and *4.4* are all formatted for zero decimal places they would appear as *2, 3,* and *4*. If these three cells are added, and the sum formatted for zero decimal places, the sum would be *10* (*10.2* rounded to no decimal places). Therefore, your worksheet would be correct, but would appear to say *2+3+4=10*!

To use the toolbar to format a number:

*   Select the cell or range of cells to be formatted.
*   Click on the **Currency Style** $, **Percent Style** %, or **Comma Style** , button.
*   If you want to change the number of decimals displayed, click on the **Increase Decimal** or **Decrease Decimal** button.

To use the Format menu to format a number:

*   Select the cell or range of cells to be formatted.

- Choose **FORMAT/Cells.**

- When the **Format Cells** dialog box is displayed, click on the **Number** tab.

- Click on the item in the **Category** list box that best describes the type of format you want to apply.

  Various list and check boxes will appear, depending on the category that you selected.

- Change the list and check boxes that appear until you have specified the format you wish to use.

- Click on **OK** to apply the number format.

Activity 2.2: Using the Toolbar to Apply Number Formats

In this activity, you will use the toolbar to format parts of your worksheet for Currency Style with two decimal places or Percent Style with one decimal place.

1. Open **employee billing**. Remember, you may need to make changes to the **Look in** box in the **Open** dialog box so that *Excel* specifies the location of your data files. If you need help doing this, refer to Activity 1.8 in Lesson 1.

2. Maximize **employee billing** if it is not already maximized.

3. To select the range **C5:D7**, point to **C5**, and click and drag the mouse across and down to cell **D7**; when the range **C5:D7** is highlighted, release the mouse button. Make sure that the mouse pointer is always this shape ⊕ .

PROBLEM SOLVER: *If you release the mouse button before the correct range is selected, use the **SHIFT+ARROW** keys to extend or contract the range. You cannot use the mouse unless you select the entire range again.*

*The range **C5:D7** will be highlighted (Figure 2 - 4). **C5** is in the **name box** (left-side of the Formula Bar) and has a white background while the rest of the range has a black background. **C5** is the active cell. If you were to begin typing, the data would be entered in **C5**. Any commands you choose will affect the entire range, **C5:D7**.*

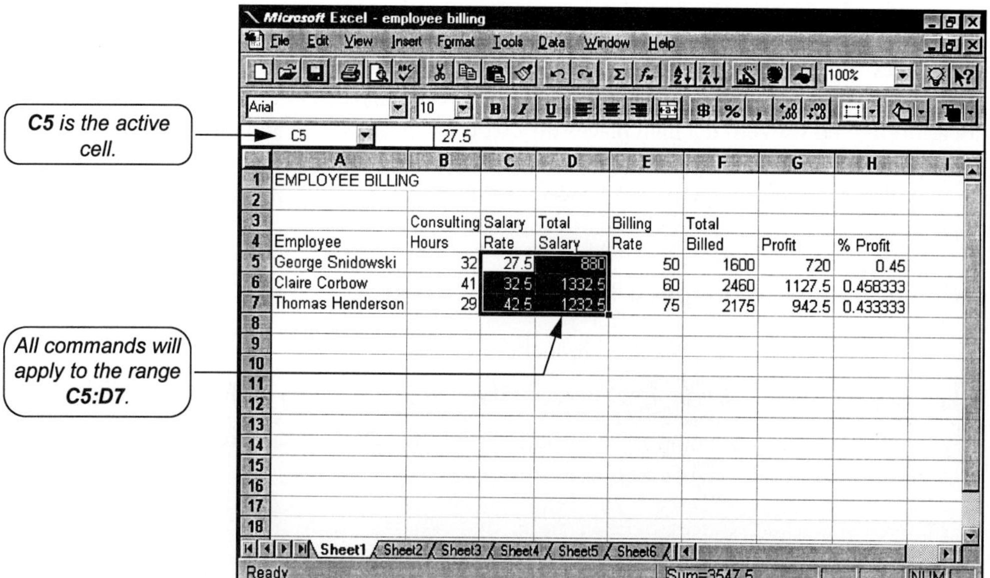

Figure 2 - 4

$ 4.   Click on the **Currency Style** button on the toolbar.

Are you surprised at what happened? All of the cells, except for the one containing George Snidowski's total salary are filled with ##### (Figure 2 - 5). As you saw in Lesson 1, when a label is too wide, it overflows into the next cell or is truncated. However, when a number is too wide to fit in a cell, the entire cell is filled with ###. To correct this you must widen the column. The easiest way to do this is to use the AutoFit feature that you learned in Lesson 1.

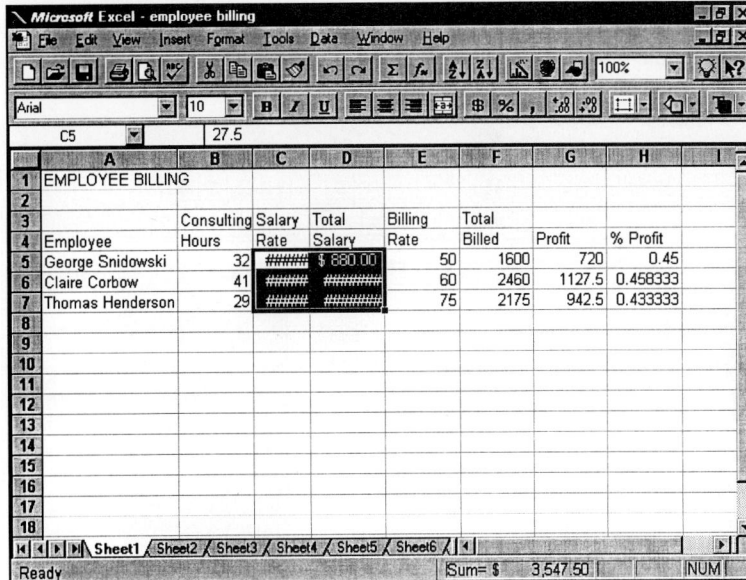

Figure 2 - 5

5.   To select both columns **C** and **D**, point to **C** in the column header, click and drag the highlight one column to the right until columns **C** and **D** are highlighted, and release the mouse button.

Make sure the mouse pointer looks like a ✛ . Columns C and D are selected (Figure 2 - 6).

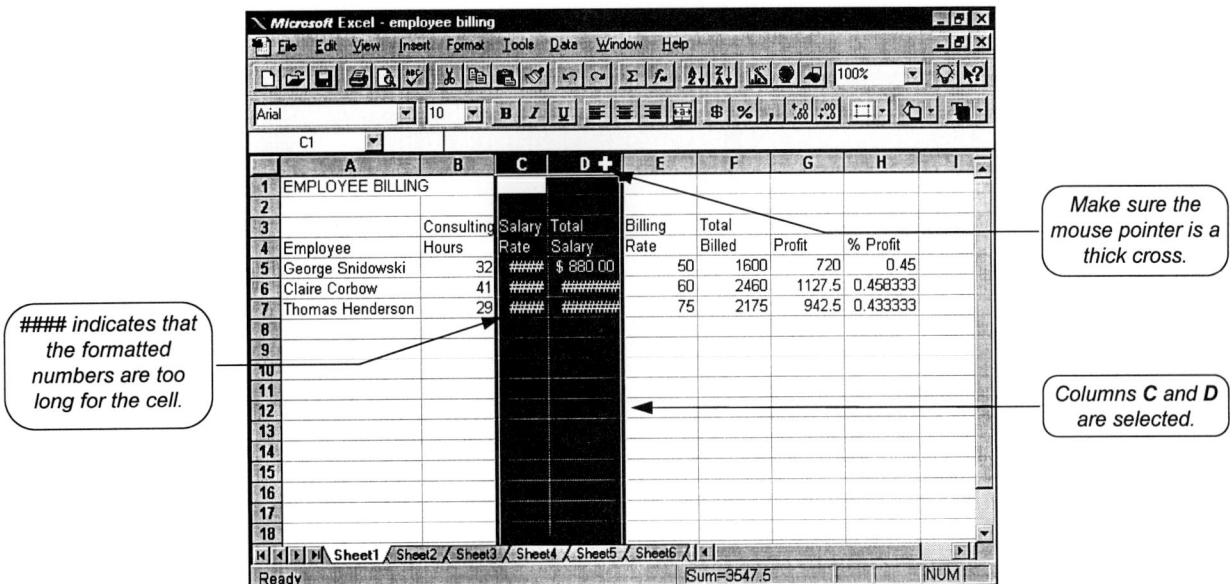

Figure 2 - 6

6.   Choose **FORMAT/Column, AutoFit Selection**.

*Columns **C** and **D** have increased in width so that all the entries are visible. All the numbers contain two decimal places even if they are zeroes. Dollar signs and commas also appear.*

7. To select the range **F5:G7**, point to cell **F5**, and click and drag the highlight to the right and down to cell **G7**.

8. Click on the **Currency Style** toolbar button.

9. Point to the **F** in the column header, and click and drag to highlight columns **F** and **G**.

10. Choose **FORMAT/Column, AutoFit Selection.** Unless someone has changed the default setting, the dollar signs will line up at the left edge of the cell (Figure 2 - 7).

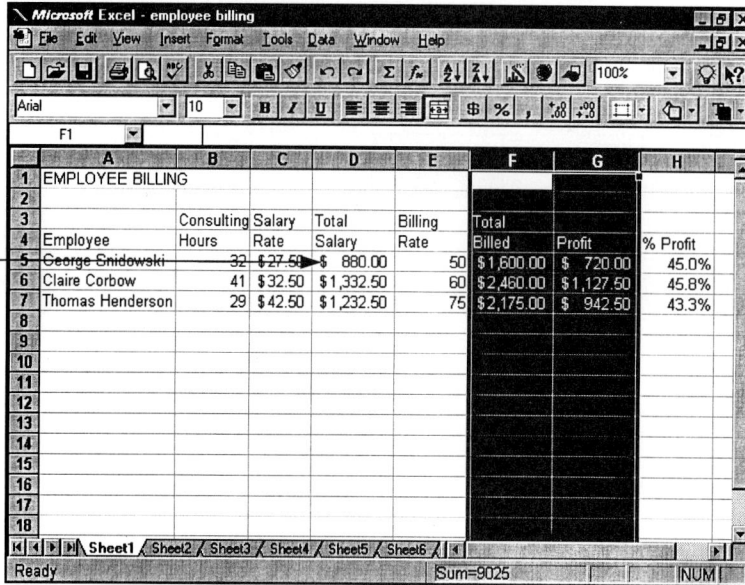

In Currency Style, $'s line up on left side of cell.

Figure 2 - 7

11. Use the mouse to select the range **H5:H7**.

12. Click on the **Percent Style** button.

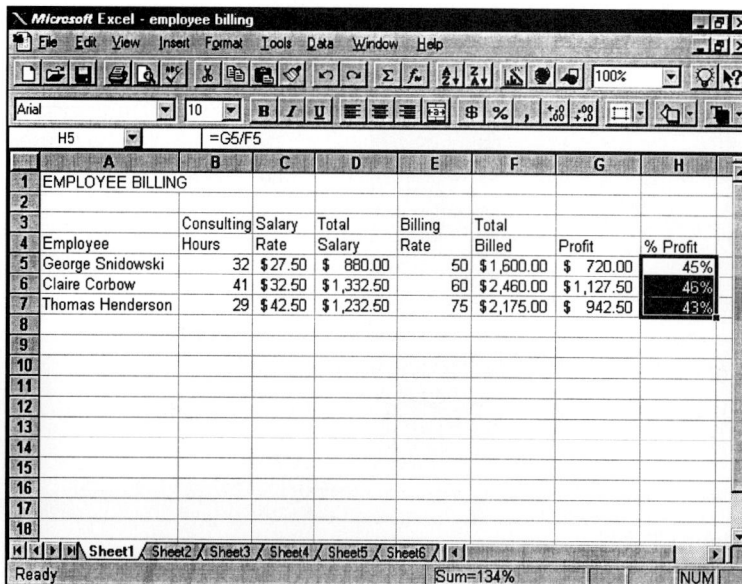

Figure 2 - 8

The cells containing the % Profit are formatted for percent with zero decimal places. All of these values are displayed because they fit within the column (Figure 2 - 8).

13. Cells **H5:H7** should still be highlighted. To display the percents with one decimal place, click on the **Increase Decimals** toolbar button once.

One decimal place will be displayed for each of the % Profits values.

14. Select **E5:E7**.

15. Format **E5:E7** for **Currency Style**. **Decrease Decimals** twice.

Currency Style, Currency Format, and Accounting Format

As you noticed in Activity 2.2, the Currency Style places the dollar sign at the left-hand side of the cell rather than next to the leftmost numeral. Since Release 5.0 of *Excel*, the **Currency Style** button applies the Accounting Format rather than the Currency Format (unless the default style has been changed on your computer). The main differences between the Currency and the Accounting Formats are that the Accounting Format aligns the $ with the left edge of the cell, displays negative numbers in parentheses, and displays zero values as a dash, while the Currency Format places the $ immediately to the left of the leftmost digit, displays zeros for a zero value, and lets you choose how to display negative numbers. In order to apply the Currency Format you must use the **Format** menu.

Activity 2.3: Using the Format Menu to Apply Number Formats

In this activity, you will use the **Format** menu to change the format of all the numbers that you previously formatted using the Currency Style.

1. Select the range **E5:E7**, if it is not already selected.

2. Choose **FORMAT/Cells**.

   *The **Format Cells** dialog box will be displayed. **Format Cells** is a **tabbed** dialog box, which means that it contains a number of related sheets. The **Number** tab will probably be highlighted and the number formatting options relating to the currently selected cells will be displayed. However, a different tab may be displayed on your screen.*

3. If the **Number** tab is not already selected, click on it to select it.

   *The **Category** list box on the **Number** tab indicates the current format of the selected cells (in this case, E5:E7). Notice that the **Custom** category has been selected. After you formatted E5:E7 for Currency Style in Activity 2.2, you decreased the number of decimal places, thus creating a "custom" format.*

4. Click on **Currency** in the **Category** list box.

   The Currency category (Figure 2 - 9)allows you to specify the number of decimal places, the use of the $, and the format for negative numbers. Since you want to format E5:E7 for 0 decimal places, the use of the $, and the use of parentheses to indicate negative numbers, you will need to make several changes to the dialog box.

5. Click on the down triangle ▼ at the right of the **Decimal Places** box until the number of decimal places to be displayed is **0**.

   *Notice that the number of decimal places in the **Negative Numbers** box changes to zero. The **Negative Numbers** box also serves as a Sample box showing you how your numbers will look with the selected formatting.*

6. Click on the **Use $** check box to mark it with a check.

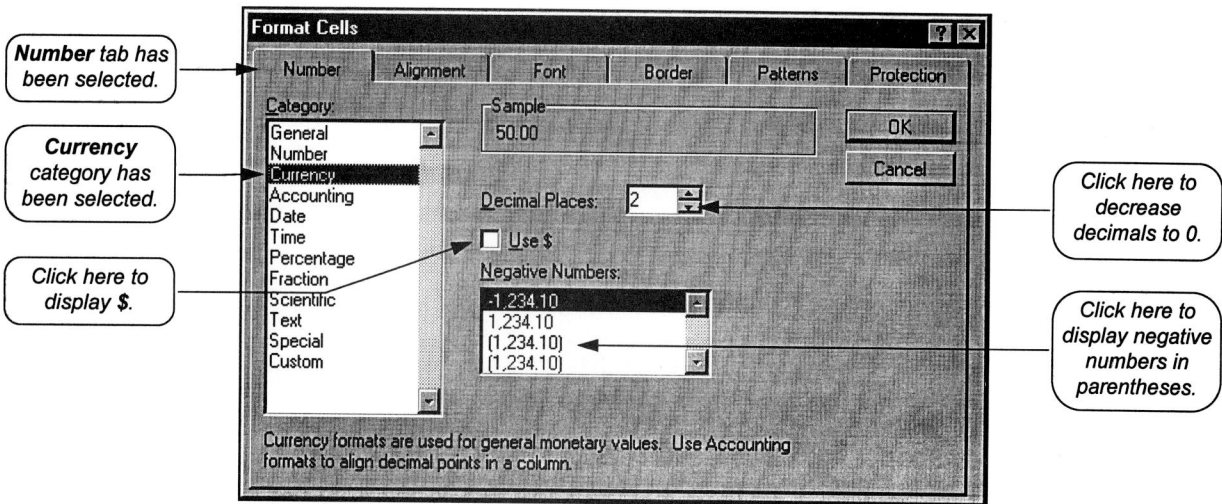

Number *tab has been selected.*

Currency *category has been selected.*

Click here to display $.

Click here to decrease decimals to 0.

Click here to display negative numbers in parentheses.

Figure 2 - 9

7. Click on the entry in the **Negative Numbers** box that indicates the use of parentheses, but *not* the color red to indicate negative numbers.

8. The **Format Cells** dialog box should resemble Figure 2 - 10. If it does not, repeat steps 5-7 until it does. Then click on **OK**.

    *Your screen should resemble Figure 2 - 11. Notice the different placement of the $ in cells with **Currency Format (E5:E7)** and **Currency Style (Accounting Format)(C5:D7, F5:G7)**.*

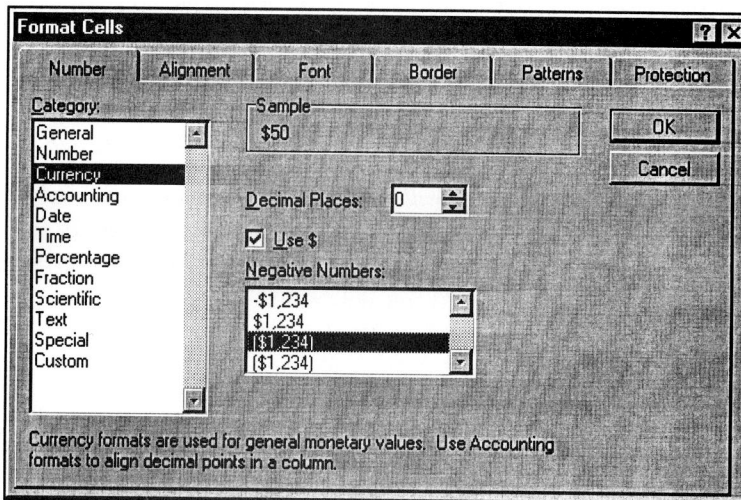

Figure 2 - 10

9. Select the range **C5:D7**.

10. Choose **FORMAT/Cells,Number**.

    *The **Accounting** category will be highlighted in the **Category** list box. **C5:D7** was previously formatted using the **Currency Style** toolbar button, which applies the **Accounting** format.*

11. Click on **Currency** in the **Category** list box.

12. The dialog box should specify **2** decimal places, the presence of the **$,** and the negative number format that uses parentheses but does not display the numbers in red. If it does, click on **OK**. If different values are selected, use the instructions in steps 6 - 7 to change them. (The dialog box should match Figure 2 - 10, except that the number of **Decimal Places** should be **2**.) Click on **OK**.

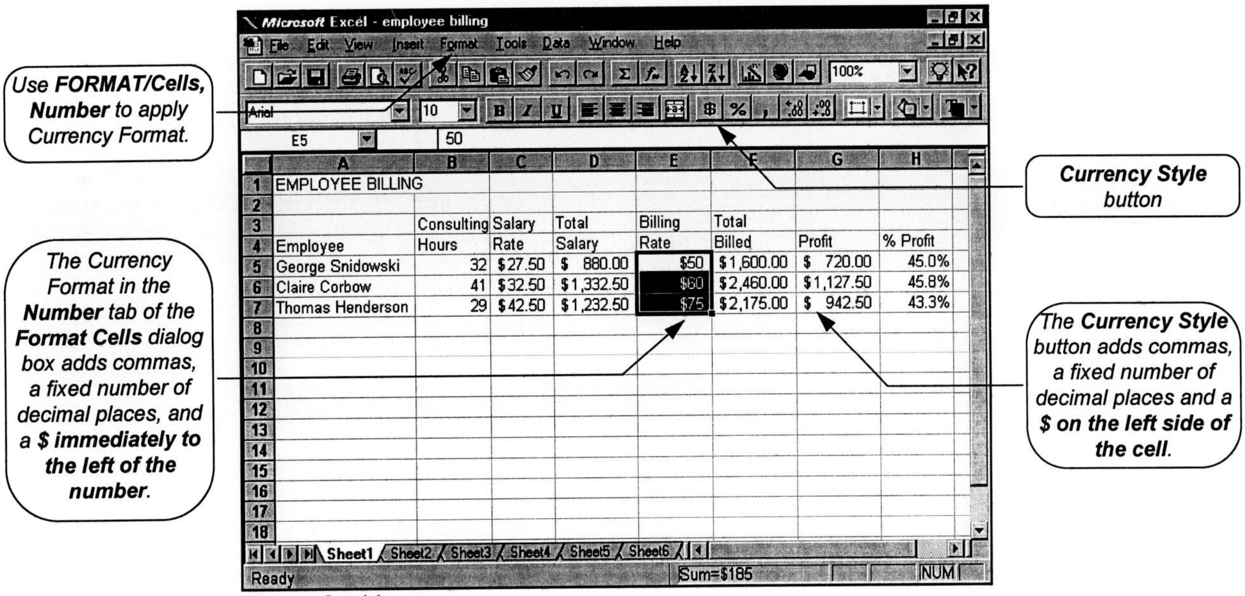

Use FORMAT/Cells, Number to apply Currency Format.

The Currency Format in the Number tab of the Format Cells dialog box adds commas, a fixed number of decimal places, and a $ immediately to the left of the number.

Currency Style button

The Currency Style button adds commas, a fixed number of decimal places and a $ on the left side of the cell.

Figure 2 - 11

13. Select the range **F5:G7** and use **FORMAT/Cells,Number** to apply the same Currency Format you applied to cells **C5:D7**. If you need help refer to steps **10 - 12**.

   All of the currency values are now formatted with Currency Format. The $ in cells C5:G7 should be immediately to the left of the number as in Figure 2 - 12.

Changing Cell Alignment

You are going to change the *horizontal alignment* of the labels in the cell. The alignment determines if the text is displayed aligned with the left or right side of the cell or centered within the cell. In addition, if a range of cells is selected and text is contained only in the leftmost cell(s) in the range, that text may be centered across the entire range.

It is possible to change the horizontal alignment of values, but this is not good to do. Values should always be right-aligned in a cell. Do you know why?

To change the horizontal alignment of text:

• Select the cell or range of cells containing the labels to be aligned. If you want to align a title over a range of cells, the title must be in the leftmost cell in the range.

• Click on the **Align Left** , **Center** , **Align Right** , or **Center Across Columns** buttons on the Formatting toolbar.

Activity 2.4: Changing Text Alignment

Since text is left-aligned and values are right-aligned automatically when they are entered, the column labels for columns containing values are not aligned with the numbers underneath them. In addition, the title of the worksheet, EMPLOYEE BILLING, is not centered over the rest of the worksheet. You will change these alignments.

1. Select the range **B3:H4**.

2. Click on the **Align Right** toolbar button.

*The labels in columns **B** through **H** are right-aligned. In columns **C:G**, the labels are closer to the right side of the cell than are the numbers under them (Figure 2 - 12). Those numbers are formatted for Currency, which displays negative numbers enclosed in right parentheses. Therefore, if the number is positive, the rightmost space in the cell is empty.*

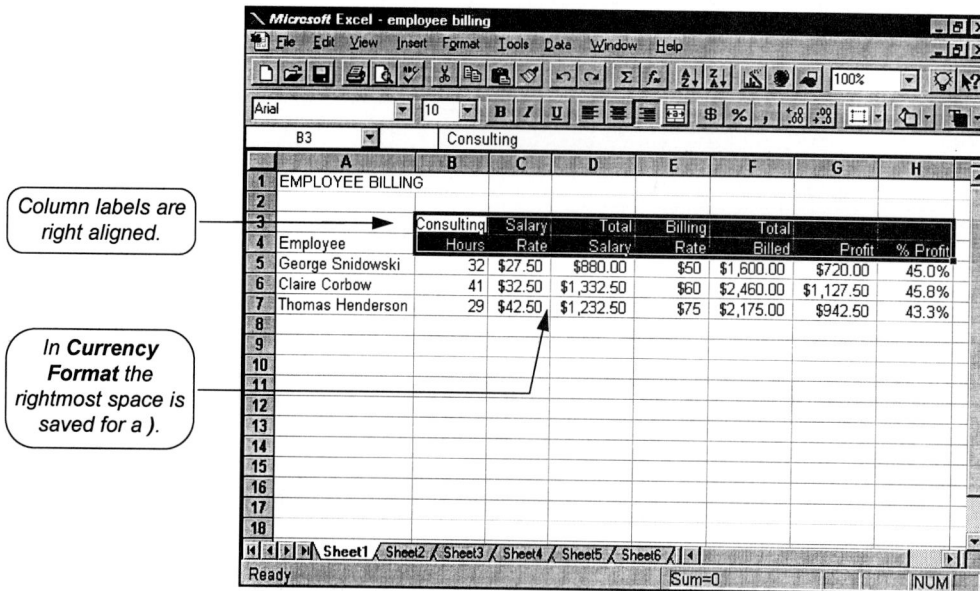

Column labels are right aligned.

In **Currency Format** the rightmost space is saved for a).

Figure 2 - 12

3. Select the range **A1:H1**.

    EMPLOYEE BILLING is in cell **A1**. The rest of the range is blank.

4. Click on the **Center Across Columns** toolbar button.

    EMPLOYEE BILLING is centered across columns **A:H**. The vertical gridlines in Row **1** in the selected range have been removed. **EMPLOYEE BILLING** also appears in the Formula Bar.

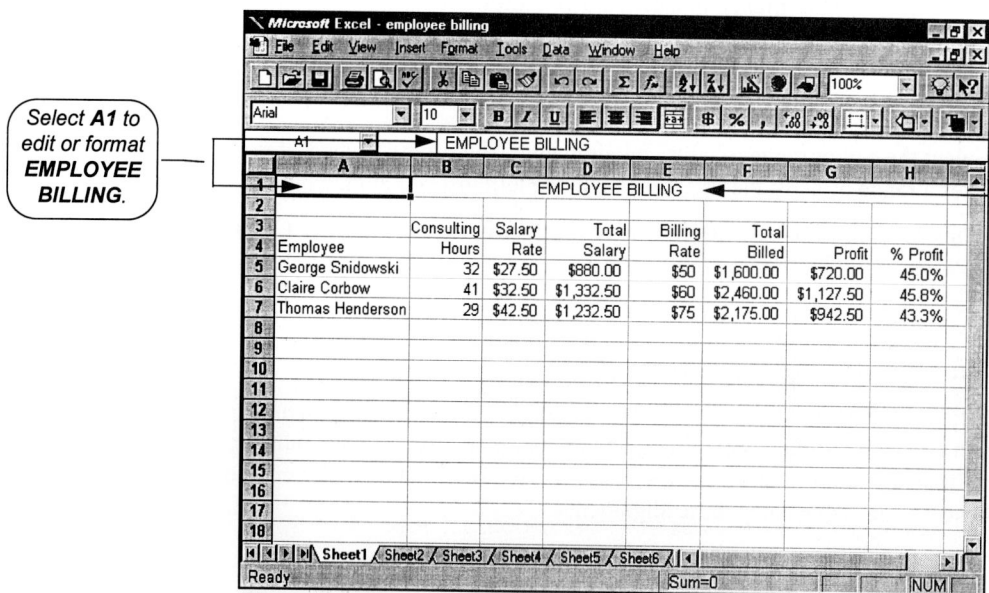

Select **A1** to edit or format **EMPLOYEE BILLING**.

Missing vertical gridlines show that **EMPLOYEE BILLING** is centered across columns.

Figure 2 - 13

> ✓ **PROBLEM SOLVER:** *If no gridlines are displayed anywhere on the worksheet, select* **TOOLS/Options.** *Click on the* **View** *tab. Click on the* **Gridlines** *check box if it is not already marked.*

5. Click on cell **D1** and look at the Formula Bar.

   The Formula Bar is empty.

6. Click on **A1** and look at the Formula Bar (Figure 2 - 13).

   EMPLOYEE BILLING *is displayed in the Formula Bar. If you want to edit or apply any other commands to* **EMPLOYEE BILLING,** *you must select A1.*

Let's save your file now, so that you won't lose any of your work.

Activity 2.5: Saving a File Using a New Name

1. To save the file to a new filename, select **FILE/Save As.**

   The **Save As** *dialog box should be displayed. The* **File name** *text box should contain the highlight (Figure 2 - 14).*

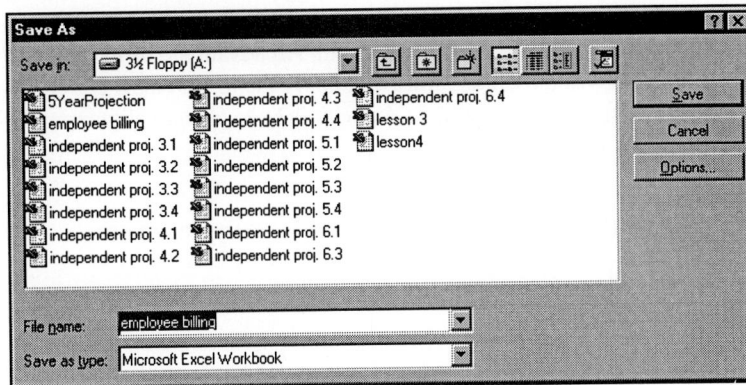

Figure 2 - 14

2. Press the **RIGHT ARROW** key on your keyboard once. This should remove the highlight and place the insertion point at the end of the current name. Type: **, rev. 1** If the **File name** box resembles Figure 2 - 15, click on **Save.**

> ✓ **PROBLEM SOLVER:** *If the file name is not highlighted, simply click at the end of the file name to correctly position the insertion point.*

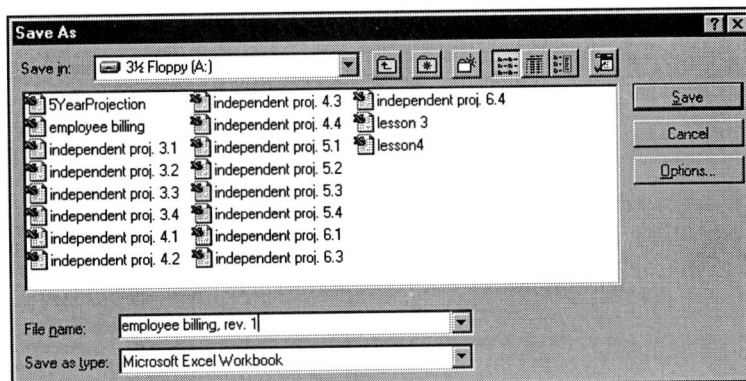

Figure 2 - 15

3. If the **Properties** dialog box appears, click on **OK.**

*The Status Bar will indicate that the file is being saved. When the save is complete, the Title Bar will say: **Microsoft Excel - employee billing, rev. 1***

Remember, anytime that you want to take a break, save your worksheet and exit Excel. Start Excel and reopen the worksheet when you are ready to continue working.

Changing Font, Font Size, and Font Style

The font is the design or typeface of the characters. Font sizes are typically measured in *points*, where each point is 1/72 of an inch. Point sizes between 10 and 12 are commonly used for the body of the worksheet, with larger fonts used for titles. Each font can be displayed in a variety of sizes and styles. The font styles are regular, **bold**, and *italics*. Bold and italics are usually used to emphasize the characters. Underlining can also be used for emphasis. The default *Excel* font is Arial, 10 point.

Windows comes with a set of fonts called TrueType fonts. These should be installed in *Windows* and then are available for all *Windows* applications to use regardless of the printer you are using. These fonts are also displayed on your screen the way they will look when they are printed. In this book we will limit our choices to TrueType fonts.

The five leftmost buttons on the Formatting toolbar control the font, font size, and font style (bold, italics, and underline) enhancements. In addition, the font, font size, and font style can be changed using the **FORMAT/Cells** command. An advantage of **FORMAT/Cells** is that you can see what the fonts will look like before you apply them. **FORMAT/Cells** can also be used to change number format (as you saw in Activity 2.3), to change alignment, and to add borders around cells.

To change font, font size, and font style using menus:

- Select the cell or range of cells to be formatted.

- Choose **FORMAT/Cells**.

- When the **Format Cells** dialog box is displayed, click on the **Font** tab.

- Use the **Font, Font Style,** and **Size** list boxes to make your changes. Use the **Underline** list box to add underlining.

- Click on **OK** to apply the format changes.

To change font, font size, and font style using the Formatting toolbar:

- Select the cell or range of cells to be formatted.

- To change the font style click on the **Bold** [**B**] , **Italic** [*I*] , or **Underline** [<u>U</u>] button.

- To change **Font Name** [Arial ▼] , or **Font Size** [10 ▼] , click on the [▼] to the right of the button, and click on your selection.

Activity 2.6: Changing Font, Font Size, and Font Style

You will use **FORMAT/Cells,Font** to change the font, font size, and font style of the employee data to Times New Roman, 10 point regular and the column headings to Arial, 12 point bold. You will then use the toolbar to change EMPLOYEE BILLING to Arial, 14 point, bold italics.

1. Select the range **A5:H7**.

2. Choose **FORMAT/Cells**.

   *If you have been following the activities in this book without closing the worksheet, the **Number** tab will be selected as it was the last one used.*

3. Click on the **Font** tab.

The font formatting choices will be displayed (Figure 2 - 16).

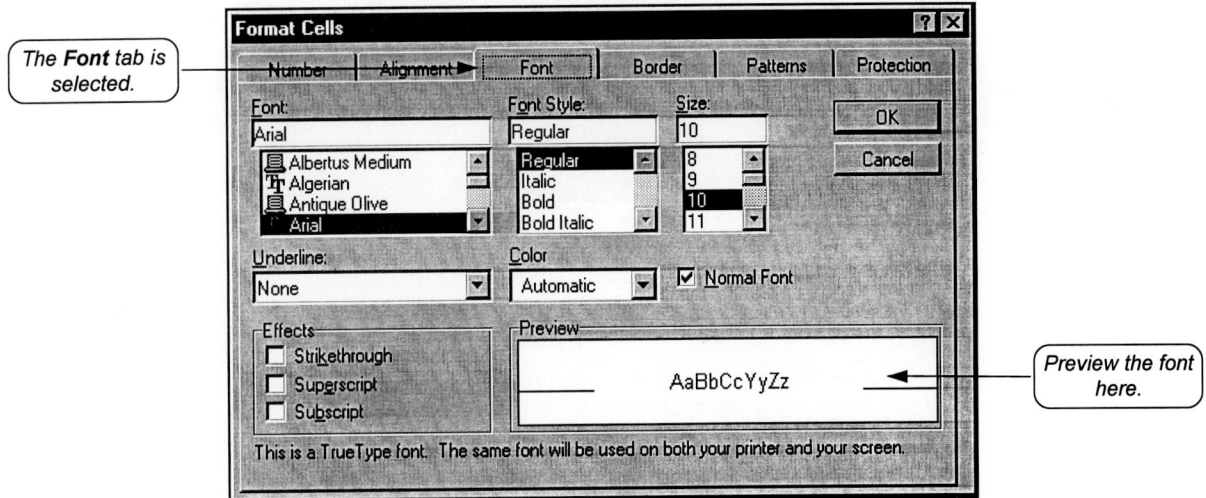

Figure 2 - 16

4. In the **Font** list box, click on **Arial**, which should already be selected (see Figure 2 - 16). Press the **DOWN ARROW** key on the keyboard. As each new font is selected, you will be able to preview it in the **Preview** area of the dialog box.

5. After previewing the fonts, use the arrow keys to select the **Times New Roman** TrueType font.

6. Click on **Regular** in the **Font Style** list box and **10** in the **Size** box (Figure 2 - 17) if they are not already selected.

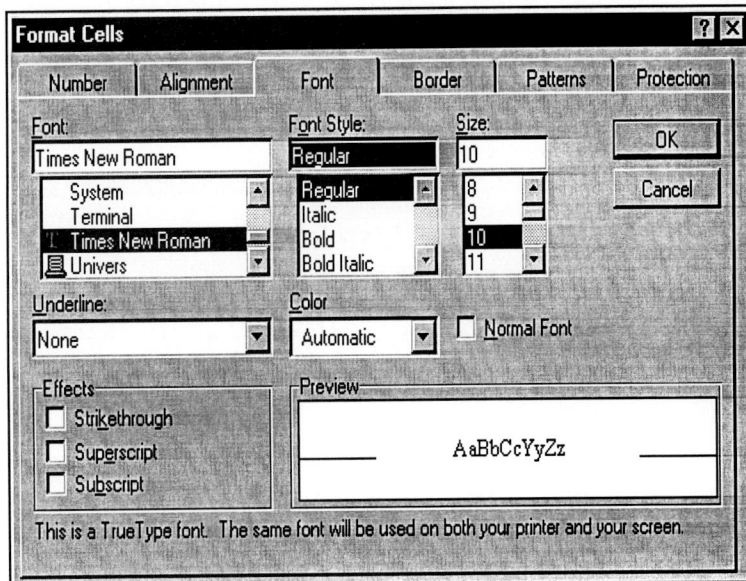

Figure 2 - 17

7. When the **Format Cells** dialog box resembles Figure 2 - 17, click on **OK** or press the **ENTER** key.

*Your screen should resemble Figure 2 - 18. Even though you changed the font using a menu command, the **Font** toolbar button changes to reflect the new font.*

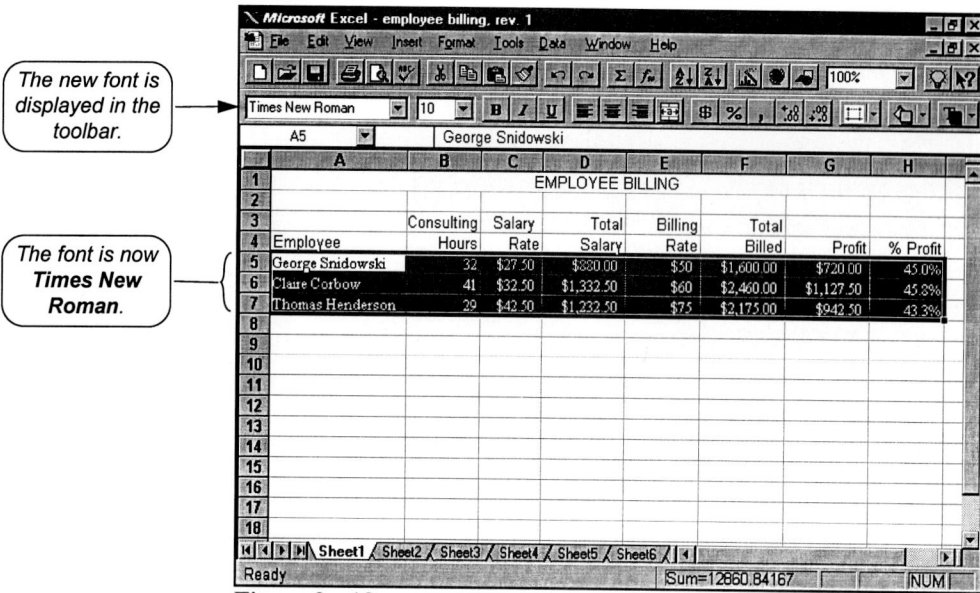

The new font is displayed in the toolbar.

The font is now *Times New Roman*.

Figure 2 - 18

8. Select the range **A3:H4**.

    Ranges must be rectangles, so you must include A3 in the range even though it is blank.

9. Choose **FORMAT/Cells**.

    The Font tab should be displayed as Excel displays the last tab used.

10. Change the font size to **12** and the font style to **Bold**. Click on **OK**.

    PROBLEM SOLVER: *If the 12 is not visible in the Size list box, click on the [▼] on the scroll bar until the 12 is visible.*

    Consulting is now too wide to fit in column B. Since it is right-aligned, it overflows into A3, the cell to its left. Parts of the other column labels may be hidden because they have no adjacent blank cells in which to overflow (Figure 2 - 19).

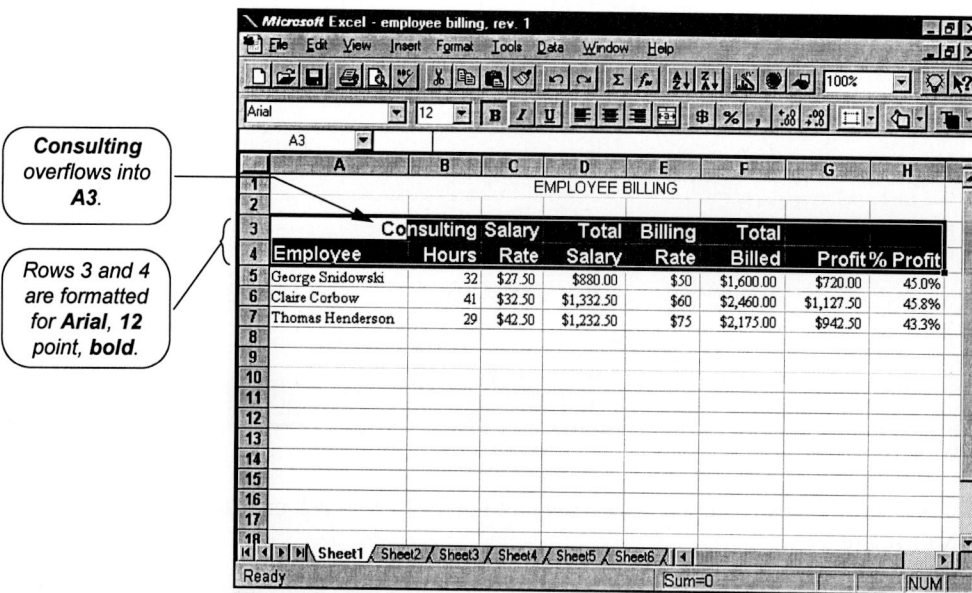

Consulting overflows into *A3*.

Rows 3 and 4 are formatted for *Arial, 12 point, bold*.

Figure 2 - 19

11. Point to the **A** in the column header, and click and drag to highlight columns **A:H**. Choose **FORMAT/Column/AutoFit Selection** to make all of the columns wide enough to display their contents.

12. To change the font size for the worksheet title, click on cell **A1**.

13. To use the toolbar to change font size, click on the ![arrow] to the right of the **Font Size** button on the Formatting toolbar. A list of font sizes is displayed (Figure 2 - 20).

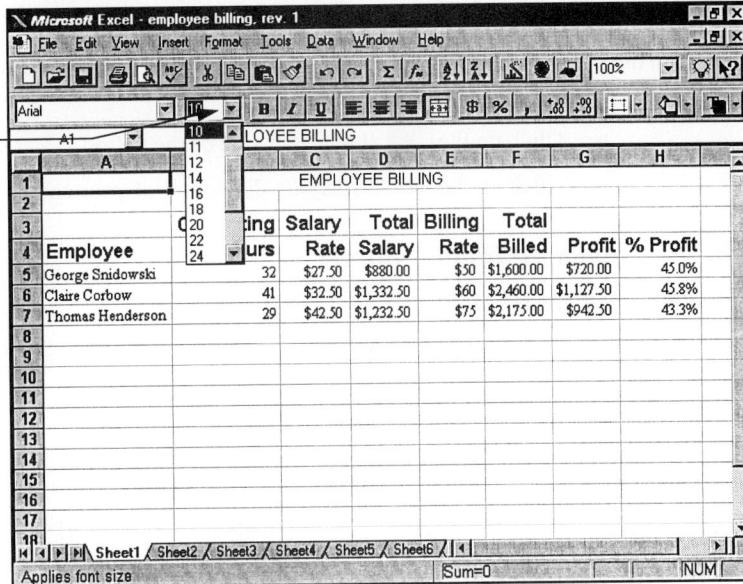

Figure 2 - 20

14. Click on **14**.

Notice that the height of the row automatically increases to fit the larger font size.

15. With your cursor still in **A1**, click on the **Bold** toolbar button.

16. Click on the **Italic** toolbar button (Figure 2 - 21).

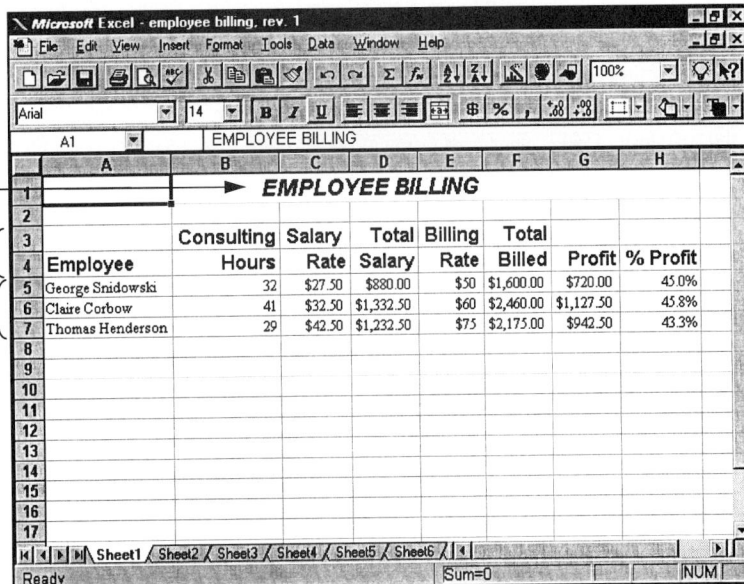

Figure 2 - 21

Adding Cell Borders

Often you want to draw a line under or around certain cells. In your worksheet, you would like a line under the column labels so that they are separated from the data. To do this you want to add a border to the bottom of the cells containing the column labels. You can do this using the **FORMAT/Cells,Borders** dialog box or by using the **Borders** toolbar button ⬛.

To add cell borders using the toolbar:

- Select the cell or range of cells.

- If the **Borders** toolbar button ⬛ shows the border you want to use, click on the button. If it does not:

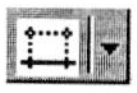

  o Click on the ▼ at the right side of the button.

  o Click on the icon displaying the border of your choice.

Activity 2.7: Adding a Bottom Border

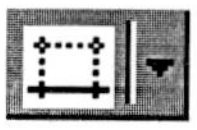

1. Select the range, **A4:H4**.

2. Click on the ▼ to the right of the **Borders** button.

   Twelve border choices will be displayed (Figure 2 - 22).

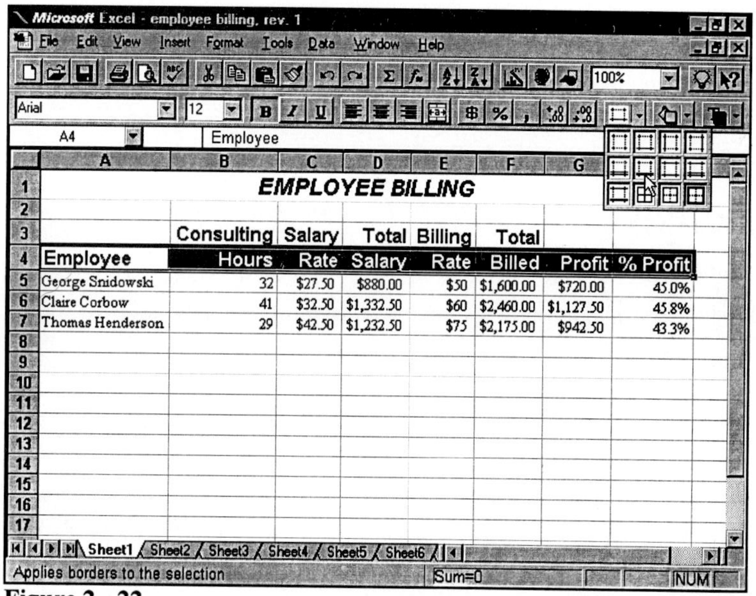

Figure 2 - 22

3. Click on the thick bottom underline border shown in Figure 2 - 22 (middle row, second from left).

4. Click on any cell in the worksheet to remove the highlight from cells **A4:H4**.

5. Click on the **Save** toolbar button to save your worksheet again using the existing file name and location.

MORE PRINTING

In Lesson 1 you printed your worksheet using the default page setup. However, parts of the printout — like the headers and footers — made the printout less attractive than it could have been. In this lesson you will learn to change the appearance of the printout. The print options are changed using the **Page Setup** command. **Page Setup** can be reached directly from the **FILE** menu or from the **FILE/Print Preview** dialog box.

Previewing a Document

Previewing a document lets you decide if you like the way it will look before you print it. If you don't, you can change it before printing.

To preview a document:

Choose **FILE/Print Preview** or click the **Print Preview** button on the Standard toolbar. The Status Bar on the bottom of the Preview Window (Figure 2 - 23) indicates the current page and the total number of pages in the printout. The screen does not contain any menus. However, it has eight buttons that can be used to work with the document:

- **Next** – displays the next page of a multi-page printout
- **Previous** — displays the previous page of a multi-page printout
- **Zoom** — switches between a magnified view and a full page view
- **Print** — displays the **Print** dialog box
- **Setup** — displays the **Page Setup** dialog box
- **Margins** — turns on or off "handles," which can be dragged to change margins
- **Close** — closes the Preview Window and displays the active worksheet
- **Help** — displays a **Help** screen

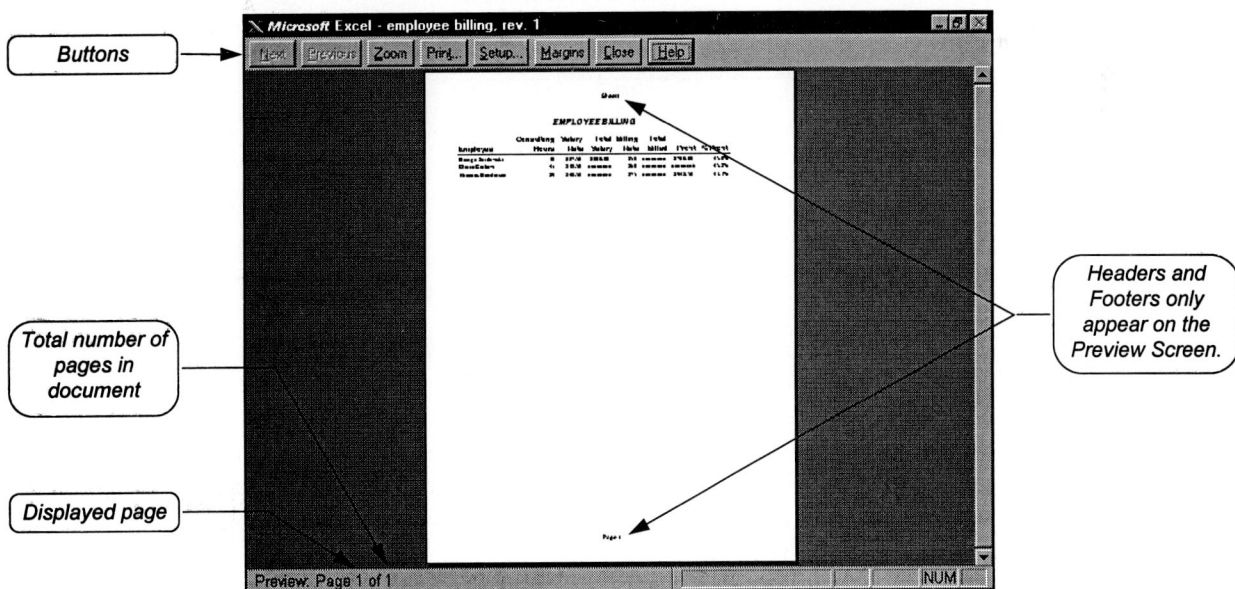

Figure 2 - 23

Activity 2.8: Previewing the Printout

1. Choose **FILE/Print Preview** or click on the **Print Preview** toolbar button.

*The **Print Preview** screen will be displayed (Figure 2 - 23). The preview shows two lines of text that did not appear on the worksheet but will appear on each page of the printout: a header that will appear on the top of each page, and a footer that will appear on the bottom of each page.*

> ✓ **PROBLEM SOLVER:** *If the Status Bar indicates that there are two pages (e.g., Preview: Page 1 of 2), click on the **Close** button. The worksheet will reappear. See if any of the columns can be made narrower so that the worksheet will fit on one page. Choose **FILE/Print Preview**.*

2. Click on the **Zoom** button.

   Even though all of the columns on the worksheet appeared wide enough to display the contents, sometimes print preview indicates that they are not wide enough for the data to be printed. If this is true, as Figure 2 - 24 indicates, part of your worksheet may contain ### instead of data. The ### shown in Figure 2 - 24 may not appear on your screen, depending on your printer.

3. If ### do not appear in **Print Preview** on your screen, go to step 6. If ### do appear click on the **Margins** button.

   Lines indicating page, header, and footer margins, and handles used to adjust the margins and column widths, appear (Figure 2 - 24).

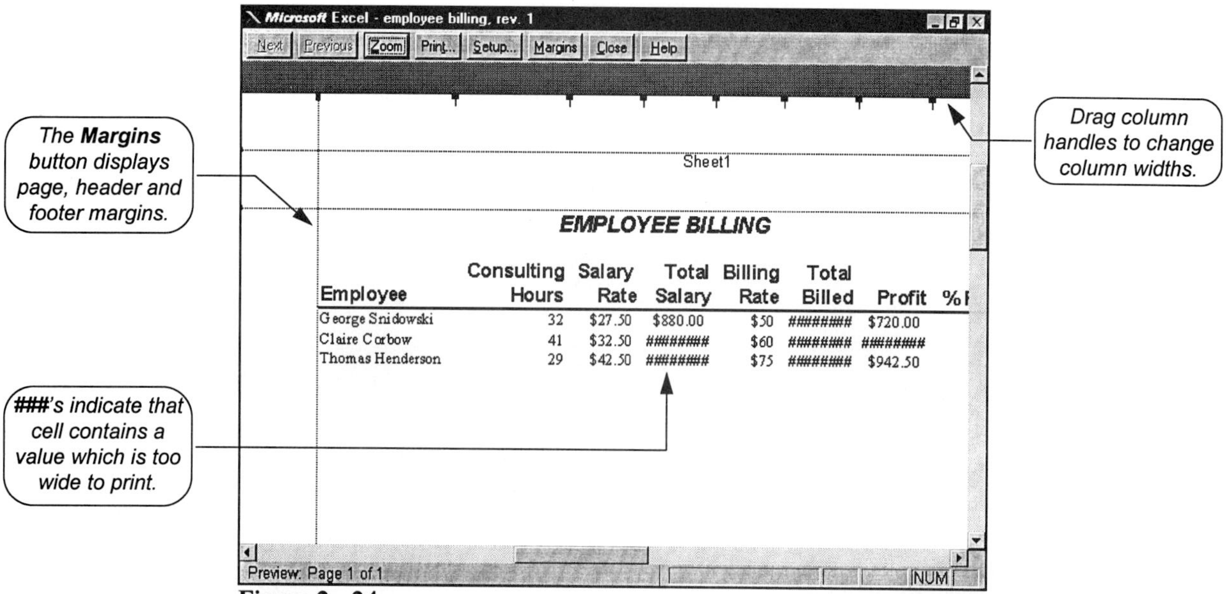

Figure 2 - 24

4. Click on the handle to the right of any column in which labels are truncated or numbers replaced by ###. When the mouse pointer changes to a crosshair ✛, click and drag slightly to the right. Repeat, if necessary, until the full contents of the column is displayed and there is minimal blank space.

   *Any margin changes made in **Print Preview** will change the column widths in the worksheet.*

> ✓ **PROBLEM SOLVER:** *If you cannot see the column handles, use the Vertical Scroll Bar to display the top of the worksheet.*

> ✓ **PROBLEM SOLVER:** *Check that the Status Bar still says Page 1 of 1. If it says Page 1 of 2 (or 2 of 2) you have increased column widths too much. Use the column handles to decrease widths.*

5. Click on **Margin** again to remove the margin lines and handles.

6. Click on **Zoom** again to return to full page view.

Changing the Page Setup

The **Page Setup** dialog box is used to change the appearance of the printout. It does not change the appearance of the worksheet itself.

To change the appearance of a printout:

*   Choose **FILE/Page Setup** or choose **FILE/Print Preview** and then click on the **Setup** button.

*   Make the desired changes in the **Page Setup** dialog box and click on **OK**.

Activity 2.9: Changing the Page Setup

1. If the Preview Window is no longer displayed, choose **PRINT/Preview.**

2. Click on the **Setup** button.

    *The **Page Setup** dialog box appears. Like the **Font** dialog box, **Page Setup** contains multiple tabs.*

3. Click on the **Header/Footer** tab.

    *The **Header/Footer** tab options are displayed (Figure 2 - 25). You will delete the current header and create a custom footer to replace the current one.*

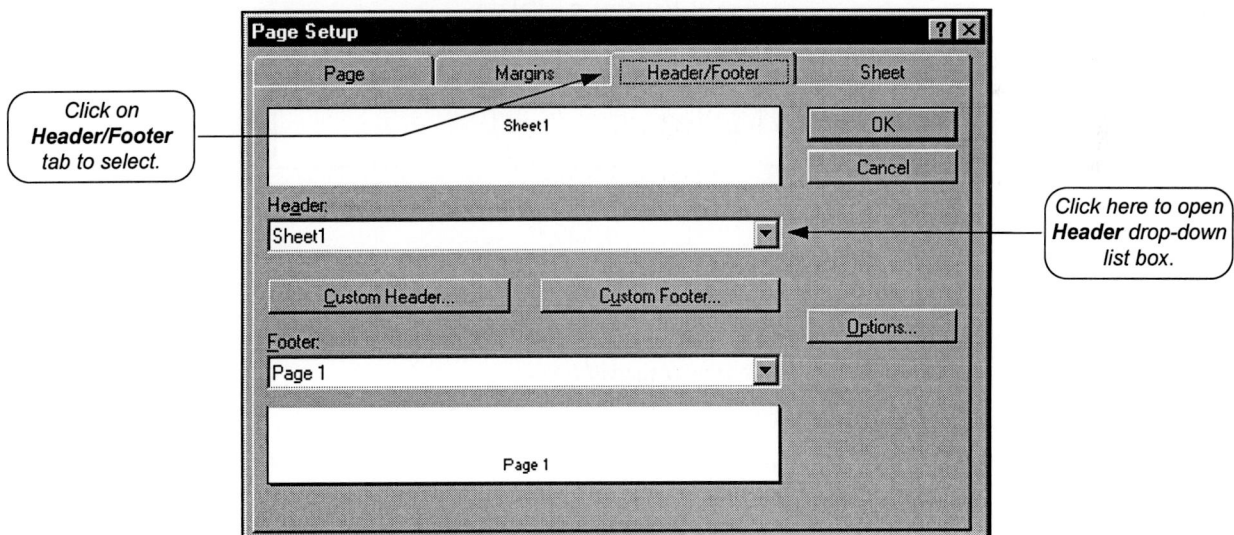

Figure 2 - 25

4. Click on the ▼ on the right side of the **Header** drop-down list box.

    The list contains built-in headers created by Excel.

5. Click on the ▲ on the scroll bar until the first item, **(none)**, is displayed (Figure 2 - 26). Click on **(none)** to select it.

6. Click on the **Custom Footer** button.

    *The **Footer** dialog box is displayed.*

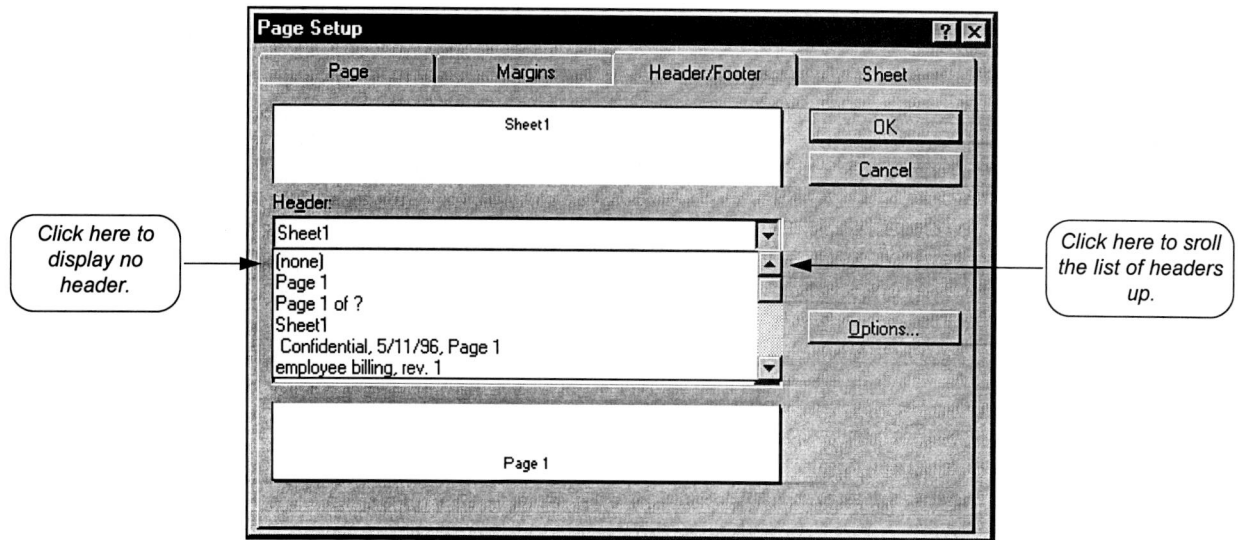

Click here to display no header. →

Click here to sroll the list of headers up. ←

Page Setup

| Page | Margins | Header/Footer | Sheet |

Sheet1

OK

Cancel

Header:

Sheet1

(none)
Page 1
Page 1 of ?
Sheet1
Confidential, 5/11/96, Page 1
employee billing, rev. 1

Options...

Page 1

Figure 2 - 26

7. Point to **Page &[Page]** in the **Center Section** text box. Click and drag the mouse across **Page &[Page]** until it is highlighted (Figure 2 - 27).

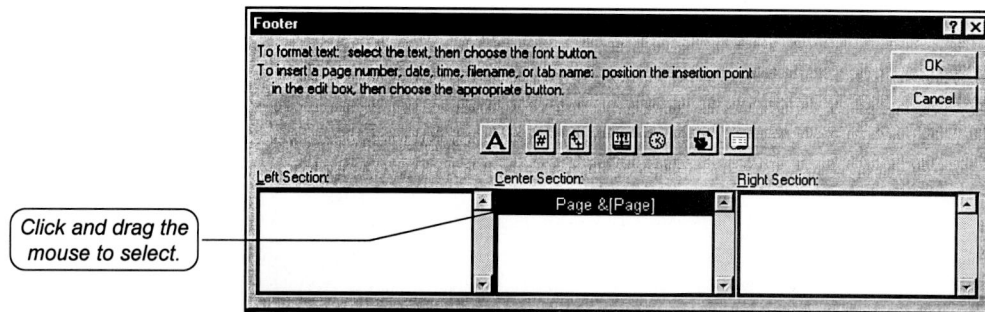

Footer

To format text: select the text, then choose the font button.
To insert a page number, date, time, filename, or tab name: position the insertion point in the edit box, then choose the appropriate button.

OK

Cancel

Left Section: Center Section: Right Section:

Click and drag the mouse to select.

Page &[Page]

Figure 2 - 27

8. Type: **Created by: (your name)**

   Created by: (your name) *will replace* **Page &[Page]** *in the center section. If your name is long Excel will continue it on a second line.*

9. Click on **OK** to leave the **Footer** dialog box.

   The **Page Setup** *dialog box will reappear on the screen. The Footer* **Created by: (your name)** *will be in the* **Footer** *text box.*

10. Click on **OK** to return to the Preview window.

   The original header should not be displayed (Figure 2 - 28). To read the **Footer,** *click on it. (The mouse pointer works like the zoom button when it is on the document.)*

11. Click on the **Print** button.

   The same **Print** *dialog box that you saw in Lesson 1 will be displayed.*

12. Click on **OK** to print your worksheet.

13. Choose **FILE/Close.**

   An alert box will be displayed asking if you want to save your worksheet.

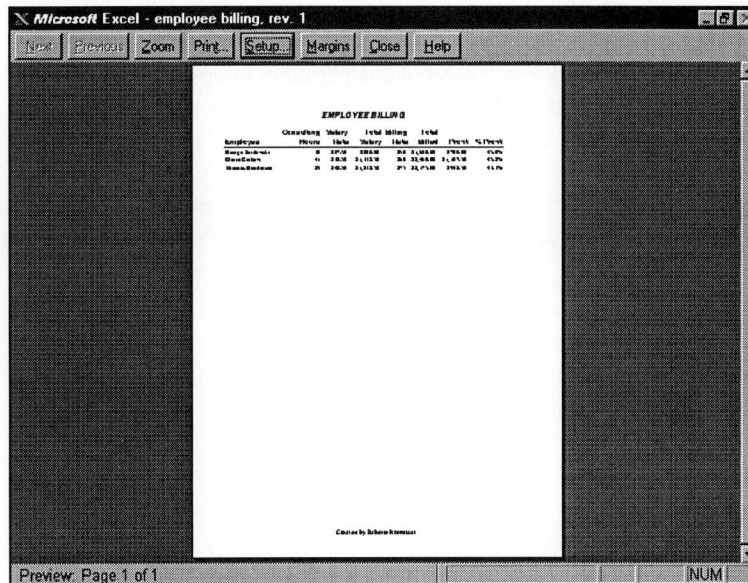

Figure 2 - 28

14. Click on **Yes** to save your worksheet again. If you do *not* save the worksheet, the page setup changes will not be saved.

SUMMARY

In this lesson you learned how to use formatting and page setup commands to enhance the appearance of your worksheet. The **employee billing, rev. 1** worksheet is now complete. However, in Lesson 6 we will add a pie chart to the worksheet so that your data can also be presented pictorially. The Independent Projects will give you practice in formatting and will introduce a new skill, spell checking.

KEY TERMS

Accounting Format	Decrease Decimals	Headers
Align left	Font	Increase decimals
Align right	Font size	Label alignment
Borders	Font style	Number tab
Center	Footers	Page setup
Center across columns	Format	Percent Style
Comma Style	Formatting toolbar	Point
Currency Format	General number format	Preview
Currency Style	Handles	Range

INDEPENDENT PROJECTS

The four independent projects allow you to practice using ranges and enhancing the worksheets that you created in the independent projects in Lesson 1. You will review formatting of value entries, changing label alignments, changing fonts, font sizes, and font styles, and adding borders to cells. You will also review the use of **Page Setup** to change the appearance of your printouts and learn a few page setup changes not introduced in this lesson. You will also learn how to check the spelling of your worksheet. You will find the spell checking procedure very similar to that used in *Windows* word processors, particularly *Microsoft Word for Windows*.

Independent Project 2.1: Enhancing Your Department Budget

In Independent Project 1.1 you created a department budget. In this project you will format the budget so that it is easier to read and more attractive. When you are finished your worksheet should resemble Figure 2 - 29.

DEPARTMENT BUDGET				
1995/1996 AND 1996/1997				
Category	1995/1996	1996/1997	Increase	% Increase
Faculty	$ 300,000	$ 338,000	$ 38,000	12.7%
Staff	$ 45,000	$ 47,500	$ 2,500	5.6%
Hardware/Software	$ 15,000	$ 40,000	$ 25,000	166.7%
Research	$ 7,500	$ 15,000	$ 7,500	100.0%
Created by:	(Your name)			
	(Your class)			

Figure 2 - 29

Use Figure 2 - 29 and the following instructions to enhance department budget, rev. 1:

1. Open the worksheet, **department budget, rev. 1**, that you created in Independent Project 1.1. If you did not complete this project, do it now using the instructions in Lesson 1.

2. **Center** the titles, **DEPARTMENT BUDGET** and **1995/1996 AND 1996/1997 across columns A:E**.

3. Make both titles **bold**.

4. Increase the **font size** of **DEPARTMENT BUDGET** to **12** points. (**HINT:** Remember that the title is in cell **A2**.)

5. Increase the **font size** of **1995/1996 AND 1996/1997** to **11** points.

6. **Right align** the column labels, **1995/1996, 1996/1997, Increase**, and **% Increase**.

7. Make the column headings in cells **A6:E6**, **bold**.

8. Place a thin bottom **border** under the column labels in cells **A6:E6**.

9. Format **B7:D10** using **Currency Style**. **Decrease decimal** places until none is displayed.

10. Use **AutoFit Selection** to increase column widths for any columns containing values that have been replaced by ###### or labels that have been truncated.

11. Format **E7:E10** using **Percent style**. **Increase decimal** places until one is displayed.

12. Make your name and other identifying information (cells **A13:B14**) **italic**.

13. **Save** the file **As: enhanced department budget**

14. To check the spelling of the document:

     a. Select a single cell.
     b. Choose **TOOLS/Spelling** or click on the **Spelling** button on the Standard toolbar.
     c. If an Alert box asking **Continue checking at beginning of sheet?** appears, click on **Yes**.
     d. If there are no spelling errors, an Alert box with the message **Finished spell checking entire sheet.** will appear. Click on **OK**.

    e.   If *Excel* finds a word that it considers to be misspelled, the **Spelling** dialog box will appear. If you have used *Microsoft Word*, this dialog box should be very familiar to you. If it is not, use the **Question Mark** button to find out what each part of the dialog box does. Do *not* use the **Add** or **AutoCorrect** buttons. It is also easier to spell check if the **Always Suggest** check box is marked.

15. Preview the printout.

16. Use the **Margins** tab in the **Page Setup** dialog box to **Center on Page Horizontally** and **Vertically.**

17. Change the **Header** and the **Footer** to **(none).**

18. **Print** the worksheet.

19. **Save** the worksheet again using the current name.

Independent Project 2.2: Enhancing Your Caseload Worksheet

In Independent Project 1.2 you created a worksheet that calculated each case worker's current caseload based on the previous month's caseload and new and closed cases within the month. In this project you will format the worksheet so that it is easier to read and more attractive-looking. When you are finished your worksheet should resemble Figure 2 - 30.

FAMILY COMMUNITY SERVICES					
July Caseload					
Case Worker	June Caseload	New Cases	Discharged Cases	July Caseload	Increase/ Decrease
Audrey Smith	33	12	7	38	5
Casey Brown	42	12	10	44	2
Jonathan Summers	36	5	6	35	-1

Figure 2 - 30

Use Figure 2 - 30 and the following instructions to enhance July caseload, rev. 1:

1. Open the worksheet, **July caseload, rev. 1,** that you created in Independent Project 1.2. If you did not complete this project, do it now using the instructions in Lesson 1.

2. **Center** the titles, **FAMILY COMMUNITY SERVICES** and **July Caseload** across columns **A:F.**

3. Increase the **Font Size** of **FAMILY COMMUNITY SERVICES** to **14** points and make it **bold.** (**HINT:** Remember that the title is in cell **A2.**)

4. Increase the **Font Size** of **July Caseload** to **12** points and make it **bold.**

5. **Right align** all of the column labels except **Case Worker.**

6. Make the column labels in cells **A5:F6 bold, italic, 11** point.

7. Use **AutoFit Selection** to increase column widths as necessary.

    MOUSE SHORTCUT: *To use the mouse to invoke AutoFit, point to the line to the right of B in the column header. When the mouse pointer changes to a* ↔ *double-click.*

8. Place a thick bottom **border** under the column labels in cells **A6:F6.**

9. Clear your name and other identifying information (cells **A11:B12**). Spell check.

10. **Save** the file **As: enhanced July caseload**

11. Use **FILE/Page Setup** to change the **Header** to **(none)**.

12. Create a **Custom Footer** that says: **Created by (your name)** in the **Left Section**. Delete the code **Page &[Page]** from the **Center Section**. In the **Right Section** insert the current date by clicking in the **Right Section** text box and then clicking on the **Date** button in the middle of the **Footer** dialog box.

     *If you don't know which button to select to enter the date, use the **Question Mark** button to find the use of each of the buttons in the **Footer** dialog box.*

13. **Print** the worksheet.

14. **Save** the worksheet again using the current name.

Independent Project 2.3: Enhancing Your Hockey Revenues Worksheet

In Independent Project 1.3 you created a worksheet that calculated the revenue from ticket and food sales at the school hockey game. In this project you will format the worksheet so that it is easier to read and more attractive. Figure 2 - 31 shows the enhanced hockey worksheet without formulas. Your worksheet may look different as you may have used a different design.

HOCKEY GAME REVENUE				
Attendance:				
		Full Price	Students	Total
	Number	182	236	
	Fee	$5.25	$3.75	
	Revenue			
Food:				
		Hot Dogs	Hamburgers	Sodas	Total
	Number	355	248	580	
	Unit Cost	$0.50	$0.75	$0.32	
	Sales Price	$1.00	$1.50	$0.75	
	Profit Per Item			
	Profit for Total Sales			
Total Hockey Game Profit:				
Created by:	Jessica Gabriel			
	Introduction to Computers			

Figure 2 - 31

Use Figure 2 - 31 and the following instructions to enhance hockey game revenue, rev. 1:

1. Open the worksheet, **hockey game revenue, rev. 1**, that you created in Independent Project 1.3. If you did not complete this project, do it now using the instructions in Lesson 1.

2. Center the title, **HOCKEY GAME REVENUE**, across all of the columns used in the worksheet.

3. Make the title **bold** and change the **font** to **14** points.

4. Make the subtitles, **Attendance** and **Food** and the label for **Total Hockey Game Profit**, **bold** and **12** points. Leave them in column **A** or center them across the columns in the section.

5. Change the **font** and **font size** for the rest of the worksheet to **Times New Roman, 11** point.

6. **Right align** all column labels for columns of numbers, and make all column labels **bold**.

7. Use the **Format** menu to format all values that represent currency with the **Currency Format** (2 decimal places).

8. Widen any columns that are not wide enough to display their full contents.

9. Format your name and any other identifying information that you put on the worksheet as **italics**. Spell check the worksheet.

10. **Save** the worksheet **As: enhanced hockey revenue**

11. Use **Page Setup** to:

    a. Remove the **Header**.

    b. Create a **Custom Footer** that contains only the **Date** in the **Center Section**.

12. **Print** the worksheet.

13. **Save** the worksheet again using the current name.

Independent Project 2.4: Enhancing Your Sports Budget

In Independent Project 1.4 you planned and created a budget for the purchase of additional sporting goods for a community athletic program (**sports equipment**). In this project you will use the skills learned in Lesson 2 to enhance the worksheet so that values are formatted correctly, labels are aligned appropriately, and font, font sizes, and font styles are applied to the worksheet title and column labels.

Make the following enhancements to your worksheet:

1. Change the font, font size, and/or font style so that the worksheet title is emphasized.

2. Change the alignment of the column labels so that they are centered or right aligned over columns of values. Use font, font size, or font style to enhance the column labels.

3. Add borders as you wish.

4. Format totals that represent currency so that they contain dollar signs. Format other values appropriately.

5. Spell check the worksheet.

6. **Save** your worksheet using the name: **enhanced sports equipment**

7. Before printing the worksheet, preview it. Change the header and/or footer as you wish, and make any other desired changes to the page setup.

8. **Print** your worksheet.

Copying and Rearranging Worksheets

Objectives

In this lesson you will learn how to:

- Move around a worksheet
- Use the **AutoSum** button to add the contents of a range of cells
- Copy cell contents to one or more adjacent cells
- Use AutoCalculate to check totals

- Copy cell contents to nonadjacent cells
- Select nonadjacent cells
- Insert and delete rows and columns
- Move cell contents
- Activate the shortcut menus

PROJECT DESCRIPTION

Nationwide Sporting Goods is a national corporation selling a variety of sports products. The file **lesson 3** contains a partially completed worksheet that summarizes 1995 sales by product and region. In this project you are going to calculate the total sales by product and region and create a separate part of the worksheet that compares the sales to previous and projected sales.

The worksheet you will complete in this project is larger than the one you used in Lessons 1 and 2. Therefore, you will learn to scroll the window to see parts of the worksheet that are not visible. In addition you will learn several shortcuts that speed up worksheet design — copying, moving, and functions. Finally you will learn how to insert and delete columns and rows so that you can modify your initial worksheet design.

In the process of completing the worksheet, you will also review:

- Entering values

- Entering formulas

- Centering titles across columns

- Formatting numbers

- Increasing column widths to display all values in the column

- Using Page Setup to change headers and footers

- Printing the worksheet

When completed, your worksheet will resemble Figure 3 - 1.

NATIONWIDE SPORTING GOODS
1995 Regional Sales Summary

Sales in Thousands of Dollars

Product	Eastern	Western	Northern	Southern	Totals
Baseball Bats	$ 8,056	$ 2,297	$ 1,768	$ 4,807	$ 16,928
Olympic Frisbees	6,017	6,647	6,926	1,474	21,064
Golf Club Sets	4,663	8,717	8,458	7,536	29,374
Athletic Wear	10,325	2,234	1,823	9,236	23,618
Kayaks	4,328	4,773	3,572	1,160	13,833
Camping Equipment	6,147	2,543	3,420	11,222	23,332
Football Pads	7,968	9,584	6,489	6,210	30,251
Boxing Gloves	1,569	2,884	3,607	1,310	9,370
Totals	$ 49,073	$ 39,679	$ 36,063	$ 42,955	$167,770

Projected vs. Actual Sales

Dollar Volume Sold (in Thousands of Dollars)

Product	1994 Sales	Projected	Actual	Variance	% Variance
Baseball Bats	$ 14,345	$ 16,000	$ 16,928	$ 928	5.5%
Olympic Frisbees	20,567	22,000	21,064	(936)	-4.4%
Golf Club Sets	28,567	30,000	29,374	(626)	-2.1%
Athletic Wear	23,145	25,000	23,618	(1,382)	-5.9%
Kayaks	10,111	12,000	13,833	1,833	13.3%
Camping Equipment	24,536	25,000	23,332	(1,668)	-7.1%
Football Pads	26,000	28,000	30,251	2,251	7.4%
Boxing Gloves	9,328	10,000	9,370	(630)	-6.7%
Totals	$156,599	$168,000	$167,770	$ (230)	-0.1%

Figure 3 - 1

MOVING AROUND THE WORKSHEET

In Lessons 1 and 2, you used a very small worksheet. The cells you wanted to go to were always visible and you could move around the worksheet by pressing the **ARROW** keys or clicking on the next cell. In this lesson all the worksheet data will not be visible on the screen at one time. Therefore, you must move, or *scroll*, the window to see different parts of the worksheet. Tables 3-1 and 3-2 describe shortcuts for moving around the screen using the mouse and the keyboard.

Key	Cell Selected	Screen Movement
↑, ↓, ←, →	The adjacent cell in the direction of the arrow	One cell in direction of arrow, only if necessary to display the selected cell
HOME	The cell in column **A** of the current row	As necessary to display column **A**
CTRL+HOME	A1	As necessary to display **A1**
CTRL+END	The cell at the intersection of the last row and the last column containing any data	As necessary to display cell
PAGE DOWN	The cell one window down from the active cell	Down one screen
PAGE UP	The cell one window up from the active cell	Up one screen
ALT+PAGE DOWN	The cell one window right from the active cell	Right one screen
ALT+PAGE UP	The cell one window left from the active cell	Left one screen

Table 3 - 1 - Using Keys to Scroll the Screen

Mouse Action (On Scroll Bars)	Screen Movement (The scroll bar changes the part of the screen displayed, but does *not* change the selected cell.)
Click the triangle at the end of the bar	One row or column in the direction of the triangle point.
Click the bar above, below, to the right, or to the left of the scroll boxes	One window above, below, to the right, or to the left
Drag the scroll box	To the position in the worksheet matching the position of the scroll box in the scroll bar (as you drag the scroll box, *Excel* displays a small box next to the scroll box that names the first column or row that will appear on the screen if you release the mouse button)

Table 3 - 2 - Using the Mouse to Scroll the Screen

Activity 3.1: Scrolling the Screen to See the Full Worksheet

In this activity you will open the worksheet **lesson 3** and scroll the window to see all parts of the worksheet.

1. Start *Excel*.

2. Open the file, **lesson 3**. If *Excel* is not maximized, click on the **Maximize** button on the right side of the *Excel* Title Bar.

3. If **lesson 3** is not maximized, click on the **Maximize** button on the right side of the **lesson 3** Title Bar.

    The worksheet shows the sales figures for the products in each of four regions. Cell A1 is the active cell (Figure 3 - 2).

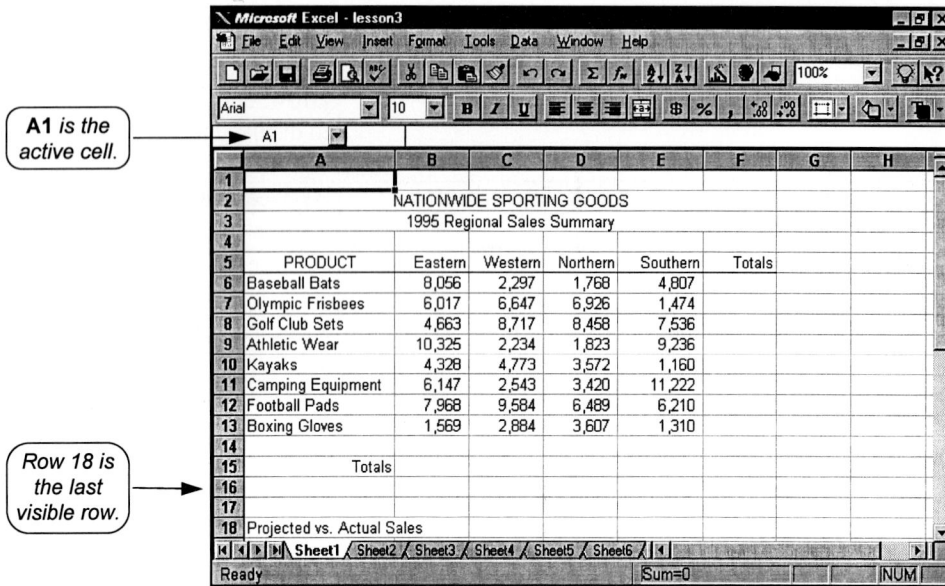

A1 *is the active cell.*

Row 18 is the last visible row.

Figure 3 - 2

4. Write down the number of the last row visible in the **lesson 3** worksheet. Press the **PAGE DOWN** key.

    The row one below the number you wrote down is now the first visible row of the worksheet. The cell one window down from the previous active cell is now active. A partially completed section of the worksheet, which will be used to compare projected and actual sales, is displayed (Figure 3 - 3).

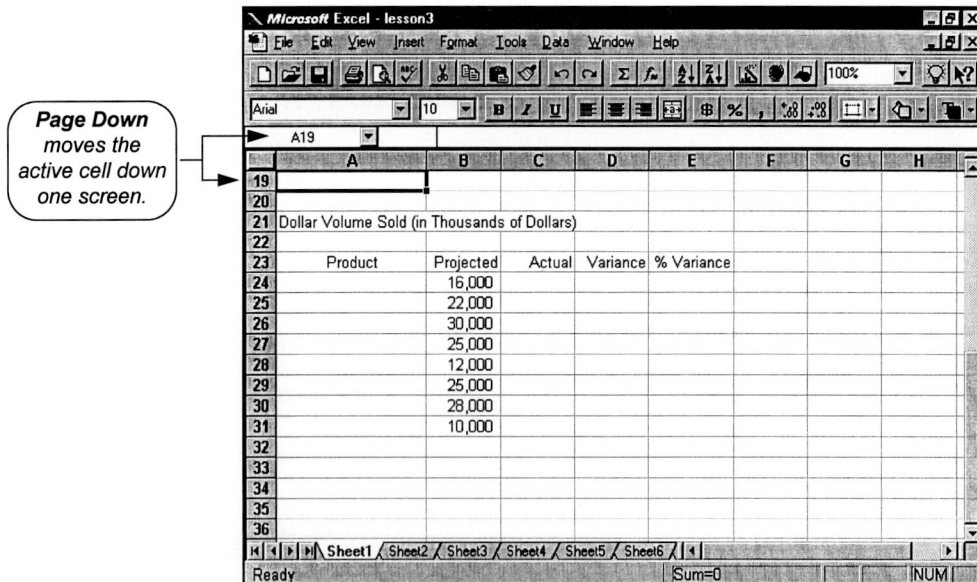

Page Down *moves the active cell down one screen.*

Figure 3 - 3

5. Press **CTRL+HOME** to jump back to the home position and make **A1** the active cell again.

6. Click on the ▼ on the vertical scroll bar until row **33** is the bottom row on the screen.

*The Projected vs. Actual part of the worksheet is displayed, but the selected cell is not visible. As the name box (on the left side of the Formula Bar) indicates, the active cell remains **A1** (Figure 3 - 4).*

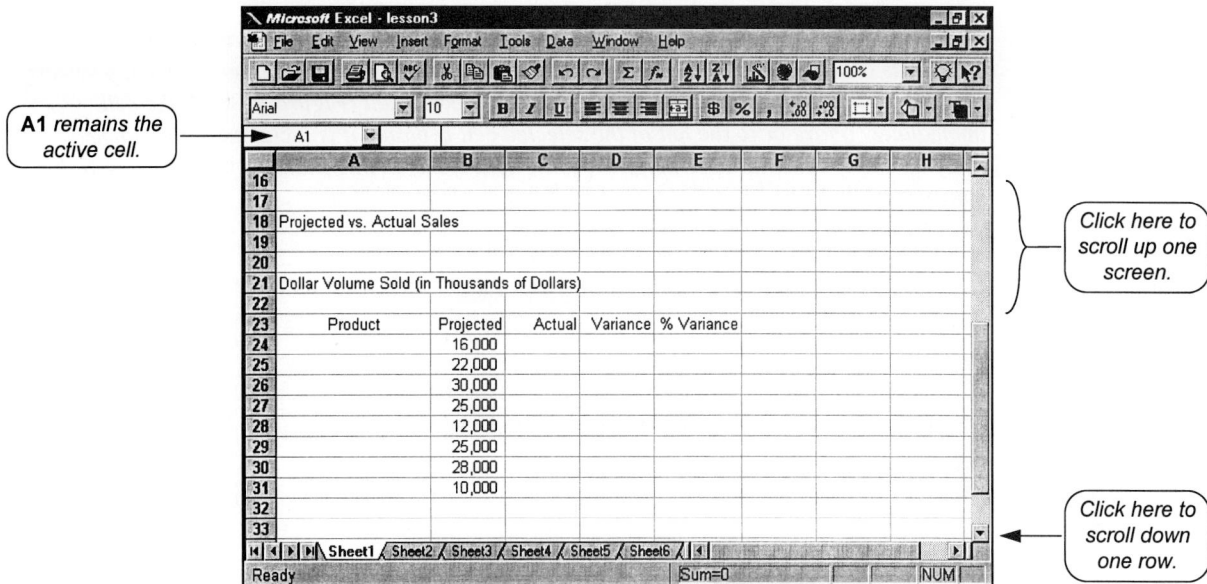

Figure 3 - 4

7. Click anywhere in the area on the scroll bar above the scroll box (Figure 3 - 4) to scroll the window up one screen.

The top part of the worksheet is displayed (as in Figure 3 - 2).

THE SUM FUNCTION

In Lesson 1 you created formulas to perform calculations. *Excel* already contains hundreds of built-in formulas that perform many calculations for you. To use a function, you enter the name of the function and the cells that contain the data needed by the function. *Excel* then performs the calculation. This process is even easier for the sum function. The sum function is used to add a range of cells. This task is performed so often in worksheets that there is a special button on the toolbar that automatically enters the sum function and even suggests a range containing the cells that you may wish to add.

> **REMEMBER** Read the bulleted list that follows, but do not actually perform the steps until you reach *Activity 3.2.*

To use the AutoSum button:

- Select the cell to contain the function.

- Click on the **AutoSum** Σ button.

- Look at the range that *Excel* has entered in the function. If it is correct, click on the **AutoSum** button again or press **ENTER**. If it is incorrect, select the correct range and then enter the function.

You will learn to use other functions in Lesson 4.

Activity 3.2: Entering Sums with the AutoSum Button

1. Select **B15**.

2. Click the **AutoSum** button.

   The function =SUM(B6:B14) is displayed in B15 and in the Formula Bar and the range B6:B14 is enclosed in a moving border. When AutoSum is used, Excel automatically selects a group of filled cells above or to the left of the selected cell (Figure 3 - 5). If the cell immediately above or to the left of the selected cell is blank, it is included in the range, since an empty cell will not change the total. Therefore, in this example, Excel selected the range B6:B14.

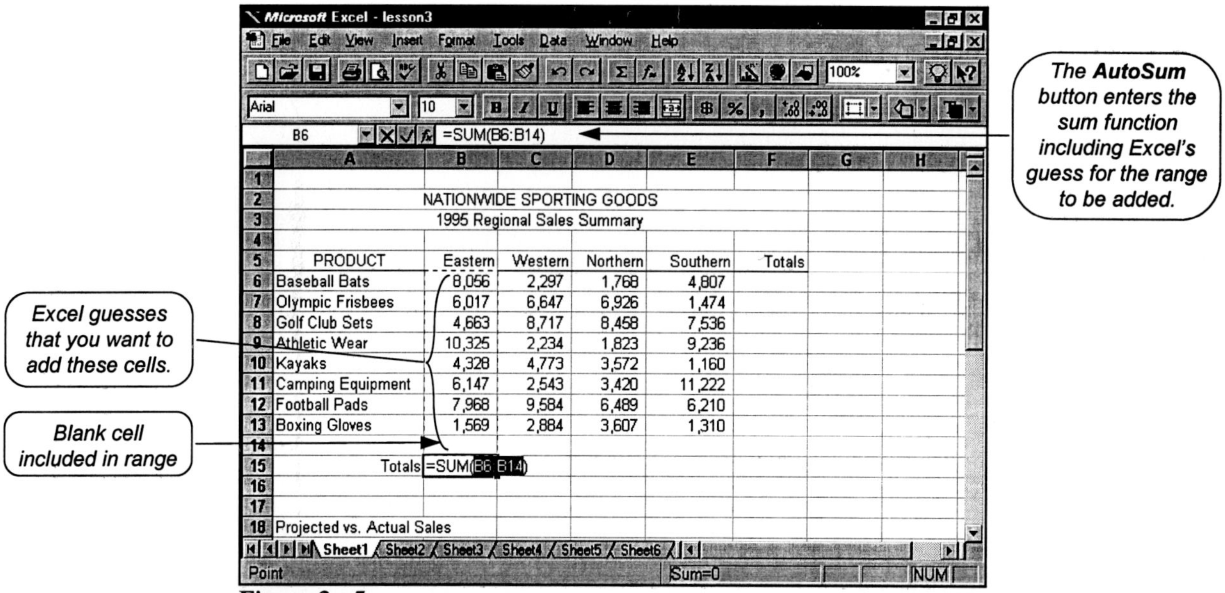

Figure 3 - 5

3. Since *Excel* has correctly selected the cells that you want to add, click on the **AutoSum** button again or click on the **enter box**.

   The total, 49073, is entered in B15, while the function =SUM(B6:B14) remains in the Formula Bar.

4. Select cell **F6**.

5. Click on the **AutoSum** button.

6. Since *Excel* has selected the cells that you want to add (**B6:E6**), click on the **AutoSum** button again or click on the **enter box** (Figure 3 - 6).

7. Select **F7**.

8. Click the **AutoSum** button, make sure the range is correct, and click again.

   The value 21064 should be displayed in F7. You could continue to enter the SUM function in the rest of the column, but as you will see in the next section, there is a quicker way to enter these formulas.

   In fact, when entering a column of similar formulas you typically only enter the formula once. You entered it twice in cells F6 and F7 only so that you could see how similar the formulas were.

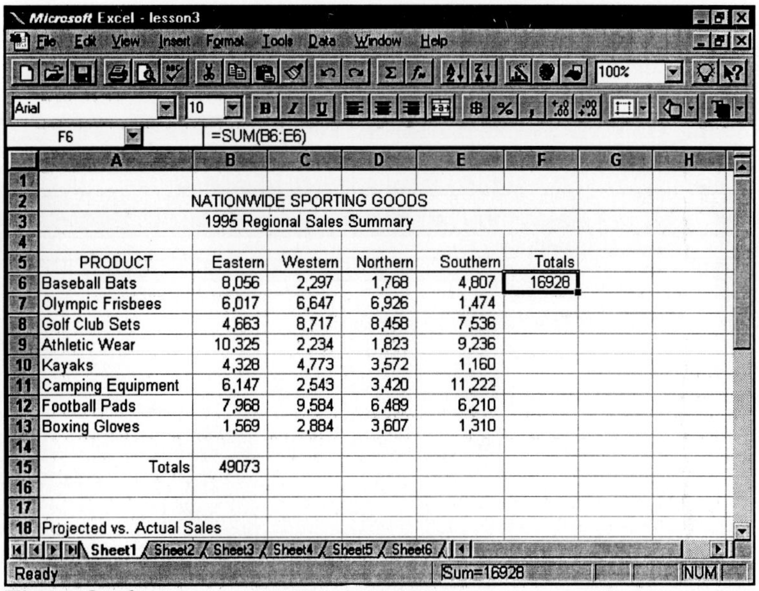

	A	B	C	D	E	F
1						
2		NATIONWIDE SPORTING GOODS				
3		1995 Regional Sales Summary				
4						
5	PRODUCT	Eastern	Western	Northern	Southern	Totals
6	Baseball Bats	8,056	2,297	1,768	4,807	16928
7	Olympic Frisbees	6,017	6,647	6,926	1,474	
8	Golf Club Sets	4,663	8,717	8,458	7,536	
9	Athletic Wear	10,325	2,234	1,823	9,236	
10	Kayaks	4,328	4,773	3,572	1,160	
11	Camping Equipment	6,147	2,543	3,420	11,222	
12	Football Pads	7,968	9,584	6,489	6,210	
13	Boxing Gloves	1,569	2,884	3,607	1,310	
14						
15	Totals	49073				
16						
17						
18	Projected vs. Actual Sales					

Figure 3 - 6

COPYING

Relative Cell Adjustment

Often you develop one formula and then discover that it will work quite well for the rest of the relationships in a specific row or column. For example, the formulas in cells **F6** and **F7** are almost the same. The only difference is that the formula has been *adjusted* to reflect the actual **row** that it is in. (The formula in cell **F6** is **=SUM(B6:E6)** while the formula in **F7** is **=SUM(B7:E7)**.)

If the contents of the cell to be copied is a formula or function, *Excel* automatically adjusts the column or row reference so that the same relationship is maintained between the cell containing the formula and the cells to which it refers. In Lesson 5 you will learn how to create a formula that should not be adjusted as it is copied.

Copying to Adjacent Cells

Excel has a special command that allows you to copy to adjacent cells in the same column or row.

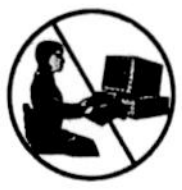

To copy cell contents to adjacent cells in the same column or row:

- Select the cell containing the information to be copied and all of the cells in the same column or row to which you want to copy.
- Choose **EDIT/Fill.**
- From the submenu, choose **Down, Right, Up,** or **Left.**

The contents and format of the initial cell will be copied to the other cell(s).

!

CAUTION: *Any existing contents of the cells you fill will be replaced.*

Activity 3.3: Copying Cell Contents to Adjacent Cells

1. Select the range **F7:F13** by clicking on **F7** and dragging the mouse down until the range **F7:F13** is highlighted.

2. Choose **EDIT/Fill**.

    *The **Fill** submenu is displayed (Figure 3 - 7).*

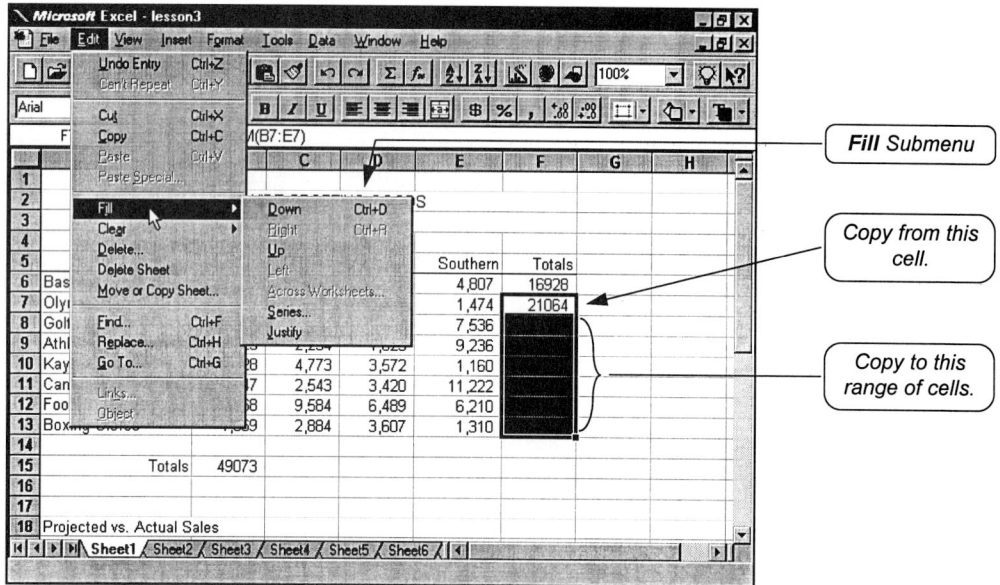

Figure 3 - 7

3. Click on **Down**.

4. Click on cell **F7**. Read the Formula Bar entry. It should say **=SUM(B7:E7)**.

5. Click on cell **F8**.

    =SUM(B8:E8) appears in the Formula Bar. When the formula was copied, the row numbers of the cells contained in the formula increased by one (from 7 to 8) as the row number of the cell containing the formula increased by one.

6. Select the range **B15:F15**.

7. Choose **EDIT/Fill**.

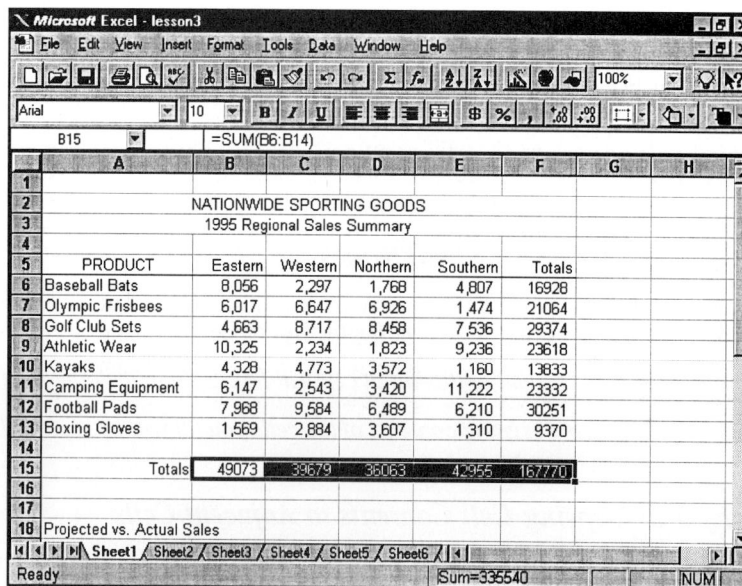

Figure 3 - 8

8. When the **Fill** submenu is displayed, choose **Right**.

    The function in cell B15 will be copied across the row (Figure 3 - 8).

9. Click, one at a time, on cells **B15** through **F15.** As you select each cell, compare the contents of the Formula Bar with Table 3-3. Note how the formulas adjust as they are copied.

Cell	Cell Entry	What the formula does
B15	=SUM(B6:B14)	Adds the values in the cells 1, 2, 3, 4, 5, 6, 7, 8, and 9 rows above **B15.**
C15	=SUM(C6:C14)	Adds the values in the cells 1, 2, 3, 4, 5, 6, 7, 8, and 9 rows above **C15.**
D15	=SUM(D6:D14)	Adds the values in the cells 1, 2, 3, 4, 5, 6, 7, 8, and 9 rows above **D15.**
E15	=SUM(E6:E14)	Adds the values in the cells 1, 2, 3, 4, 5, 6, 7, 8, and 9 rows above **E15.**
F15	=SUM(F6:F14)	Adds the values in the cells 1, 2, 3, 4, 5, 6, 7, 8, and 9 rows above **F15.**

Table 3 - 3: The Effects of Relative Cell Adjustment

10. Choose **FILE/Save As**. Save the file using the new File Name: **nationwide sales**

USING AUTOCALCULATE TO CHECK TOTALS

AutoCalculate, a new feature of *Excel 7.0*, allows you to temporarily display totals, minimums, maximums, averages and counts simply by highlighting a range. If you follow the activities in this book and match your screen to each screenshot, you know that all of the formulas are correct. However, when you are using worksheets in real life situations, you do not know what the answer should be. The ability to cross-check totals is one way of helping to ensure that your work is correct.

To use AutoCalculate to total a range temporarily:

*   Select the range containing the data to be added.

*   Look at the AutoCalculate box on the Status Bar. If it begins **Sum=**, the number following the sum is the total of the data in the highlighted range. If it begins with another term, such as **Average=**, point to that term and click with the right mouse button. Click on **Sum** in the shortcut menu which appears. (You will learn more about shortcut menus later in this chapter.)

Activity 3.4 Using AutoCalculate to Sum a Range Temporarily

In Activity 3.3 the formula in **F15** calculates the total sales for all of the products in all of the regions by summing the totals for all of the regions for each of the products (i.e., summing the row totals). You can check this total by calculating a temporary sum of the totals for all of the products in each of the regions (i.e., summing the column totals).

1. Click on cell **F15.** Look at the formula in the Formula Bar. It should say **=SUM(F6:F14)**. This sums the row totals which are in cells **F6** through **F14.**

2. Highlight the range **B15:E15.** The range includes the column totals for columns **B** through **E.**

3. Look at the AutoCalculate Area on the Status Bar to determine the sum. It should be the same as the contents of **F15** (Figure 3 - 9).

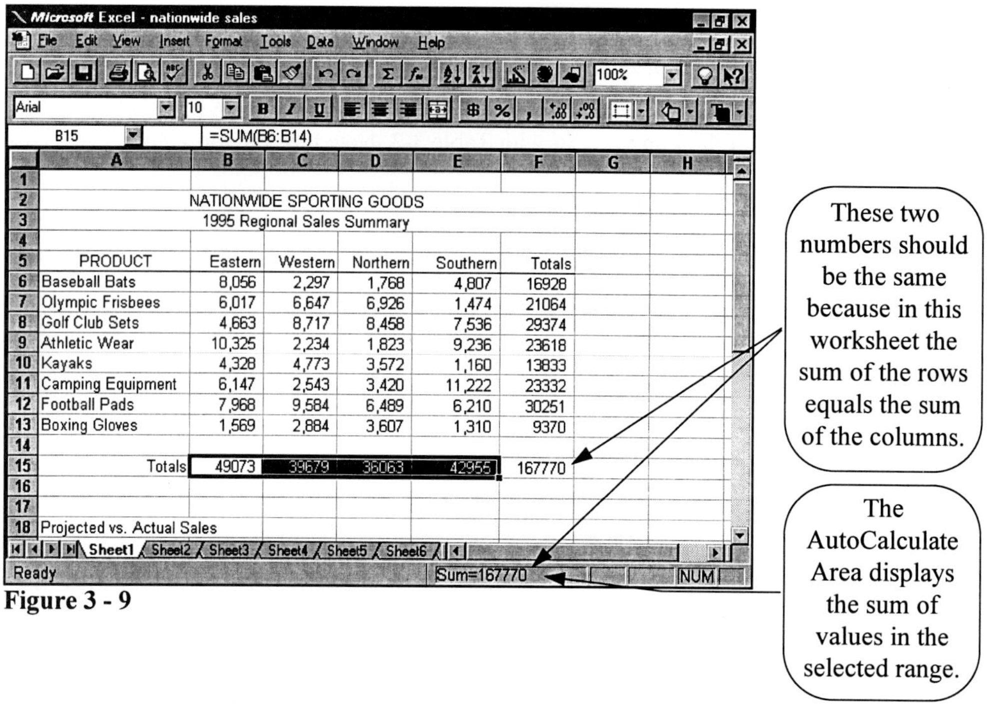

These two numbers should be the same because in this worksheet the sum of the rows equals the sum of the columns.

The AutoCalculate Area displays the sum of values in the selected range.

Figure 3 - 9

MORE COPYING

Copying to Nonadjacent Cells

Sometimes worksheet contents can be reused in a part of the worksheet that is not adjacent to the current location. *Excel* uses the **EDIT/Copy** command to start the copying process. When you choose **EDIT/Copy** the highlighted range is copied to the *Windows* clipboard, where it remains until something else is cut or copied. The cells are then *pasted* to the new location. The cell contents can be pasted anywhere in the worksheet or even to other sheets in the workbook or to other programs. As with **EDIT/Fill** the cell contents and format are copied and formulas are adjusted relatively.

To copy cell contents to nonadjacent locations:

- Select the cell(s) to be copied.

- Choose **EDIT/Copy** or click the **Copy** button on the Standard toolbar.

  The range to be copied is surrounded by a moving border.

- Select the upper-left cell of the range to which the cell contents are to be copied.

- Press **ENTER** to copy the cell contents and remove the moving border.

  ALTERNATE METHOD: *If you want to paste the cell contents in more than one location, choose **EDIT/Paste** or click the **Paste** button instead of pressing **ENTER**. After you have copied the data for the last time, press **ESC** to remove the moving border.*

Activity 3.5: Copying to Nonadjacent Cells

In this activity you will copy the product names from the top part of the worksheet to the **Projected vs. Actual Sales** section.

1. Select the range **A6:A15**.

2. Click on the **Copy** button or choose **EDIT/Copy**.

   *A moving border should appear around cells A6:A15. The message **Select destination and press ENTER or choose Paste** appears on the Status Bar.*

3. Press **PAGE DOWN** or scroll down until row **A24** is visible.

4. Select **A24** if it is not already the active cell.

5. Press **ENTER**.

   *The product names and **Totals** should be copied to cells A24:A33 (Figure 3 - 10). **Totals** is right aligned because the copy command copies cell formats as well as cell contents.*

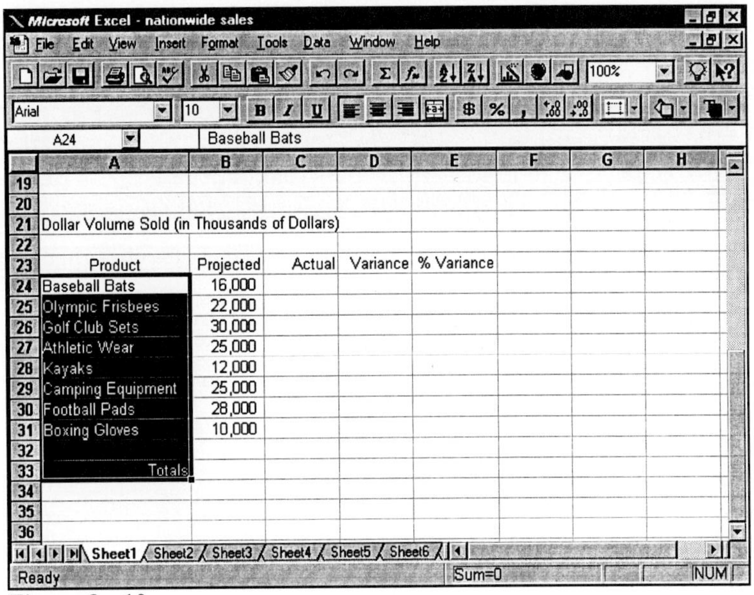

Figure 3 - 10

A MOUSE SHORTCUT FOR THE EDIT/FILL COMMAND

EDIT/Fill,Down and **EDIT/Fill,Right** are so commonly used that there is a mouse shortcut for them. When a cell or range of cells is selected, the lower-right corner of the heavy border around the cell or range of cells has a small square, which is called the *fill handle*. Dragging the fill handle copies the data in the selected cell or range.

To use the fill handle in copying:

- Select the cell or range of cells containing the data to be copied.

- Point to the **fill handle**. The mouse pointer will change to a crosshair **+** .

- Making sure the pointer remains a **+** , drag the **fill handle** across the cells you want to fill and then release the mouse button.

   CAUTION: *Dragging the **fill handle** back over the selected cells erases the cell contents. If this happens immediately choose **EDIT/Undo** or click on the **Undo** button.*

Activity 3.6: Reviewing Entering and Copying Formulas and Functions

In this activity you will enter the formulas needed for the bottom section of the worksheet and copy them to the appropriate cells.

1. Select cell **C24**.

2. The **Actual** value of the **Baseball Bats** sales is equal to the total **Baseball Bats** sales at the top of the worksheet. To enter this as a formula:

    a. Begin the formula by typing: =

    b. Click the ▲ on the scroll bar until **F6** is visible and select the cell containing total baseball sales, **F6**.

    c. Click on the **enter box** or press **ENTER**.

    The screen scrolls down to display row 24. The value of the baseball bats' total sales, 16928, appears in C24 (Figure 3 - 11).

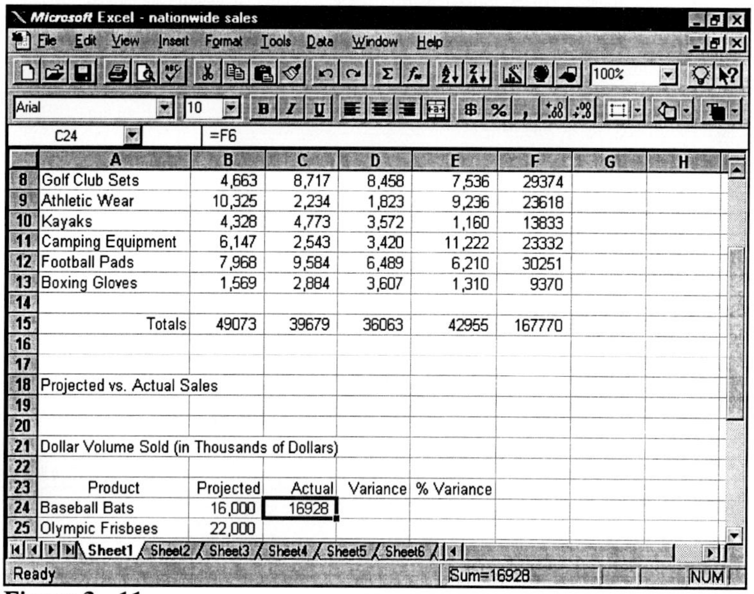

Figure 3 - 11

3. Select **D24**. Use pointing to enter a formula for the **Variance**. The **Variance** is equal to the **Actual** sales minus the **Projected** sales.

4. In **E24** enter a formula for the **% Variance**. The **% Variance** is equal to the **Variance** divided by the **Actual** sales.

    Cell D24 should contain the value 928; cell E24 should contain 0.0548204.

5. To copy all three formulas at one time, select the range **C24:E31**.

    HINT: *Point to C24, click and drag the mouse across row 24 and down to row 31. As the highlight hits the bottom edge of the window, the screen will scroll. If you have trouble selecting the entire area, release the mouse button. Use SHIFT+ARROW keys to extend or contract the selected area.*

6. Choose **EDIT/Fill, Down**.

    If cells in more than one column are selected, EDIT/Fill, Down copies the contents of the first cell in each column to the other cells in the same column (Figure 3 - 12).

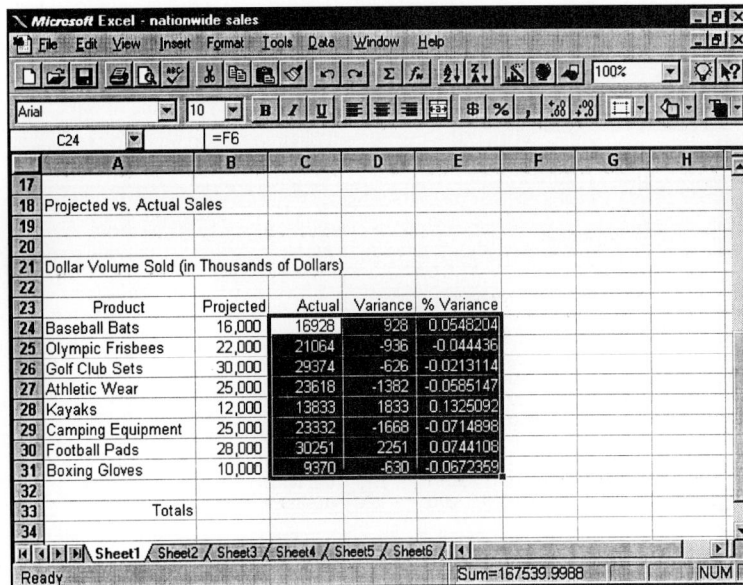

Figure 3 - 12

7. If row **33** is not displayed, click on the [icon] on the vertical scroll bar until row **33** is displayed.

8. Select **B33** and use the **AutoSum** button to create a total of the **Projected** sales.

9. Point to the **fill handle**. When the mouse pointer changes to a **+**, drag the **fill handle** (Figure 3 - 13) to copy the function to cells **C33** and **D33**. Do NOT copy the function to **E33**.

    The contents of B33 (the SUM function) and its format are copied to the other cells.

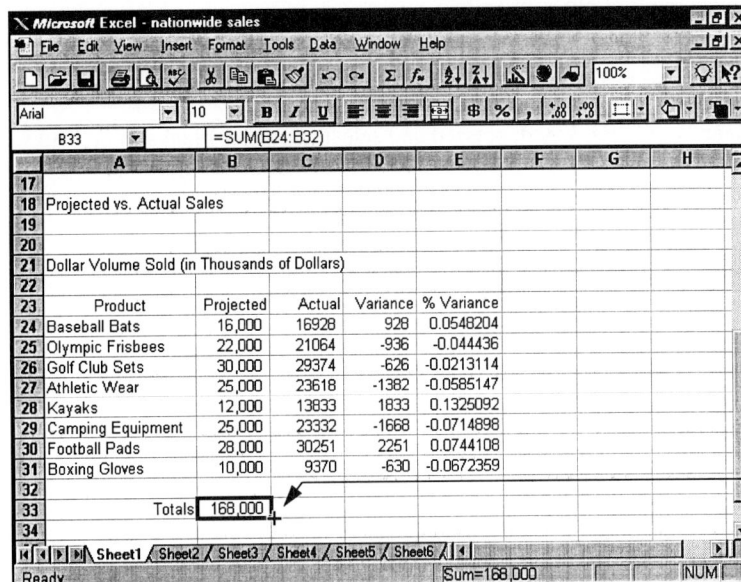

Figure 3 - 13

10. Use **EDIT/Copy** or the **Copy** button to copy the variance formula from **E31** to **E33**.

    Your worksheet should resemble Figure 3 - 14.

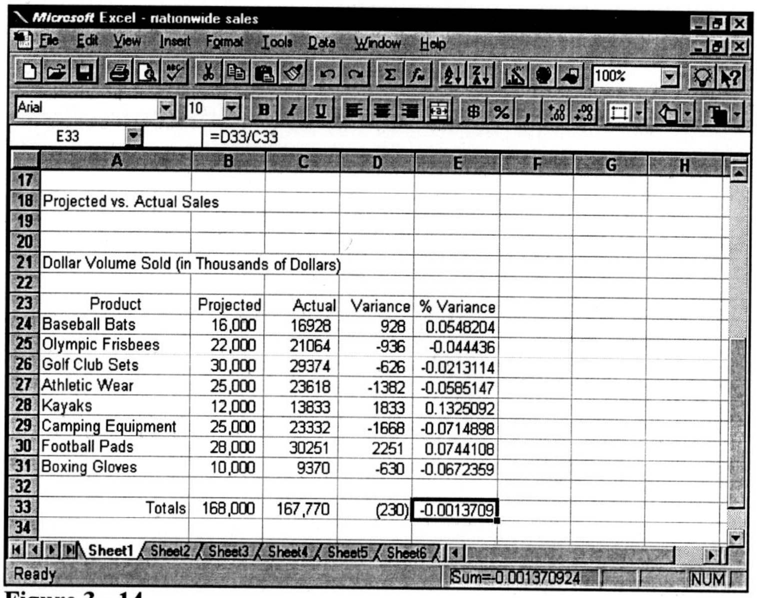

Figure 3 - 14

SELECTING NONADJACENT RANGES

As worksheets get larger, you often want to apply the same command to groups of cells that are not next to each other.

To select nonadjacent ranges:

- Select the first block of cells.

- Press the **CTRL** key and *while keeping it depressed* use the mouse to select the second range.

- Keep the **CTRL** key depressed and select any other blocks of cells to which you want to apply the command. Release the **CTRL** key when all blocks are selected.

Activity 3.7: Formatting

In this activity you will use the number formatting skills you learned in Lesson 2 to format the worksheet.

1. Select **C24:D31**.

2. Use the **Comma Style** button to format the range.

    Remember, if any of the formatted numbers are too wide to fit in the cell they will be replaced by ###. You will fix this in a moment.

3. Use the **Decrease Decimal** button to display the numbers with no decimal places.

4. Use the **Percent Style** and **Increase Decimal** buttons to format **E24:E33** for **Percent** with one decimal place.

    The Comma and Currency Styles use parentheses to indicate negative numbers; the Percent Style uses the minus sign (Figure 3 - 15).

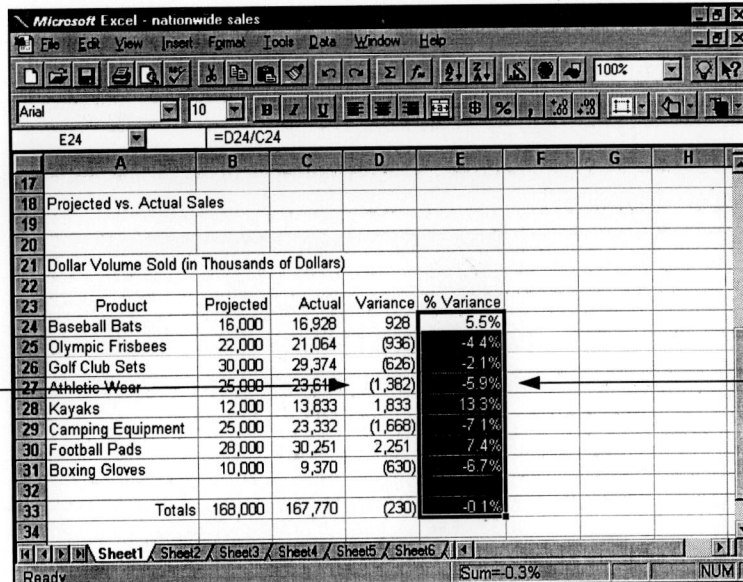

Figure 3 - 15

Parentheses indicate negative number in the Comma and Currency Styles.

Minus sign indicates negative number in Percent Style.

5. To format **B24:D24** and **B33:D33** for Currency Style with no decimal places.

   a. Select **B24:D24**.

   b. Press the **CTRL** key and *while keeping it depressed,* use the mouse to select **B33:D33**.

   c. Release the **CTRL** key and click the **Currency Style** button; then click the **Decrease Decimal** button twice.

6. If any of the columns are too narrow to display the formatted cell contents, use **FORMAT/Column,AutoFit** to increase the column width.

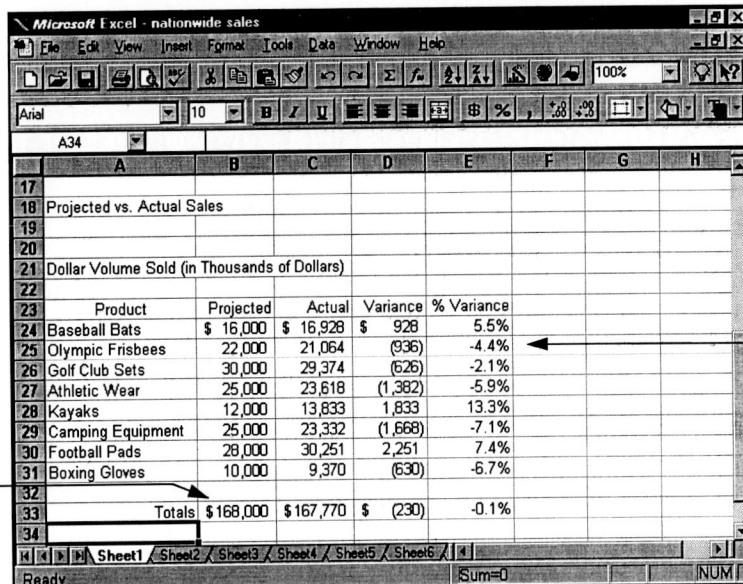

Figure 3 - 16

Percent Style; Increase Decimals once

Currency Style; Decrease Decimals twice

7. Compare the **Projected vs. Actual Sales** part of the worksheet with Figure 3 - 16 and make any formatting changes necessary to match the figure.

8. Press the **PAGE UP** key to move up one screen.

9. Format **B6:F6** and **B15:F15** using **Currency Style** with no decimal places.

10. Format **F7:F13** using **Comma Style** with no decimal places.

11. Increase column widths as necessary.

Use Figure 3 - 17 to make sure that you made all of the formatting changes.

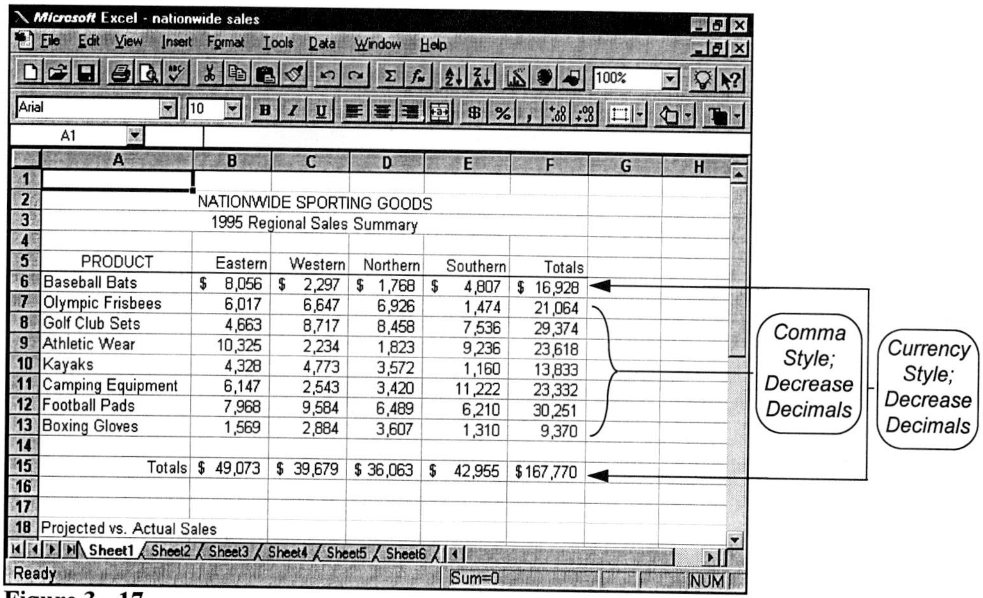

Figure 3 - 17

You've worked long enough. It's time to save the document, but let's use a new name so that you still have the original if you need to go back to it.

12. Choose **FILE/Save As**.

13. In the **File name** box, type the new file name: **nationwide sales, rev. 1** and click on **OK**.

REARRANGING A WORKSHEET BY DELETING AND INSERTING

Inserting and Deleting Rows

Sometimes after you have designed a worksheet you find that you want to add information that should be included in its own row or delete blank rows or rows that contain information. The easiest way to insert or delete rows is to use the *shortcut menus*. A *shortcut menu* is a list of commands relevant to a particular item. The contents of the shortcut menu depends on what actions you have just taken and what part of the screen you are working with. Therefore, you display one shortcut menu if the mouse pointer is pointing at a toolbar, another if it is pointing to a range that you have just selected, and so on. Shortcut menus are activated using the **right** mouse button instead of the left button.

To insert a row:

- Select the entire row below the one to be inserted by clicking on the row header.

- Point anywhere in the selected row and click the **right** mouse button.

- Choose **Insert** from the shortcut menu.

ALTERNATE METHOD: *After selecting the row, choose **INSERT/ Row** from the regular menus in the menu bar.*

To delete a row:

- Select the entire row to be deleted by clicking on the row header.
- Point anywhere in the selected row and click the **right** mouse button.
- Choose **Delete** from the shortcut menu.

ALTERNATE METHOD: *After selecting the row, choose **EDIT/Delete** from the regular menus in the menu bar.*

CAUTION: *A row is deleted for the entire width of the worksheet, including parts that are not currently visible on the screen. Make sure that the row does not contain any information that you want to keep. To check that the row is blank, click on the cell in that row in column A. Press the **CTRL+RIGHT ARROW** keys. If the pointer moves to the cell in the same row in column **IV** (the last column in the worksheet) the row is empty. If it stops on any other cell, check to see if that cell contains information that you need.*

Activity 3.8: Inserting and Deleting Rows

In this activity you want to insert a row for an extra title line and delete several blank lines. When rows are inserted or deleted, *Excel* automatically adjusts all cell references in formulas that refer to data that now have new cell addresses.

1. Click on cell **B15**. It contains the formula **=SUM(B6:B14)**.

2. Point to row heading **5**. Make sure the mouse pointer is a ✚ and click the mouse button to select the entire row (Figure 3 - 18).

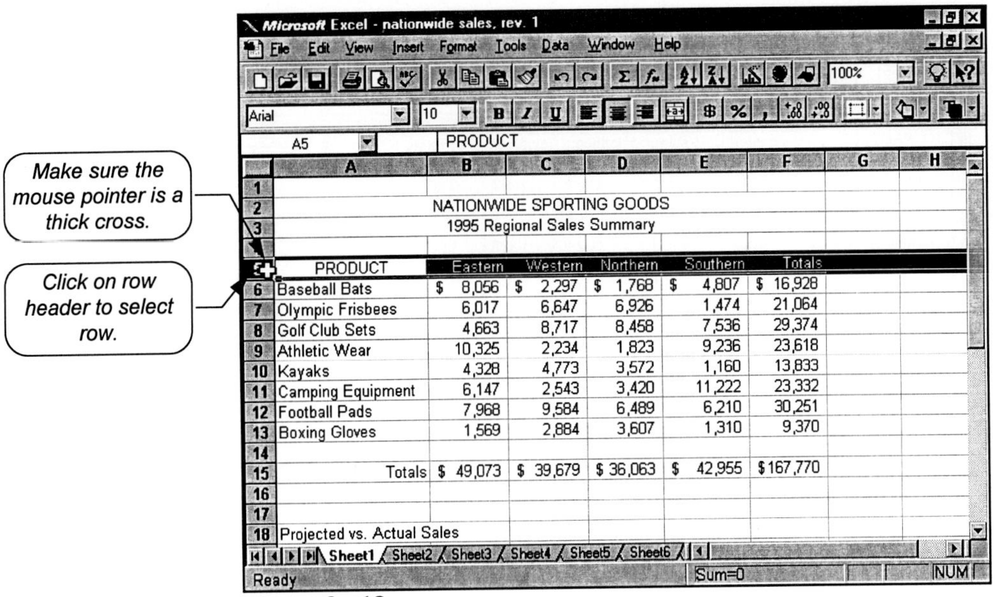

Make sure the mouse pointer is a thick cross.

Click on row header to select row.

Figure 3 - 18

3. Continue to point at the row **5** header and click the **right** mouse button.

   The shortcut menu listing activities that are commonly used with selected rows is displayed (Figure 3 - 19).

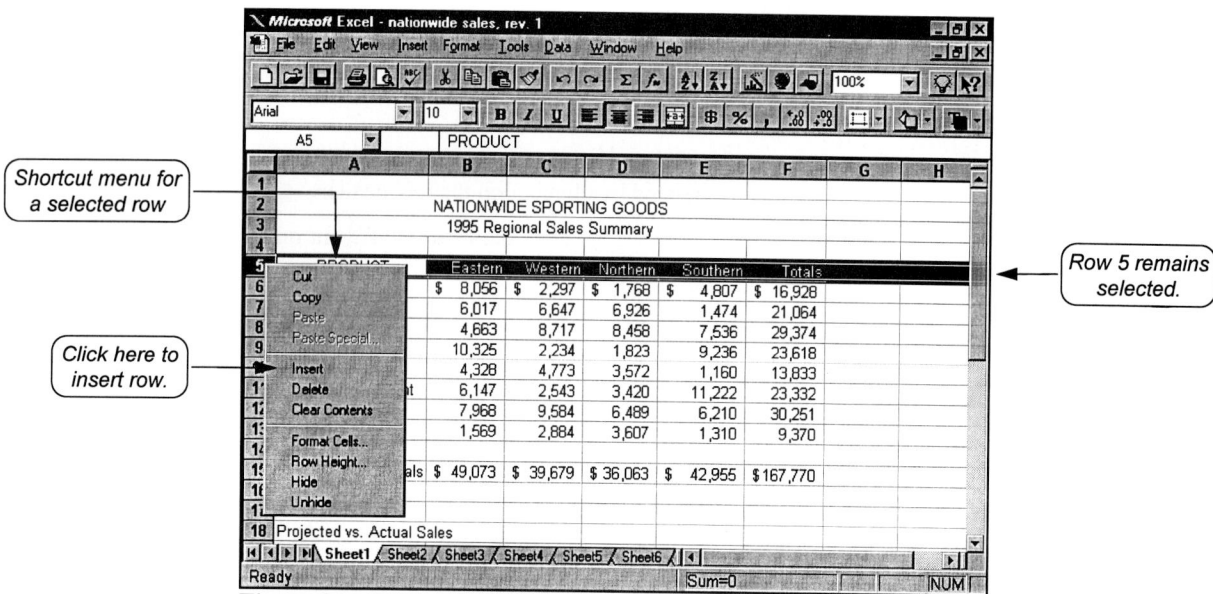

Figure 3 - 19

4. Watch the screen carefully as you click on **Insert**.

   If you are watching the screen, you can see Excel inserting a blank row. The new blank row is now labeled row 5 and the original row 5 is now row 6 (Figure 3 - 20).

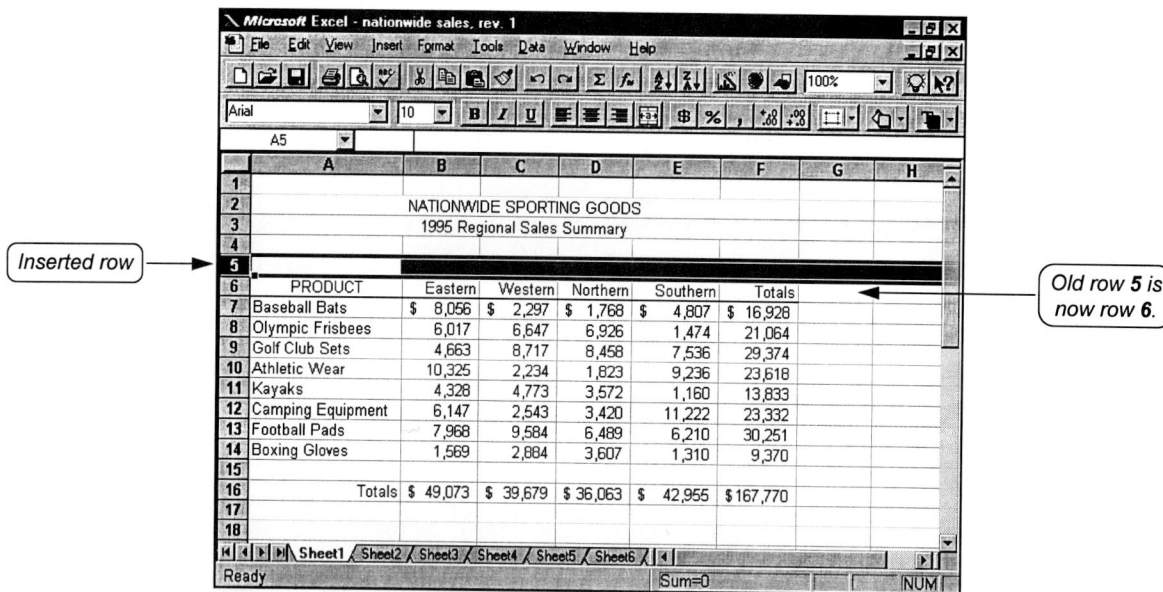

Figure 3 - 20

5. Click on the cell **B16**. The names of the cells it sums have changed, so the formula now reads **=SUM(B7:B15)**.

6. Select **B5** and enter: **Sales in Thousands of Dollars**

7. Select the range **B5:F5** and click on the **Center Across Columns** button.

8. Scroll the screen until row **21** is visible.

9. Click on the row heading **21** to select the entire row. Row **21** should be blank.

10. While still pointing at the row, click the **right** mouse button.

11. Choose **Delete** from the shortcut menu.

> *The previous row **21** is deleted. The row containing **Dollar Volume Sold (in Thousands of Dollars)** is now row **21** (Figure 3 - 21).*

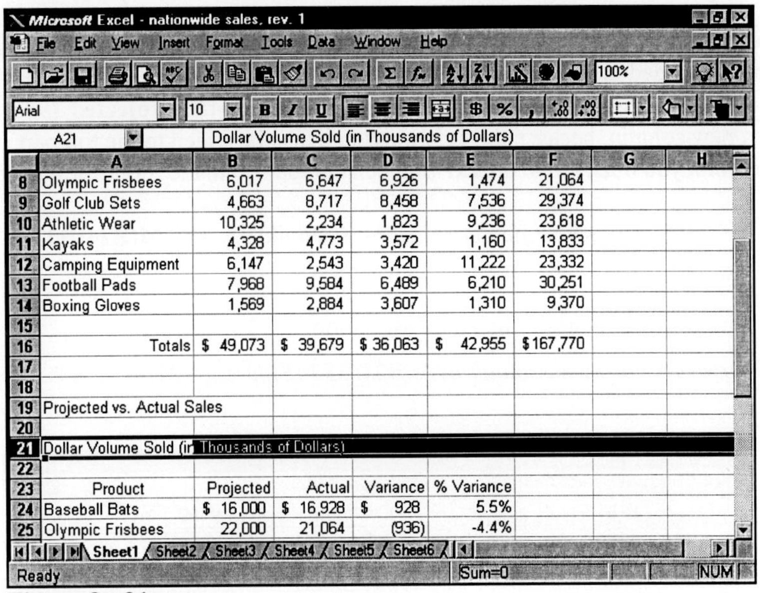

Figure 3 - 21

Inserting and Deleting Columns

The same procedure is used to insert and delete columns, except that the column heading is selected instead of the row heading.

To insert or delete multiple columns or rows, click on the first column or row heading and drag the highlight across the other column or row headings. When inserting columns, one column is inserted for each highlighted column. The columns are inserted to the left of the first highlighted column.

REARRANGING A WORKSHEET BY MOVING CELL CONTENTS

When you insert rows or columns, the row or column is added for the full width or length of the worksheet. Sometimes, you want to add a new column of data in one part of your worksheet without disturbing the rest of the worksheet. In this case, you must move the existing cell contents. The procedure for moving cells is similar to that for copying cells but the effect is very different. When cells are moved the original location becomes blank. In addition if the cell contains a formula, it is not adjusted in the same way that copied cells are.

To move cell contents:

- Select the cell(s) containing the information to be moved.

- Choose **EDIT/Cut** or click the **Cut** button  on the Standard toolbar.

  The range to be moved is surrounded by a moving border.

- Choose the upper-left cell of the range to which the cell contents are to be moved.

- Press **ENTER** to move the cell contents. The original cells will be empty.

> **CAUTION:** *When the cut cells are pasted in their new location, they will overwrite any existing cell contents.*

Activity 3.9: Adding New Data to Part of the Worksheet

After you have completed your worksheet, you are told that the 1994 actual sales figures should also be included in the **Projected vs. Actual Sales** part of your worksheet. You want to include the **1994 Sales** figures between the **Product** names and the **Projected** 1995 figures. You cannot add a new column, because the column would also be added to the top part of the worksheet. Therefore, you must move the existing cell contents to make room for the new data.

1. Select **B33.** Look at the Formula Bar. It should say =**SUM(B24:B32)**.

2. Select **B23:E33**.

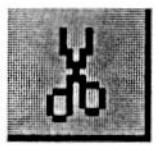

3. Choose **EDIT/Cut** or click the **Cut** button.

   A moving border surrounds cells B23:E33 (Figure 3 - 22).

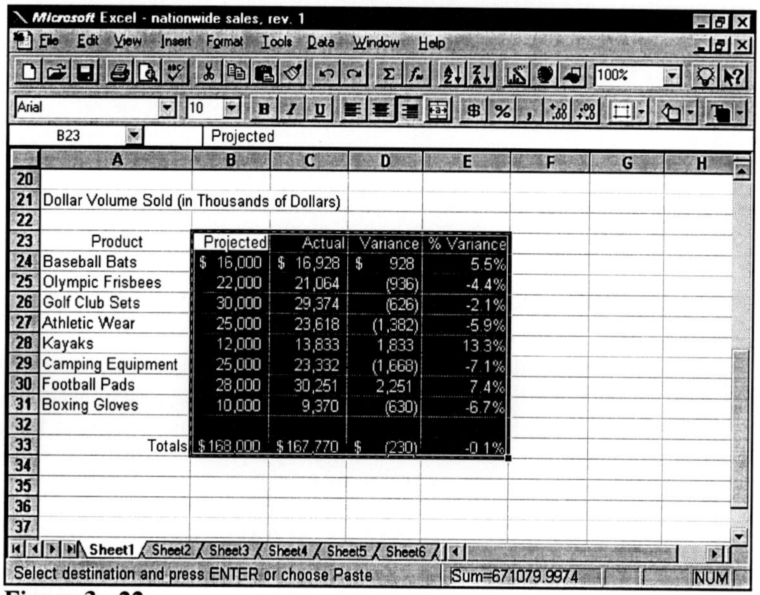

Figure 3 - 22

4. Select the top left cell of the new range, **C23**.

5. Press **ENTER**.

   The selected range is moved to C23:F33. Some numbers may be replaced by ### because they are wider than the column they are now in.

6. Increase column widths if necessary to display cell contents.

7. Select **C33** and look at the Formula Bar.

   When a formula and the cells referenced in the formula are both moved, the formula adjusts to reflect the new locations of the referenced cells (Figure 3 - 23). Therefore, the formula is now =SUM(C24:C32) instead of =SUM(B24:B32).

8. In **B23** enter the label for the new column: **1994 Sales**

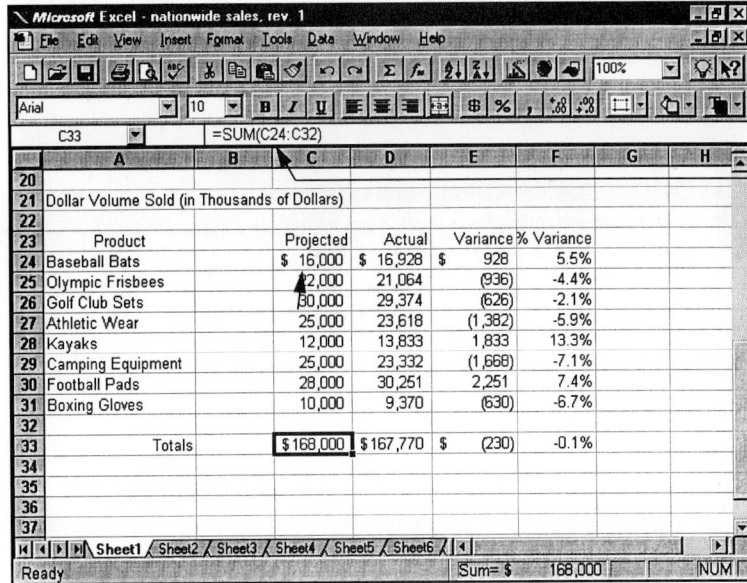

Figure 3 - 23

9. In cells **B24:E31** enter the data below. Only type the numbers. The row labels are only included to keep you from getting lost while entering the data.

Existing Row Headings	Data to enter:
Baseball Bats	14345
Olympic Frisbees	20567
Golf Club Sets	28567
Athletic Wear	23145
Kayaks	10111
Camping Equipment	24536
Football Pads	26000
Boxing Gloves	9328

*Notice that the new numbers are not formatted. **EDIT/Cut** and **Paste** move cell formatting along with cell contents. The original cells revert back to general format.*

10. In cell **B33** enter the **SUM** function to add up the 1994 sales.

   *The value **156599** should appear in **B33**. If your sum is different, check that you entered the correct values for **1994 Sales**.*

Activity 3.10: Finishing Touches

1. Format **B24:B33** to match **C24:C33**.

2. Center **Projected vs. Actual Sales** and **Dollar Volume Sold (in Thousands of Dollars)** over columns **A:F**. (**HINT:** Select **A19:F21** and then click on the **Center Across Columns** button).

3. Select **A23:F23** and use the **Borders** button to add a thin line as a bottom border (i.e., the border should match the one under row **6** at the top of the worksheet).

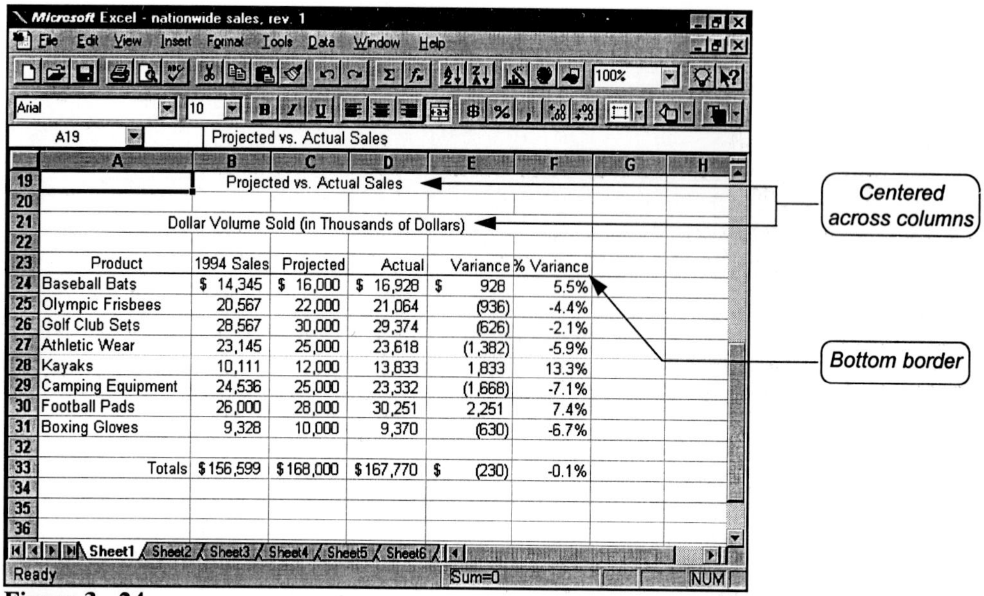

Figure 3 - 24

4. When your screen resembles Figure 3 - 24, scroll to the top of the worksheet and edit cell **A5** so that only the first letter in **PRODUCT** is in uppercase (i.e., it should match cell **A23** as shown in Figure 3 - 24.)

5. Use the **Save** button to save the file again using the existing name.

6. Choose **FILE/Page Setup**.

7. Choose the **Header/Footer** tab and choose **(none)** from the **Header** drop-down list.

8. Choose the **Print** button from the **Page Setup** dialog box. When the **Print** dialog box appears, click on **OK** to print the document.

9. Press **CTRL+`** to display formulas.

10. Use **FILE/Print** to print the worksheet again with formulas displayed.

11. Press **CTRL+`** to reset the worksheet to display values.

12. **Save** the file again to save the page setup changes. **Close** the file.

SUMMARY

In this lesson you have learned to use copying to automate worksheet creation. Although it is important to plan a worksheet before you create it, you often need to change your original design. The ability to move data and insert and delete columns and rows makes worksheet modification much easier. In Lesson 6 you will further modify this project by adding a chart to represent part of the worksheet visually.

KEY TERMS

AutoCalculate	Deleting rows	Inserting rows
AutoSum	Fill Down	Paste
Clipboard	Fill handle	Relative cell adjustment
Copy	Fill Right	Scroll
Cut	Function	Shortcut menu

INDEPENDENT PROJECTS

Independent Project 3.1: Completing a Sales Worksheet

You work for a mail order company. You have been given a worksheet that lists a number of invoices, the amount of each sale, and the shipping cost. You need to add the formulas to compute the tax and the total due, and to sum the total sales, tax, shipping, and amount due. In addition you find that some of the clients have two-part invoices, but only one part has been entered. You need to insert rows and add the new data.

When you finish this project, your worksheet should resemble Figure 3 - 25.

SALES					
Invoice Number	Name	Amount of Sale	Tax (6.75%)	Shipping	Total Due
00115	Peter Lynch	842.40	56.86	5.00	904.26
00116	Nancy Smith	597.78	40.35	5.00	643.13
00117	Jacklyn Jones	779.33	52.60	5.00	836.93
00117a	Jacklyn Jones	112.65	7.60	4.00	124.25
00118	Barry Turko	997.41	67.32	5.00	1,069.73
00119	Samuel Patter	647.03	43.67	5.00	695.71
00119a	Samuel Patter	98.53	6.65	3.00	108.18
00120	Jerry Gerald	181.65	12.26	3.00	196.91
00121	Kurry Hirray	22.37	1.51	3.00	26.88
00122	Nurnak Rumold	758.20	51.18	5.00	814.38
00122a	Nurnak Rumold	89.60	6.05	4.00	99.65
00123	Stan Williams	293.73	19.83	3.00	316.56
00124	Jennifer Lewis	75.48	5.10	3.00	83.58
00125	Sharon Jeeves	975.94	65.88	5.00	1,046.82
00126	Willie White	152.04	10.26	3.00	165.31
	Totals	6,624.15	447.13	61.00	7,132.28

Figure 3 - 25

Use Figure 3 - 25 and the following instructions to help you complete the project:

1. Open the file **independent proj. 3.1**.

2. In cell **D4** enter a formula to compute the tax. The formula should multiply the **Amount of Sale** by **6.75%**.

3. Check the result of your formula with Figure 3 - 25. If it is correct, use the **fill handle** or **EDIT/Fill down** to copy the formula down column **D** through row **15**.

4. While **D4:D15** is still selected, format the values using **Comma Style**, two decimal places.

5. In cell **F4**, enter a formula to calculate the sum of the **Amount of Sale, Tax**, and **Shipping** for the first invoice. You may use a formula that adds the three amounts or you may use the **AutoSum** button to let *Excel* insert the **sum** function.

6. Copy the formula down column **F** to row **15**.

7. Add a **Bottom Border** to cells **A15:F15**.

8. In cell **B16** add the label: **Totals**.

9. Right align and bold **Totals**.

10. In cell **C16** use **AutoSum** to total the sale amounts.

    Your total will not agree with the total shown in Figure 3 - 25. You will be adding data in the next few steps.

11. Copy the function across row **16.**

12. Save the worksheet using the name: **sales**

13. To add the second part of the invoice for **Jacklyn Jones**:

    a. Insert a row between rows **6** and **7.**

    b. Add the following data in the correct columns:

Invoice Number	**0117a**
Name:	**Jacklyn Jones**
Amount of Sale:	**112.65**
Shipping:	**4.00**

    NOTE: *As soon as you type the first two letters of **Jacklyn Jones**, or any other name already present in a list of names, Excel enters the rest of the name. You can press **ENTER** without typing the rest of the name. This is an example of AutoComplete, a new Excel 7.0 feature. To find out more about AutoComplete, choose **What's New** from the **Contents** tab of the **Help Topics** dialog box.*

    c. Copy the formulas for the **Tax** and **Total Due** from cells **D6** and **F6.**

14. Add the second part of the invoices for **Samuel Patter** and **Nurnak Rumold** in an inserted row beneath each of their current invoices. Copy the appropriate formulas from the preceding row. Use the following data:

Invoice Number:	**00119a**	**00122a**
Name:	**Samuel Patter**	**Nurnak Rumold**
Amount of Sale:	**98.53**	**89.60**
Shipping:	**3.00**	**4.00**

    Your totals should now agree with those shown in Figure 3 - 25.

15. Use **Page Setup** to delete the header and create a custom footer that includes your name, course name, and the current date. Print the worksheet.

16. Save the file again using the name: **sales, rev. 1**

17. Print the worksheet again displaying formulas. Close the worksheet.

Independent Project 3.2: Rearranging Data by Country

You have been given a worksheet that analyzes sales of several American, British, German, and Japanese cars in seven states. Currently the sales for each country's cars are presented next to each other. You have been asked to reorganize the worksheet so that the sales for each country's cars are separated. Once this is completed you will also add totals for each state and for the total number of each car sold in the included states.

When you finish this project, your worksheet should resemble Figure 3 - 26 except for font size and column spacing.

Use Figure 3 - 26 and the following instructions to help you complete the project:

1. Open the file, **independent proj. 3.2.**

1		**AUTO SALES BY STATE**				
2						
3		American Manufacturers				
4	State:	Ford	GM	Chrysler	Totals	
5	Florida	12,349	78,924	13,454	104,727	
6	Georgia	45,675	12,372	24,344	82,391	
7	S. Carolina	89,017	87,459	2,345	178,821	
8	N. Carolina	23,453	34,250	14,548	72,251	
9	Pennsylvania	56,786	67,337	14,456	138,579	
10	New Jersey	87,658	123,395	45,665	256,718	
11	New York	15,230	64,544	45,660	125,434	
12	Totals	330,168	468,281	160,472	958,921	
13						
14						
15		UK Manufacturers				
16	State:	Jaguar	Rolls Royce	Totals		
17	Florida	1,257	5,668	6,925		
18	Georgia	89	3,000	3,089		
19	S. Carolina	154	569	723		
20	N. Carolina	887	1,220	2,107		
21	Pennsylvania	2,167	0	2,167		
22	New Jersey	980	3,453	4,433		
23	New York	1,336	12,909	14,245		
24	Totals	6,870	26,819	33,689		
25						
26						
27		German Manufacturers				
28	State:	BMW	Mercedes	Volkswagen	Totals	
29	Florida	2,267	5,512	1,229	9,008	
30	Georgia	984	983	5,403	7,370	
31	S. Carolina	127	3,380	4,812	8,319	
32	N. Carolina	1,176	2,945	8,882	13,003	
33	Pennsylvania	2,365	1,287	22,445	26,097	
34	New Jersey	4,002	5,005	8,110	17,117	
35	New York	5,910	12,760	23,800	42,470	
36	Totals	16,831	31,872	74,681	123,384	
37						
38						
39			Japanese Manufacturers			
40	State:	Honda	Toyota	Mazda	Nissan	Totals
41	Florida	52,378	5,436	3,429	1,355	62,598
42	Georgia	5,572	23,234	559	3,452	32,817
43	S. Carolina	9,030	4,564	4,312	2,356	20,262
44	N. Carolina	12,988	5,673	6,780	5,664	31,105
45	Pennsylvania	66,800	7,855	23,678	23,445	121,778
46	New Jersey	43,811	3,453	36,890	4,534	88,688
47	New York	59,802	34,532	12,765	34,555	141,654
48	Totals	250,381	84,747	88,413	75,361	498,902

Figure 3 - 26

2. Move the data on the **UK Manufacturers** from **E3:F11** to an area of the worksheet beginning in cell **B15**.

3. Move the data on the **German Manufacturers** from **G3:I11** to an area of the worksheet beginning in cell **B27**.

4. Move the data on the **Japanese Manufacturers** to an area of the worksheet beginning in cell **B39**.

5. You need labels for the UK, German, and Japanese cars. Copy the **State** names from **A4:A11** to areas beginning in cell **A16, A28,** and **A40**.

6. In **E4** enter the column label: **Totals**

7. Right align **Totals** and add a bottom border to the cell that matches the one used in the rest of the line.

   SHORTCUT: *Instead of manually changing the format of cell E4 to match the rest of the row you can use the Format Painter button to copy the format from a previous cell. To do this, select cell D4 (the cell with the format that you want to copy), click on the Format Painter button   , and then click on E4 (the cell to which you want to copy the format).*

8. In **E5** use **AutoSum** to total the **Florida** sales for the three American Manufacturers. Copy the formula down the column.

9. Enter the same labels and totals for the other three countries.

10. In cell **A12** enter the row label: **Totals** and right-align it.

11. In cell **B12** use **AutoSum** to total the sales for **Ford**. Copy the formula across the row through column **E**.

12. Enter the same labels and totals for the other three countries.

13. Add a thick **Bottom Border** to the row above all of the totals lines. Increase any column widths for columns where all of the values or labels are not displayed. Make any other formatting changes necessary so that your worksheet resembles Figure 3 - 26.

14. Save your file as: **auto sales by state**

15. Preview the worksheet. In preparation to print your document remove the footer and create a custom header that contains only your name, class, and the current date.

16. Print the worksheet.

17. Save the worksheet using the current name so that you save your page setup.

18. Print the worksheet again displaying formulas. Close the worksheet without saving.

Independent Project 3.3: Rearranging Data to Facilitate Projections

The travel agency that you work for has a simple worksheet that analyzes the sales of its special vacation packages to five different locations. The travel agency wants you to compare sales in the peak summer season, June through August, with the two bordering periods, spring (April/May) and autumn (September/October) so that you can make projections for next year's sales. You decide that it would be easier for you to do this if you separate the current worksheet into three sections — one for each of the time periods. Then you will total the sales figures for each destination and each month in each time period.

   Use Figure 3 - 27 as a general guide to completing your worksheet, but your worksheet need not be an exact copy. (Font sizes and spacing may differ from your worksheet.)

THE BEST TRAVEL AGENCY IN THE UNITED STATES

Summer Vacation Package Sales

Destination	June	July	August	Totals
New York	125	165	154	444
Disney World	653	754	558	1,965
Alaska	425	552	425	1,402
Yellowstone National Park	332	425	411	1,168
LA/San Francisco	199	210	205	614
Totals	1,734	2,106	1,753	5,593

Spring Vacation Package Sales

Destination	April	May	Totals
New York	85	60	145
Disney World	500	335	835
Alaska	100	200	300
Yellowstone National Park	175	160	335
LA/San Francisco	150	130	280
Totals	1,010	885	1,895

Autumn Vacation Package Sales

Destination	September	October	Totals
New York	135	86	221
Disney World	350	290	640
Alaska	225	65	290
Yellowstone National Park	190	123	313
LA/San Francisco	175	148	323
Totals	1,075	712	1,787

Figure 3 - 27

Use Figure 3 - 27 and the following instructions to help you complete the project:

1. Open the file **independent proj. 3.3**.

2. To begin the part of the worksheet that will look at spring sales, add the title, **Spring Vacation Package Sales**, in column **A** a few rows below the current filled cells.

3. Move the labels and values that deal with **April** and **May** sales to the new section of your worksheet. Remember to leave a blank column for the destination names.

4. Label a section for autumn sales and move **September** and **October** data to this section.

5. Copy the destinations for your vacation packages from the original section of the worksheet to the two new sections.

6. Move the remaining summer months next to the destinations.

7. Label the remains of the first part of your worksheet **Summer Vacation Package Sales**.

8. For each section of the worksheet total the sales for each destination and each month. Format the labels to match existing labels. Format all values for comma with no decimal places. Separate the bottom row of totals from the values above it with a line.

9. Format the names of the sections any way you wish, as long as you use a different font, font size, or font style from the rest of the labels on the worksheet.

10. Center titles across columns if you wish.

11. **Save** the file as: **vacation**

12. Preview your file. Change the header to include identifying information about you, and make any other formatting changes to the printout that you wish.

13. **Print** the worksheet.

14. **Save** the file again using the current name.

15. **Print** the worksheet with formulas displayed.

Independent Project 3.4: Creating a Payroll

ECAP Corporation has decided to computerize its payroll. As the first step in the process, you have been given a worksheet that contains the raw data for last week's payroll. You have been asked to add all of the necessary formulas to the worksheet and do some basic formatting. You have also been asked to separate the exempt and hourly employees.

Use the following guidelines while completing your project:

1. Open the file **independent proj. 3.4**.

2. Separate the sections for hourly and exempt employees. You can create the second section by moving the data on each exempt employee to a row under those of all of the hourly employees. The section should have a label and each of the columns should have the same labels as already included in the worksheet. Figure 3 - 28 shows you the organization of the worksheet after it has been divided into two sections and step 3 has been completed. (Some of the exempt employees are not shown.) Use moving and copying to reorganize the worksheet or use the shortcut directions that follow.

ECAP CORPORATION							
Hourly Employees							
		Hourly	Gross		Taxes		Net
Employee	Hours	Wage	Pay	FICA	State	Federal	Pay
Albert, Joel	80	6.5					
Boyenga, Gladys	80	5					
Dodd, Doris	78	3.8					
Eisenberg, Sun-Wong	80	5.5					
Harrison, Wilbert	80	4.5					
King, John	76	5.5					
Raymond, Frank	80	4.5					
Stoddard, James	80	6.5					
Thompson, Frederic	75	7					
Exempt Employees							
	Gross			Taxes		Net	
Employee	Pay	FICA	State	Federal	Pay		
Cruz, Elinor	636						
Farrell, Dudley	1650						
Glass, Cynthia	1850						
Major, John	1200						
Nelson, Charles	580						
Paige, Carol	750						
Wagner, George	1800						
Zandonetta, Bjorn	2000						

Figure 3 - 28

SHORTCUT: *It is hard to move all of the data on the exempt employees because these employees are scattered throughout the employee list. A shortcut involves the use of the **Sort Ascending** button ▲▼, one of the data features that is not covered in this book. To use **Sort Ascending**:*

    a.   Select **B6**, one of the cells in the column that includes the word **exempt**.

    b.   Click on the **Sort Ascending** button on the Standard toolbar. *Excel* automatically selects all of your data and puts it in order according to the entries in the **Hours** column. The exempt workers are at the end because values are sorted before labels.

    c.   Insert **4** rows before the first exempt worker.

    d.   Copy the existing column labels to the two rows immediately above the first exempt employee.

    e.   To alphabetize the names of the hourly employees, select a cell containing a name of an hourly employee and click on the **Sort Ascending** button.

    f.   To alphabetize the names of the exempt employees, select a cell containing a name of an exempt employee and click on the **Sort Ascending** button.

    *For further information on sorting use **Help**.*

3.   The exempt employee part of the worksheet should not include the **Hours** or **Hourly Wage** columns (as indicated in Figure 3 - 28).

4.   Include formulas for the **Gross Pay** for the hourly (nonexempt) workers, and **FICA, State** and **Federal** taxes, and the **Net Pay** for all workers. To compute these values, we will use the following simplified assumptions:

        Gross Pay (for hourly workers) equals hours times hourly wages
        FICA equals 7.65% of gross pay
        State taxes equal 4.5% of gross pay
        Federal taxes equal 28% of gross pay
        Net pay equals gross pay minus FICA, and state and local taxes

5.   Total the **Gross Pay** and **Net Pay** for the hourly employees and for the exempt employees.

6.   Format the worksheet appropriately.

7.   Save the worksheet using the name: **payroll**

8.   Print the worksheet using a page setup that includes identifying information about you in the header or footer.

9.   Print the worksheet with formulas displayed.

Lesson 4 More Formulas and Functions

Objectives

In this lesson you will learn how to:

- Let *Excel* help you create a series
- Adjust column widths to fit part of a column
- Create more complex formulas
- Change the range inserted by the **AutoSum** button
- Create multi-line labels in one cell

- Use the statistical functions, **AVERAGE, MIN, MAX**
- Use the **TODAY** function to enter the current date
- Use the **Function Wizard** to enter functions
- Use nonadjacent cells in a function

PROJECT DESCRIPTION

In this lesson you will create an expense report. While on your business trip, you used your Notebook computer to enter your expenses quickly. In this project you will finish entering data and then will calculate your daily expenditures in each category to determine the amount that you should be reimbursed. In addition, your company, ECAP Corporation, is reconsidering its expense account guidelines for meals. Therefore, it has requested that you analyze your meal expenses. When finished, your worksheet will resemble Figure 4 - 1 except for the submission date.

The focus of this lesson is to increase your ability to use formulas and functions. However, you will also review the formatting skills learned in Lesson 2 and learn about an extension of *Excel's* **Fill** command—**Fill Series**.

CREATING A SERIES

In Lesson 3 you used the **fill handle** or **EDIT/Fill** to copy a cell or range of cells to adjacent cells. However, if the filled cell contains a day of the week, a month, a date, or other data that *Excel* recognizes as the beginning of a *series* (see Table 4-1), *Excel* assumes that you want to create a series of entries rather than make an exact copy of the cell contents.

CONTENTS OF CELL(S) TO BE COPIED	NEXT TWO VALUES OF SERIES
January	February, March
Nov	Dec, Jan
Tue	Wed, Thu
1/1/96	1/2/96, 1/3/96
Division 1	Division 2, Division 3
1/1/96, 1/8/96	1/15/96, 1/22/96

Table 4 - 1 Results of Filling a Series

ECAP Corporation Travel Expense Report

Submitted by: Jessica Gabriel
Date: 2/10/96

Categories	2/1/96	2/2/96	2/3/96	2/4/96	2/5/96	Total
Breakfast		7.89	8.99	6.50	4.50	27.88
Dinner		15.50	20.00	22.75	12.00	70.25
Tips		4.21	5.22	5.27	2.97	17.66
Air Fare	358.00					358.00
Car Rental	49.00	49.00	49.00	49.00		196.00
Hotel	119.00	119.00	119.00	119.00		476.00
Miscellaneous	5.00	3.50	8.00	2.75	15.00	34.25
Daily Total	$ 531.00	$ 199.10	$ 210.21	$ 205.27	$ 34.47	$ 1,180.04

Expense	Minimum Spent	Maximum Spent	Average Spent
Breakfast	4.50	8.99	6.97
Dinner	12.00	22.75	17.56
Total	$ 16.50	$ 31.74	$ 24.53

Figure 4 - 1

To create a series:

- Enter a day, a month, a date, or other data that implies a series.

- Select the cell(s) containing the series starting point(s).

- Drag the **fill handle** to fill adjacent cells with the next entries in the series.

ALTERNATE METHOD: *EDIT/Fill,Series can also be used to fill a range with a series. More customized series can also be created with this command. Click on the **Help** menu and choose **Answer Wizard**. In the **Type your request** text box of the **Help Topics** window, type **How do I create a custom autofill list** and click the **Search** button. Click on **Create a custom AutoFill list** in the **How Do I** section, and click the **Display** button for further instructions.*

Activity 4.1: Creating a Series of Days

In this activity you will use the **fill handle** to help you replace the column labels Day 1 through Day 5 with the actual dates. Then you will use the **fill handle** to copy the daily hotel and car rental fees to the rest of the week.

1. Start *Excel* and open **Lesson4**. If necessary, maximize the *Excel* and **Lesson4** windows (Figure 4 - 2).

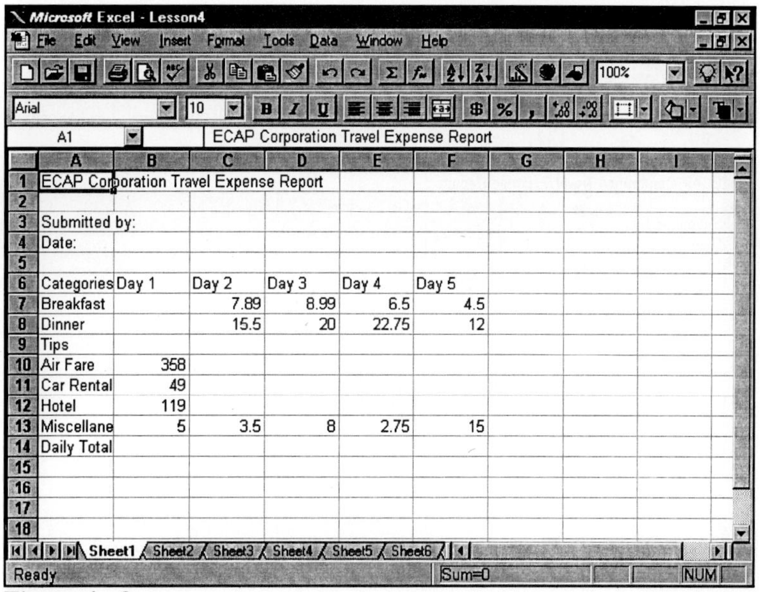

Figure 4 - 2

2. Select cell **B6** and enter the date: **2/1/96**

   *2/1/96 will replace **Day 1** as soon as you press **ENTER** or click on the **enter box**.*

3. Point to the **fill handle**. When the mouse pointer changes to a ✚, press the left mouse button and slowly drag to the right to select cells **B6:F6**. Before you release the mouse button, look at the **name box** in the Formula Bar. It will say **2/5/96**. Release the left mouse button.

   Excel automatically fills the range with the series of dates that follows 2/1/96 (Figure 4 - 3).

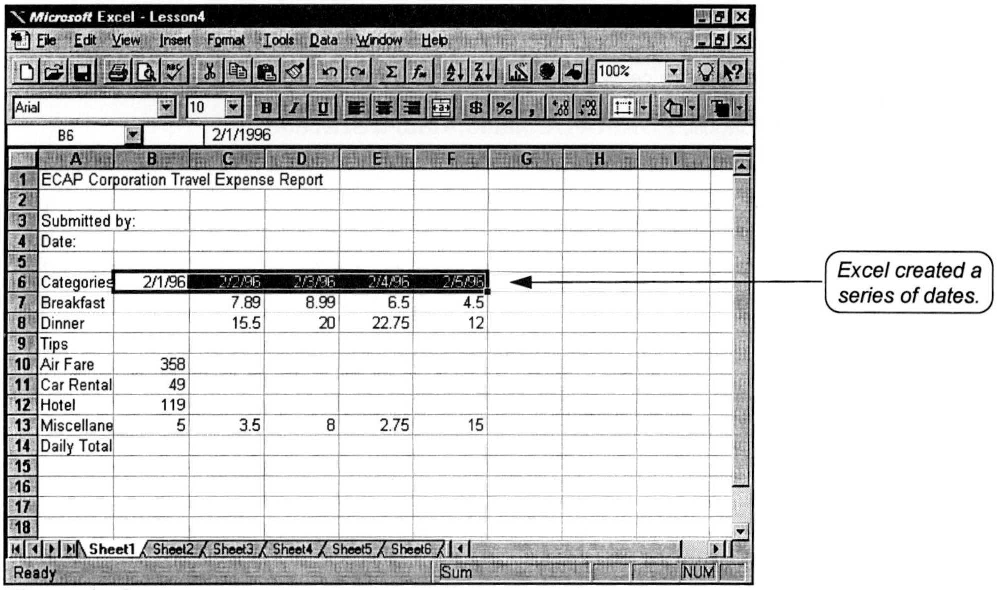

Excel created a series of dates.

Figure 4 - 3

4. Select the range **B11:B12**.

5. To copy the daily car rental and hotel charges to the rest of the row, drag the **fill handle** to **E12**. Look at the **name box** in the Formula Bar as you drag the mouse. The number **49** remains in the **name box** because that number is being copied instead of incremented. When the range **B11:E12** is highlighted, release the left mouse button (Figure 4 - 4).

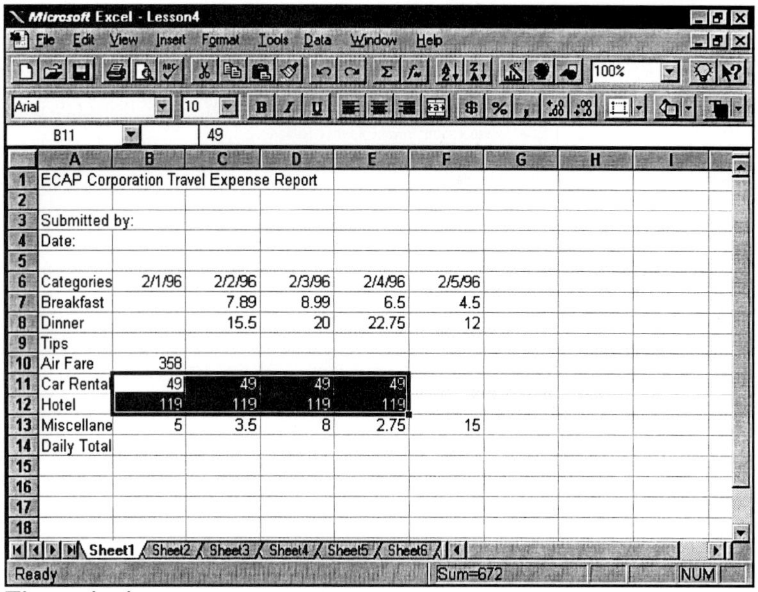

Figure 4 - 4

AUTOMATICALLY ADJUSTING COLUMN WIDTHS FOR PART OF A COLUMN

As you saw briefly in Lesson 3, occasionally you want *Excel* to adjust the column width to fit some, but not all, of the entries in a column. This is most often used when the column contains titles for the worksheet or a section of the worksheet.

To adjust the column width to fit some of the entries in a column:

- Select the cells containing the data that you want to be fully displayed within the column.

- Choose **FORMAT/Column,AutoFit Selection.**

Activity 4.2: Changing Column Widths

In this activity you will change the width of column **A** to accommodate the expense categories. Since you do not want the column width to accommodate the worksheet title, you will select the expense categories before applying **AutoFit Selection.**

1. Select the part of column **A** to which you want to adjust the column, **A6:A14.**

2. Choose **FORMAT/Column,AutoFit Selection** (Figure 4 - 5).

ORDER OF OPERATIONS IN FORMULAS

In Lessons 1 and 3 you created simple formulas that contained only one mathematical operator in each formula. When a formula contains more than one operator, *Excel* must decide which operation to perform first. You probably learned rules for the *order of operations* when you took algebra. *Excel* follows those same rules. In a formula, *Excel* moves from left to right, first performing all operations contained within parentheses, then performing all exponentiation (^), then all multiplications (*) and divisions (/), and finally additions (+) and subtractions (-). You must use parentheses to change the normal order of operations. See Table 4 - 2 for examples of how this works.

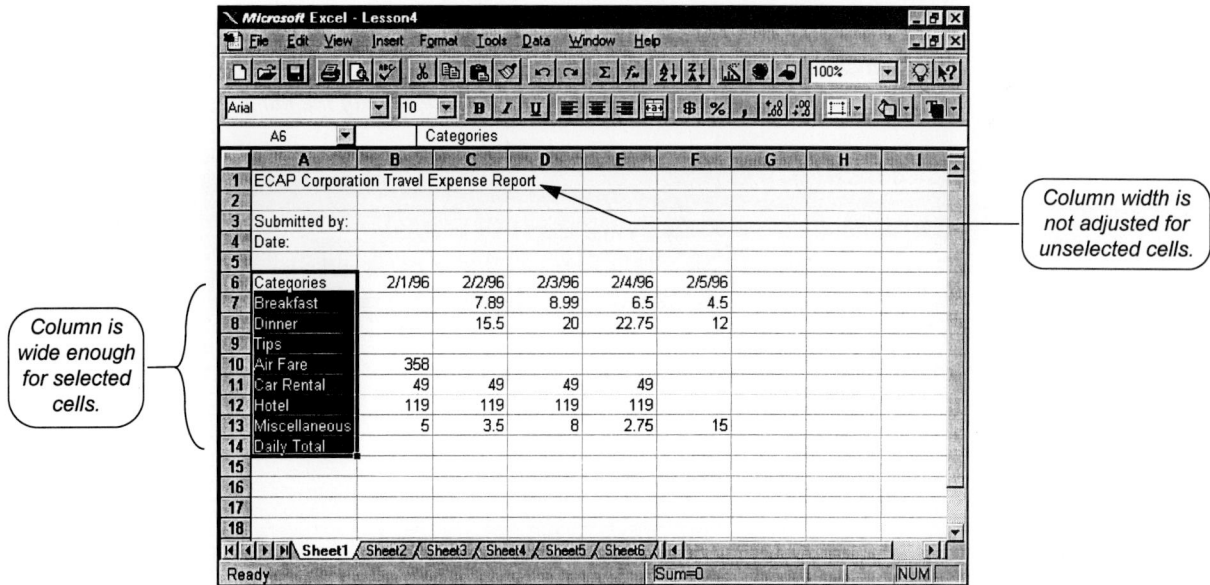

Figure 4 - 5

Formula	Order of Operations	Result (Assuming A1=3, B1=4, C1=5 and D1=6)
=2*A1+B1	Multiply 2 times A1(3); then add B1 (4)	=6+4 =10
=2*(A1+B1)	Add A1 (3) and B1 (4); then multiply the sum by 2	=2*7 =14
=A1+B1*C1	Multiply B1 (4) by C1 (5); then add A1 (3)	=3+20 =23
=A1+B1*C1+D1	Multiply B1 (4) by C1 (5); then add A1 (3); then add D1 (6)	=3+20+6 =23+6 =29
=(A1+B1)*(C1+D1)	Add A1 (3) and B1 (4); then add C1 (5) and D1 (6); then multiply the two sums	=7*(5+6) =7*11 =77

Table 4 - 2 Order of Operations

Activity 4.3: Using Parentheses to Change Order of Operations

In this activity you will create a formula to calculate the allowable tip. For expense account purposes, ECAP defines the tip as 18% of the total amount paid for breakfast and dinner.

1. To enter a formula to calculate 18% of the total spent on breakfast and dinner:

    a. Select **C9**.

    b. Type: **=18%*(**

        *You may type **18 percent** as **.18** or as **18%**. If you type **18%**, Excel automatically divides 18 by 100 and uses .18 in the calculations.*

    c. Click on cell **C7**.

    d. Type: **+**

    e. Click on cell **C8**.

f.   Type: **)** and press **ENTER** or click on the **enter box**.

*Excel calculates .18 (18%) times the sum of (7.89+15.5) and enters the result, **4.2102** in C9 (Figure 4 - 6). Don't worry about the appearance of the number; you'll format it later.*

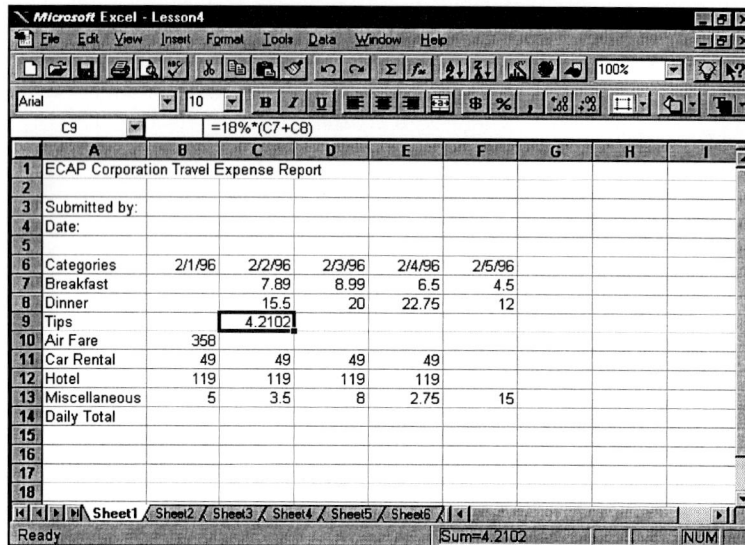

Figure 4 - 6

2.   Use the **fill handle** to copy the formula to cells **D9:F9**.

Activity 4.4: Changing the Range Inserted by the AutoSum Button

Next, you want to calculate the totals for each category and for each day. The easiest way to do this is to use the **AutoSum** tool that you used in Lesson 3.

1.   In **G6** enter the column label: **Total**

2.   Select cell **G7**.

3.   Click the **AutoSum** button once.

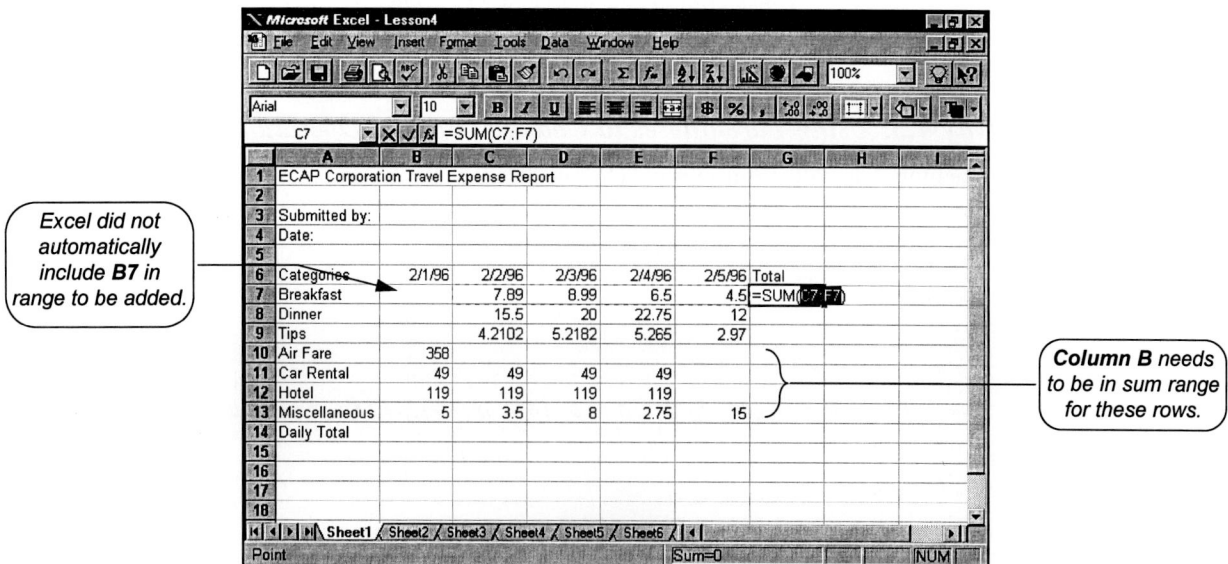

Excel did not automatically include B7 in range to be added.

Column B needs to be in sum range for these rows.

Figure 4 - 7

The function =SUM(C7:F7) will be entered (Figure 4 - 7). Excel did not include B7 in the range because it is empty. Since you want to copy the function down column G, you must include B7 in the function. Even though B7 is empty, column B does contain data in the other rows to which you will copy the function.

4. Select the correct range, **B7:F7**.

    B7:F7 *replaces* **C7:F7** *in the function in cell* **G7** *and in the Formula Bar (Figure 4 - 8).*

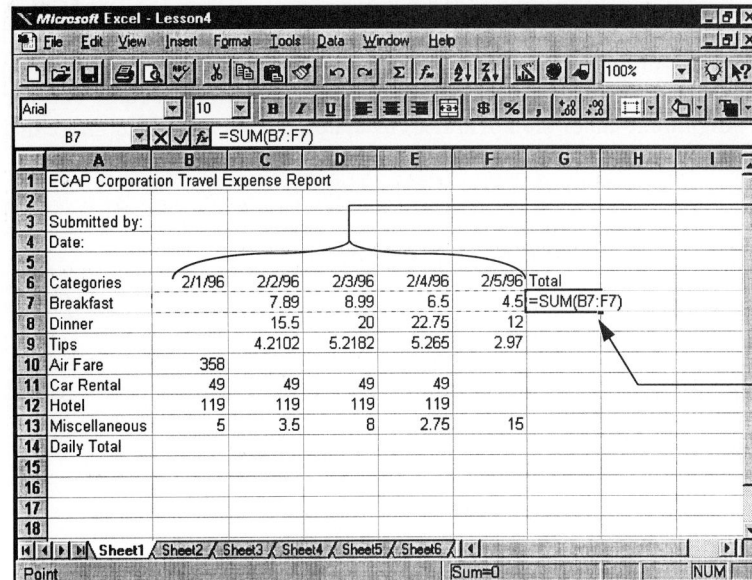

Figure 4 - 8

5. Click on the **AutoSum** button again or press **ENTER** to enter the corrected function.

6. Use the **fill handle** to copy the function down column **G** through cell **G13**.

7. Use the **AutoSum** button to enter the sum of the daily expenses in cell **B14**. Be sure to adjust the range that *Excel* suggests for the function to **B7:B13** so that the formula will copy correctly.

8. Use the **fill handle** to copy the sum function across row **14** to column **G** (Figure 4 - 9).

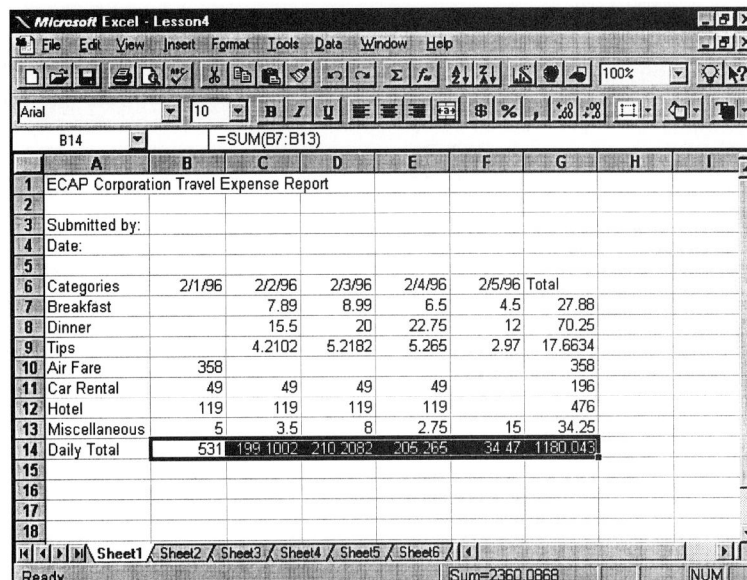

Figure 4 - 9

9. Now you want to use **AutoCalculate** to check your total expenses for the week. Select **B14:F14**. Look at the AutoCalculate area of the Status Bar. It should display **Sum=1180.0434**, which is the same value displayed in cell **G14**.

10. Use **FILE/Save As** to save the worksheet using the file name: **travel**

CREATING MULTI-LINE LABELS IN ONE CELL

Next you are going to create a new section of the worksheet. The section will analyze the amount spent on meals. In previous projects when a column label was wider than the width you wanted the column to be, you typed each part of the label into different cells. The **Wrap Text** check box on the **Alignment** tab of the **Format Cells** dialog box lets you enter more than one line of text in a single cell.

To create a multi-line label in one cell:

*   Enter the label into the cell.

*   Choose **FORMAT/Format cells** from the Menu Bar or display the shortcut menu and choose **Format Cells**.

*   Choose the **Alignment** tab if it is not already selected.

*   Check the **Wrap Text** check box and click on **OK**.

Activity 4.5: Creating Multi-line Column Labels in One Cell

1. Select cell **A19**. (HINT: Press **CTRL+HOME** and then press **PAGE DOWN**. Move the cursor if necessary.)

2. In cells **A19, B19, C19,** and **D19**, enter the column labels from Table 4 - 3 for the section of the worksheet analyzing the food costs. Since the column labels are too wide for a single cell, they will overflow into the next cell (Figure 4 - 10) or be truncated if that cell is filled. You will fix that by using an alignment option that you have not yet used.

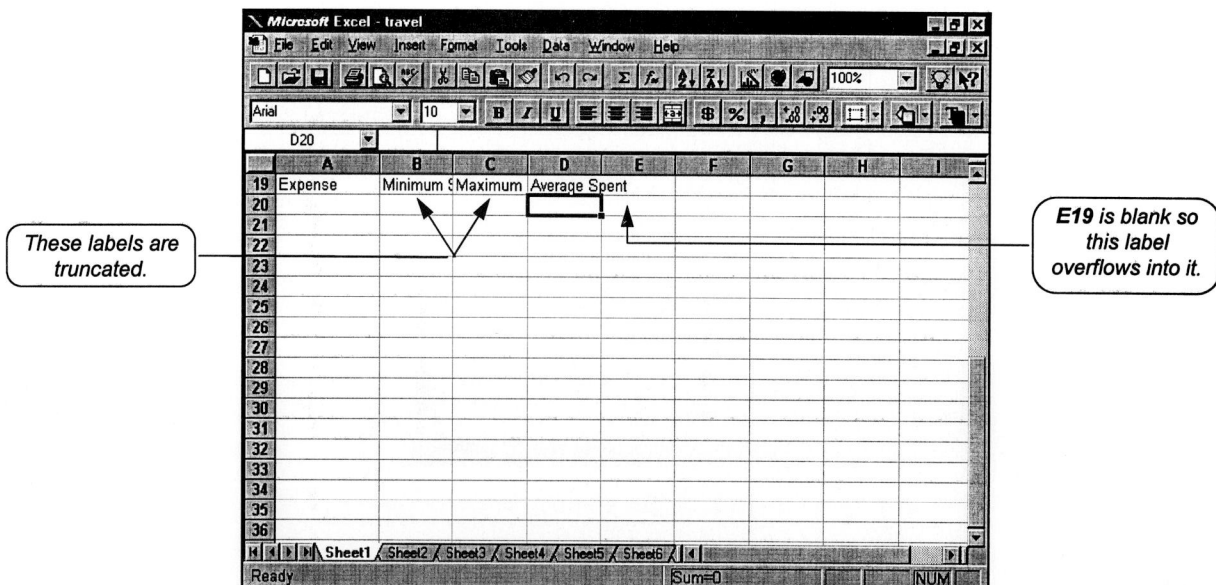

These labels are truncated.

E19 is blank so this label overflows into it.

Figure 4 - 10

Cell	Label
A19	**Expense**
B19	**Minimum Spent**
C19	**Maximum Spent**
D19	**Average Spent**

Table 4 - 3

3. Select cells **B19:D19**.

4. While pointing somewhere in the range **B19:D19**, click the right mouse button.

   The shortcut menu for a range of cells appears (Figure 4 - 11).

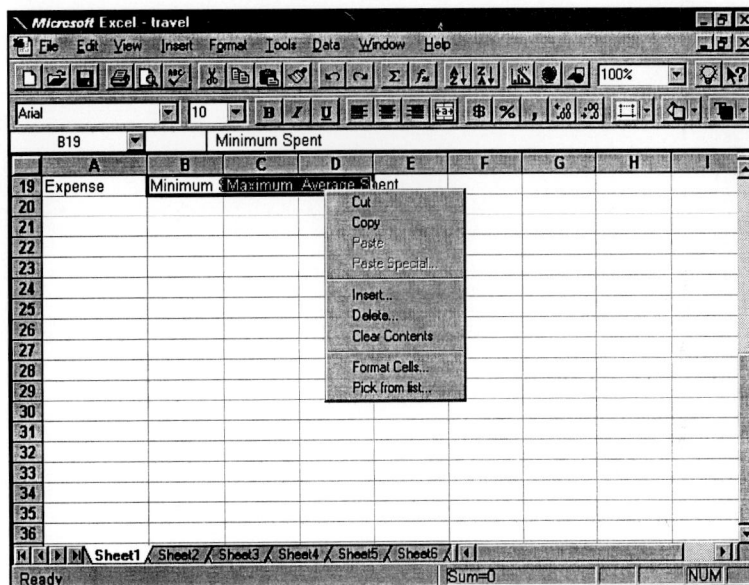

Figure 4 - 11

5. Choose **Format Cells**.

6. Click on the **Alignment** tab in the **Format Cells** dialog box.

7. Click on the **Wrap Text** check box to mark it (Figure 4 - 12).

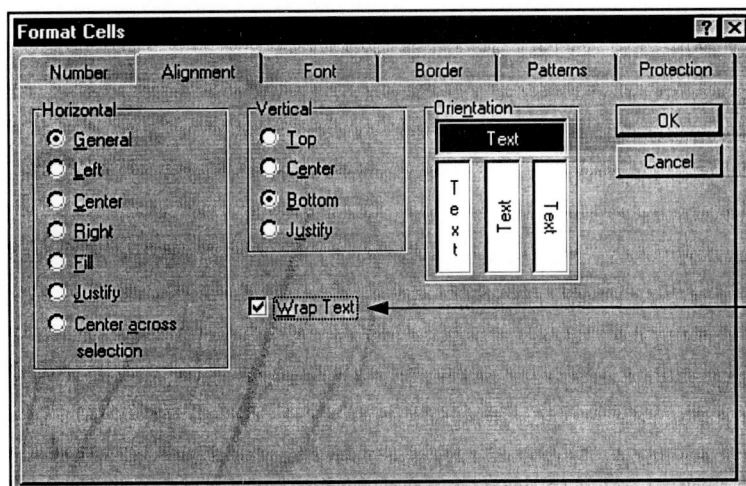

Click on Wrap Text to select.

Figure 4 - 12

8.   Click on **OK**.

Notice that the row automatically got taller to accommodate the multiple lines of text.

9.   Copy cells **A7:A8** to **A20:A21** (Figure 4 - 13).

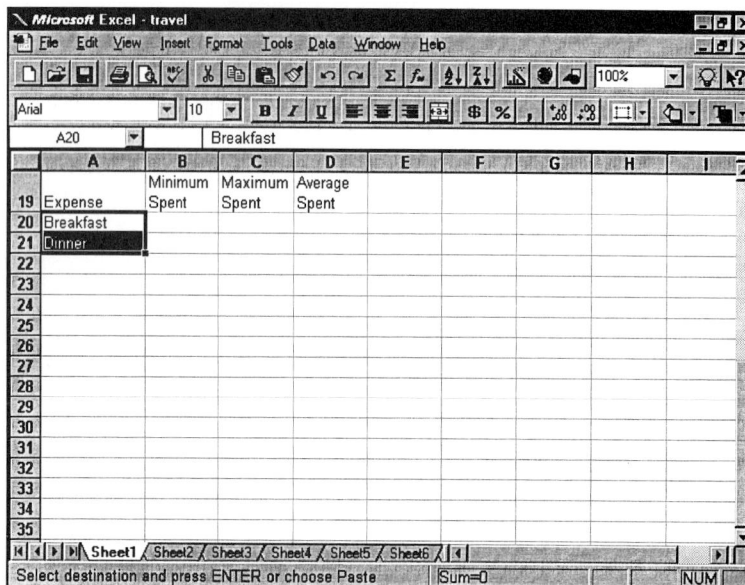

Figure 4 - 13

FUNCTIONS

Analyzing Data with the MIN, MAX, and AVERAGE Functions

You've finished your basic expense calculations. Now you are ready to do some analysis on your expense accounts. ECAP corporation sets a $20 limit on the amount spent daily for breakfast and dinner. (Lunch expenditures are not reimbursed since they are considered normal daily expenses.) To see how reasonable this limit is, you want to find the least, most, and average amount spent on meals each day.

Among the more than 400 functions included with *Excel* are statistical functions that let you find the minimum (=**MIN**), maximum (=**MAX**), or average (=**AVERAGE**) value of a range. All functions have the same format as the **SUM** function. They begin with an equal sign (=) followed by the function name. The function name is then followed by a set of parentheses that contains the values that the function will use in its predefined calculations. The values included within the parentheses are called the *arguments* of the function. The arguments of the **MIN, MAX,** and **AVERAGE** functions, like those of the **SUM** function, are the range(s) of cells to be added or averaged or from which the minimum or maximum value is to be found.

To enter the MIN, MAX, or AVERAGE functions manually:

• Type an equal sign followed by the name of the function and a left parenthesis.

• Use pointing to select the range to be used in the function. (If more than one range is included, select the first range and keep the **CTRL** key depressed while pointing to the next range(s).)

• Type the closing right parenthesis and press **ENTER** or click on the **enter box**.

Activity 4.6: Using the MIN, MAX and AVERAGE Functions to Analyze Data

1.   Select cell **B20**.

2. Type: **=min(**

3. Scroll the screen up until row 7 is visible. Select the range containing the daily breakfast costs, **C7:F7** (Figure 4 - 14).

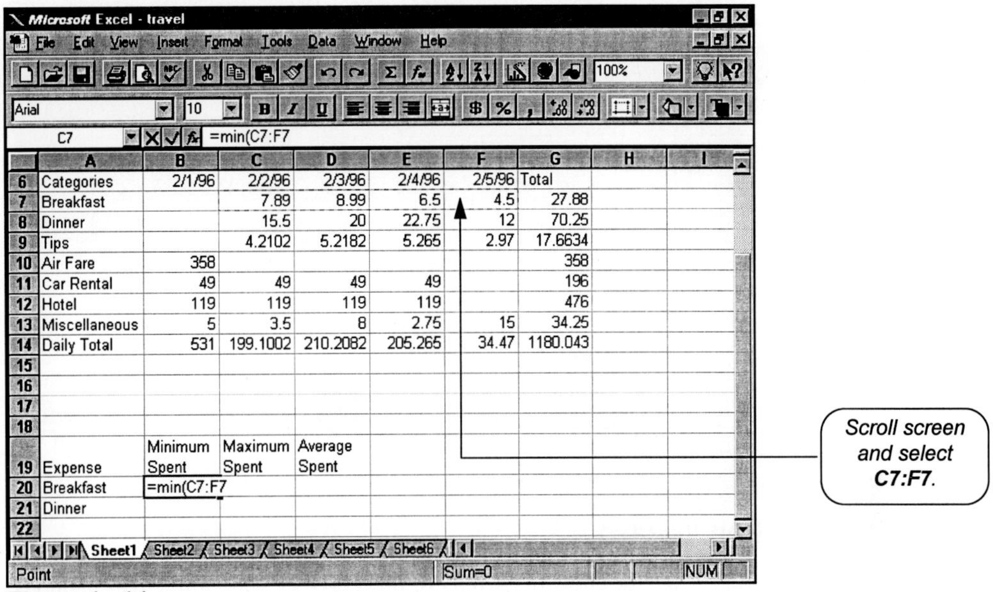

Figure 4 - 14

4. Type: **)** and click on the **enter box** or press **ENTER**.

    The function =MIN(C7:F7) appears in the Formula Bar. The smallest value (4.5) in the range C7:F7 appears in cell B20.

5. Use the same procedure to enter the formula for the maximum spent for breakfast (**=max**) in cell **C20**.

    When C20 is selected, =MAX(C7:F7) appears in the Formula Bar and the maximum amount in the range (8.99) appears in the cell.

6. Enter the formula for the average spent for breakfast (**=average**) in **D20**.

7. Select the range containing the three functions, **B20:D20**.

8. Use the **fill handle** to copy the formulas down to cells **B21:D21** (Figure 4 - 15).

9. In **A22** enter the row label: **Total**

10. Use the **AutoSum** tool to calculate the sum of the minimum spent in cell **B22**.

11. Use the **fill handle** to copy the sum formula from **B22** to **C22** and **D22**.

12. **Save** the file again using the existing name.

Entering the System Date

Often you want to include the completion date on your worksheet. The **TODAY** function allows you to enter the *system date* on your worksheet. The system date is a preset date, which is automatically updated and which should be set to the current date. The date entered by the **TODAY** function is updated whenever you open the worksheet so that it will always display the current date.

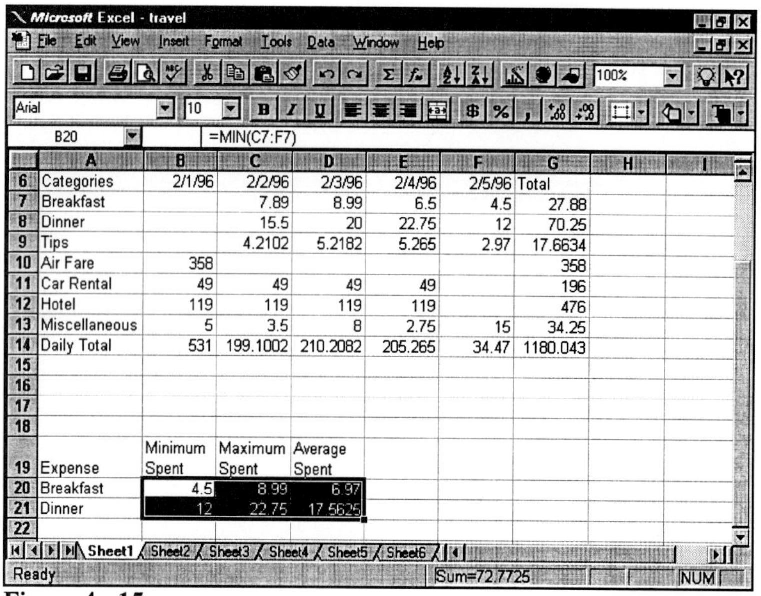

Figure 4 - 15

Using the Function Wizard

You don't have to know the syntax of the **TODAY** function. *Excel* includes a number of aids, called *wizards*, which guide you through the basic steps required to complete a task. The **Function Wizard** button on the Standard toolbar aids you in entering functions. It is useful for entering functions that you have never used before, or for entering functions with complicated syntax, or anytime you have forgotten the exact name or format of a function. Since the definition of the selected function is displayed in the **Function Wizard** dialog box, the **Function Wizard** can also be used to familiarize yourself with *Excel*'s many functions.

To use the Function Wizard to enter a function:

*   Select the cell to contain the function.
*   Click on the **Function Wizard** button f_x or select **INSERT/Function**.
*   Click on the function category. If you are unsure of the category, select **All**. Select **Most Recently Used** if you have used the function recently.
*   Click on the function name.
*   Click on the **Next** button.
*   Enter values for each of the arguments. If the argument is a range of cells, you may type the range or highlight the range on the worksheet. When an argument box is active, a description of the argument is displayed. Press the **TAB** key or click in the next box to move from box to box.
*   Click on the **Finish** button.

Activity 4.7: Using the Function Wizard to Enter the System Date

You want to include the System Date in cell **B4** so that the date the worksheet is printed appears on the worksheet.

1. Select **B4**.

f_∞

2. Click on the **Function Wizard** button or select **INSERT/Function.**

    *The **Function Wizard - Step 1 of 2** dialog box will appear (Figure 4 - 16). The **Most Recently Used** category will probably be selected in the **Function Category** list box. **TODAY** may or may not appear in the **Function Name** box, depending on whether or not someone has recently used the **TODAY** function on your computer.*

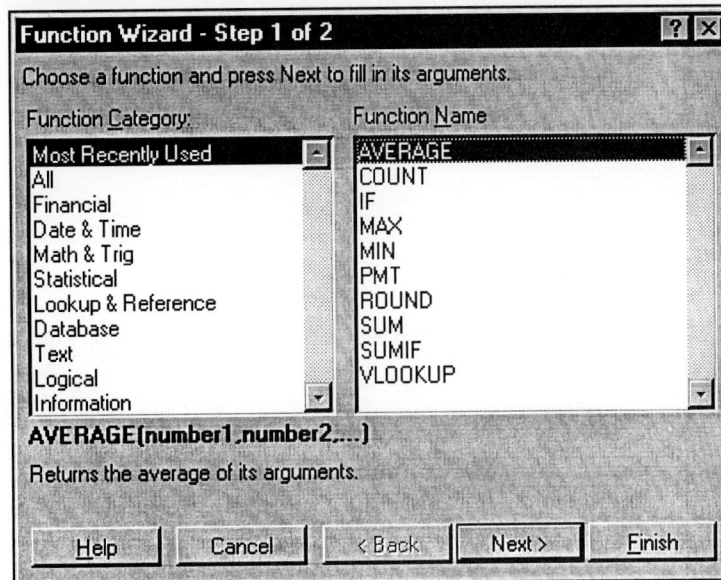

Figure 4 - 16

3. Click on **Date & Time** in the **Function Category** list box.

    *The date and time functions will be displayed in the **Function Name** list box (Figure 4 - 17).*

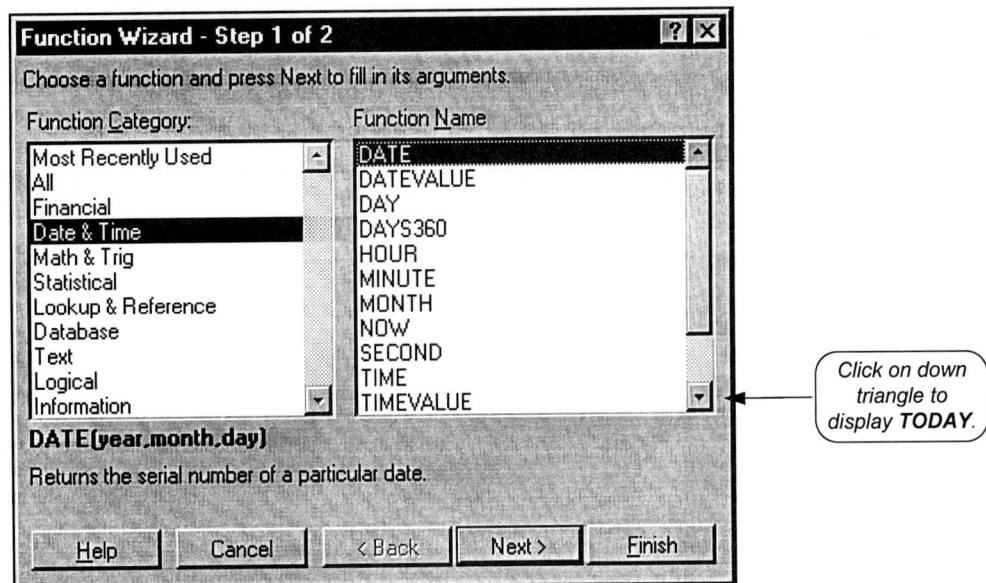

*Click on down triangle to display **TODAY**.*

Figure 4 - 17

4. Click on the ▼ on the vertical scrollbar of the **Function Name** list box until **TODAY** is visible. Click on **TODAY**.

5. Click on the **Next** button.

    *The **Function Wizard-Step 2 of 2** dialog box is displayed (Figure 4 - 18).*

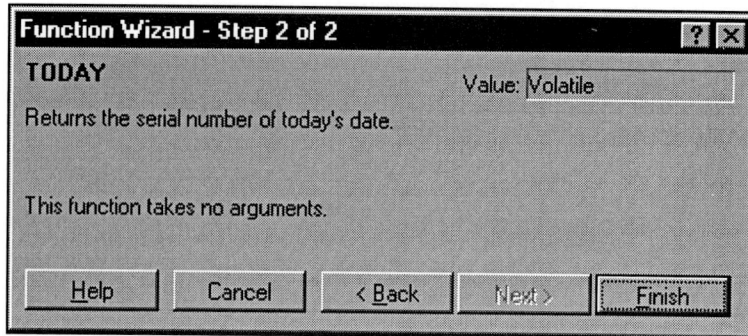

Function Wizard - Step 2 of 2 [?] [X]

TODAY   Value: Volatile

Returns the serial number of today's date.

This function takes no arguments.

| Help | Cancel | < Back | Next > | Finish |

Figure 4 - 18

6. The **TODAY** function is very simple—it contains no arguments. You have finished entering the function, so click on **Finish**.

    *The function =TODAY() is entered in the Formula Bar. Notice that Excel has begun the function with an equal sign and that the function name is followed by a set of parentheses even though they are empty. The current date should appear in cell **B4**. If the date is not today's date, tell your lab instructor so that the system date on your computer can be changed.*

Activity 4.8: Formatting the Worksheet

In this activity you will format and print the worksheet.

1. Change the font size of the worksheet title, **ECAP Corporation Travel Expense Report** to **12** point. Make the title **Bold. Center** the title **across columns A:G**.
2. Type your name into cell **B3**.
3. Make the column labels in row **6 bold. Right align** the column label **Total**.
4. Format **B7:G13** using the **Comma Style** with two decimal places.
5. Format **B14:G14** using the **Currency Style** with two decimal places.
6. Increase column widths if necessary.
7. Add a bottom border under rows **6** and **13** (Figure 4 - 19).
8. Format the second section of the worksheet in cells **A19:D22** to match **A6:G14** as in Figure 4 - 20.
9. **Save** the worksheet using the current name.

Activity 4.9: Printing the Worksheet

1. Use **FILE/Page Setup** to change the **Header** to **None**.
2. **Print** the worksheet.
3. Press **CTRL+`** to display formulas.
4. **Print** the worksheet again with formulas displayed.
5. Press **CTRL+`** again to redisplay values.
6. **Save** the worksheet again.

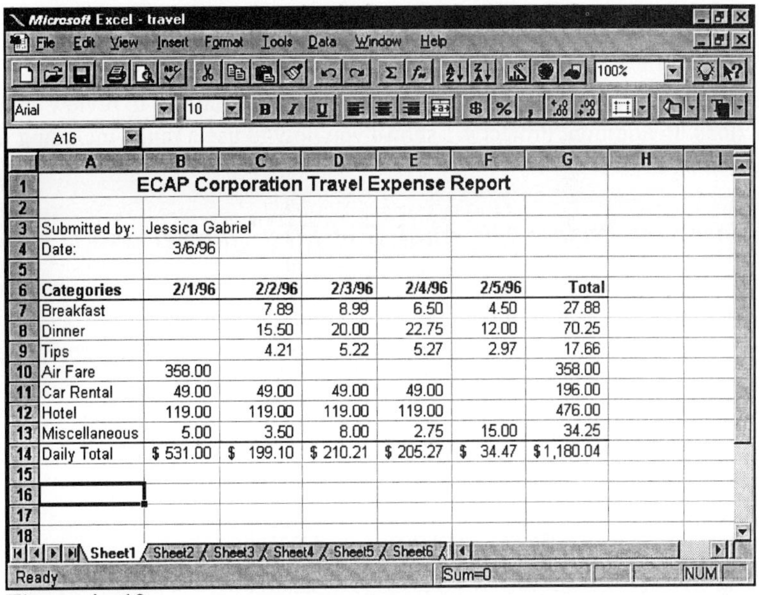

	A	B	C	D	E	F	G
1	ECAP Corporation Travel Expense Report						
2							
3	Submitted by:	Jessica Gabriel					
4	Date:	3/6/96					
5							
6	**Categories**	**2/1/96**	**2/2/96**	**2/3/96**	**2/4/96**	**2/5/96**	**Total**
7	Breakfast		7.89	8.99	6.50	4.50	27.88
8	Dinner		15.50	20.00	22.75	12.00	70.25
9	Tips		4.21	5.22	5.27	2.97	17.66
10	Air Fare	358.00					358.00
11	Car Rental	49.00	49.00	49.00	49.00		196.00
12	Hotel	119.00	119.00	119.00	119.00		476.00
13	Miscellaneous	5.00	3.50	8.00	2.75	15.00	34.25
14	Daily Total	$ 531.00	$ 199.10	$ 210.21	$ 205.27	$ 34.47	$1,180.04

Figure 4 - 19

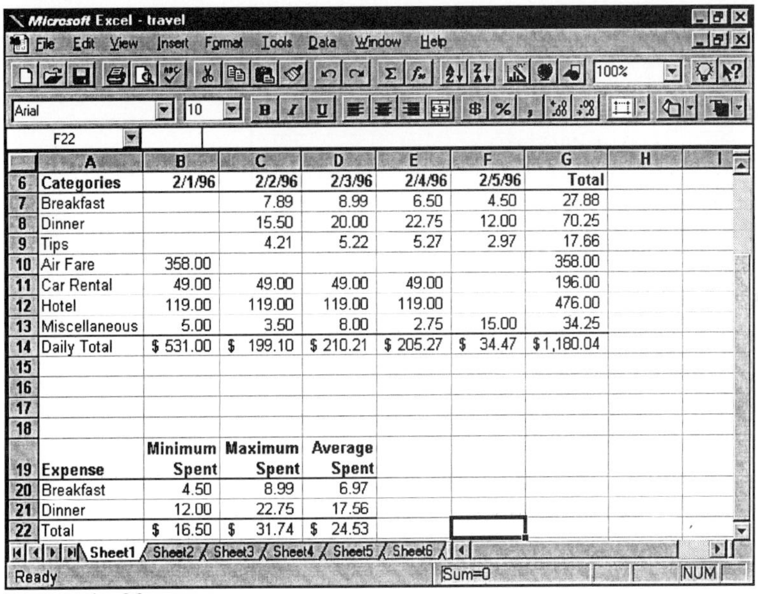

	A	B	C	D	E	F	G
6	**Categories**	**2/1/96**	**2/2/96**	**2/3/96**	**2/4/96**	**2/5/96**	**Total**
7	Breakfast		7.89	8.99	6.50	4.50	27.88
8	Dinner		15.50	20.00	22.75	12.00	70.25
9	Tips		4.21	5.22	5.27	2.97	17.66
10	Air Fare	358.00					358.00
11	Car Rental	49.00	49.00	49.00	49.00		196.00
12	Hotel	119.00	119.00	119.00	119.00		476.00
13	Miscellaneous	5.00	3.50	8.00	2.75	15.00	34.25
14	Daily Total	$ 531.00	$ 199.10	$ 210.21	$ 205.27	$ 34.47	$1,180.04
19	**Expense**	**Minimum Spent**	**Maximum Spent**	**Average Spent**			
20	Breakfast	4.50	8.99	6.97			
21	Dinner	12.00	22.75	17.56			
22	Total	$ 16.50	$ 31.74	$ 24.53			

Figure 4 - 20

SUMMARY

In this lesson you learned how to use parentheses to change the order in which calculations are performed in a formula. You also learned how to use a few of *Excel's* more than 400 functions. Use the **Function Wizard** on your own to explore some of *Excel's* other functions.

KEY TERMS

- Argument
- AVERAGE
- Function Wizard
- MAX
- MIN
- Order of operations
- Series
- System Date
- TODAY
- Wizards
- Wrap Text

INDEPENDENT PROJECTS

The independent projects will provide you with opportunities to review creating formulas and functions. In addition, Project 4.1 shows you how to use a range including nonadjacent cells in a function.

Independent Project 4.1: Analyzing First Quarter Sales

Your company has branches in seven cities. You have been given a worksheet that contains the sales for the seven cities for the first quarter and have been asked to perform some analyses on the data. When you have completed the project your worksheet should resemble Figure 4 - 21.

FIRST QUARTER SALES			
Branch	**January**	**February**	**March**
Boston, MA	$ 897,453	$ 723,432	$ 632,143
New York City, NY	567,345	765,435	764,621
Philadelphia, PA	154,325	123,234	175,276
Pittsburgh, PA	234,516	256,473	321,456
Richmond, VA	983,214	765,456	832,435
Washington, D.C.	345,123	476,587	432,435
White Plains, NY	164,361	324,156	123,456
Total Sales:	$ 3,346,337	$ 3,434,773	$ 3,281,822
Average Sales:	$ 478,048	$ 490,682	$ 468,832
Minimum Sales:	$ 154,325	$ 123,234	$ 123,456
Maximum Sales:	$ 983,214	$ 765,456	$ 832,435
Range of Sales:	$ 828,889	$ 642,222	$ 708,979
1st Quarter Total Sales:	$ 10,062,932		
1st Quarter PA Sales:	$ 1,265,280		
1st Quarter NY Sales:	$ 2,709,374		

Figure 4 - 21

Use Figure 4 - 21 and the instructions below to complete the project:

1. Open the file **independent proj. 4.l**.

2. In **B13** enter a function to total the **January** sales. Copy it across the row.

3. In **B14** enter a function to calculate the **Average January** sales. Copy it across the row.

4. In **B15** enter a function to calculate the **Minimum January** sales. Copy it across the row.

5. In **B16** enter a function to calculate the **Maximum January** sales. Copy it across the row.

6. In **B17** enter a formula to calculate the range of **January** sales (i.e., the difference between the highest and lowest sales). Copy it across the row.

7. In **B19** enter a function to calculate the total of the first quarter sales (January, February, and March) for all of the cities.

8. In **B20** enter a function to calculate the total of the first quarter sales for both of the Pennsylvania cities. (What range will you use in the formula?)

9. In **B21** enter a function to calculate the total of the first quarter sales for both of the New York cities. (**HINT:** *This is harder than the previous step because the New York cities are not next to one another. Therefore, to select a range that has nonadjacent parts, you can highlight the first part and then depress the* **CTRL** *key while you highlight the second part of the range.*)

10. When you create a formula, the result of the formula usually is formatted to match the first cell in the formula range. Therefore, the total, average, minimum, and maximum were all formatted with Currency Style while the PA and NY totals used the comma style. Format the PA and NY values using the **Currency Style**, 0 decimal places.

11. **Save** your worksheet using the name: **quarter1**

12. **Print** your worksheet. Include your name and other identifying information in the header in place of **sheet 1**.

13. **Print** your worksheet again displaying formulas. Close and save the worksheet.

Independent Project 4.2: Analyzing Weather Information

You work for a home heating company. You are given a worksheet that contains the high and low temperatures and the amount of snowfall for the past week. You must enter formulas and functions to calculate the average temperature for each day in Fahrenheit and Centigrade. They also want you to calculate the degree days for each day. Degree days is a concept used by heating companies to see how far the average temperature was above or below 65 degrees Fahrenheit. You have also been told to calculate the average of each of the measurements for the week and the total number of degree days and snowfall. When completed, compare your worksheet to Figure 4 - 22.

	Weather Information					
	Temperature (Fahrenheit)			Degree	Average	Snowfall
Day	Low	High	Average	Days	Centigrade	(inches)
5-Dec	15	35	25.0	40.0	-3.9	0.75
6-Dec	26	43	34.5	30.5	1.4	5.00
7-Dec	28	42	35.0	30.0	1.7	1.50
8-Dec	10	38	24.0	41.0	-4.4	0.00
9-Dec	-2	10	4.0	61.0	-15.6	0.25
10-Dec	-5	8	1.5	63.5	-16.9	0.00
11-Dec	10	25	17.5	47.5	-8.1	0.00
Average	11.7	28.7	20.2	44.8	-6.5	1.1
Low for Week	-5					
High for Week	43					
Total Degree Days	313.5					
Total Snowfall	7.50					

Figure 4 - 22

Use Figure 4 - 22 and the instructions below to complete the project:

1. Open the file **independent proj. 4.2**.

2. First, you will replace the days of the week by dates. Beginning in cell **A7** enter the series of dates beginning with: **12/5**

   The date will appear in the default date format for a date containing only a month and a day.

3. Left-align all of the dates that you have just entered.

4. In **D7** enter a function to compute the average of the **Low** and **High** temperatures for the day.

5. In **E7** enter a formula to compute the **Degree Days**. The degree days is equal to **65** minus the **Average** temperature of the day.

6. In **F7** enter a formula to convert the **Average Fahrenheit Temperature** to the **Average Centigrade** temperature. The average Centigrade temperature is equal to **5/9** of the difference between the **Average Fahrenheit** temperature and **32**.

7. Copy all of the above functions and formulas to the appropriate cells.

8. You need to format the new numbers. Since you want to display negative numbers with a minus sign rather than in parentheses, use **FORMAT/Cells,Number** instead of the **Comma Style** button. Make sure the **Number** tab of the **Format Cells** dialog box is active. Choose **Number** from the **Category** list box. Make the appropriate changes so that one decimal place is displayed and negative numbers are preceded by a minus sign. Click on **OK**.

9. In **B15** enter a function to calculate the average **Low** temperature. Copy the function across the row. Format the numbers as you did in step 8.

10. In **B16** enter a function to calculate the lowest Fahrenheit temperature of the week.

11. In **B17** enter a function to calculate the highest Fahrenheit temperature of the week.

12. In **B18** enter a function to calculate the total number of degree days for the week.

13. In **B19** enter a function to calculate the total snowfall for the week.

14. Save your worksheet using the name: **weather**

15. Print your worksheet. Include your name and other identifying information in the header in place of **sheet 1**.

16. Print your worksheet again displaying formulas.

17. Close and save the worksheet.

Independent Project 4.3: Analyzing Stock Sales

You have been asked to analyze the success of an investment portfolio. You have sold a number of stocks in 1995 and you want to analyze the profitability of the stocks that you sold. In completing this project you will create some complex formulas and explore date arithmetic. When complete your worksheet should resemble Figure 4 - 23, although the spacing may be different.

Purchase Date	Number of Shares	NAME	Cost per Share	Total Cost	Date of Sale	Sales Price per Share	Proceeds	Gain (Loss)	Years Held	% Annual Return on Investment
		INVESTMENT PORTFOLIO								
		STOCKS SOLD IN 1995								
10/12/92	100	Jiffy Data Processing	56.26	5,626	10/15/95	65.25	6,525	899	3.0	5%
9/30/85	100	Books Galore	109.12	10,912	11/12/95	62.50	6,250	(4,662)	10.1	-4%
12/15/88	500	Dinosaurs, Inc.	29.58	14,790	12/5/95	45.50	22,750	7,960	7.0	8%
10/2/92	200	My Life Insurance	22.12	4,424	4/2/95	75.87	15,174	10,750	2.5	97%
1/5/91	300	Toys, Toys, Toys	20.21	6,063	1/19/95	32.50	9,750	3,687	4.0	15%
9/4/88	500	Best Travel Agency	68.38	34,190	7/15/95	62.25	31,125	(3,065)	6.9	-1%
6/24/89	250	Strawberry Fields	10.28	2,570	8/27/95	21.50	5,375	2,805	6.2	18%
7/6/93	1,000	Fly By Night Airlines	19.45	19,450	11/7/95	12.50	12,500	(6,950)	2.3	-15%
5/5/95	600	ECAP, Corp.	9.74	5,844	7/23/95	17.75	10,650	4,806	0.2	380%
12/8/90	400	Nationwide	109.73	43,892	5/16/95	125.50	50,200	6,308	4.4	3%
10/4/84	800	Best Buys	54.87	43,896	12/17/95	62.50	50,000	6,104	11.2	1%
		Total Gain (Loss)	$28,642							
		Maximum Gain (Loss)	$10,750							
		Minimum Gain(Loss)	($6,950)							
		Average % Return on Investment	46%							
		Maximum % Return on Investment	380%							
		Minimum % Return on Investment	-15%							

Figure 4 - 23

1. Open **independent project 4.3**.

2. In **E5** enter a formula to compute the **Total Cost** of the stocks. The Total Cost is equal to the **Number of Shares** multiplied by the **Cost per Share**. Copy the formula down the column.

3. In **H5** calculate the **Proceeds**, which is equal to the **Number of Shares** multiplied by the **Sales Price per Share**.

4. In **I5** calculate the **Gain(Loss)**, which is the difference between the **Proceeds** and the **Total Cost** and should be positive if the **Proceeds** are higher than the **Total Cost**.

5. In **J5** calculate the **Years Held**. In *Excel* every date you enter is associated with a number, so you can use dates in calculations. When you subtract dates, the answer is the number of days between the two dates. Therefore, to find the **Years Held** you must divide the difference between the **Date of Sale** and **Purchase Date** by **365**.

6. In **K5** calculate the **% Annual Return on Investment** (without considering compounding). The **% Annual Return on Investment** equals the **Gain(Loss)** divided by both the **Total Cost** and the **Years Held**.

7. Copy the formulas in **H5:K5** down the columns.

8. In cell **D17** use a function to calculate the total **Gain (Loss)**.

9. In cell **D18** use a function to calculate the maximum **Gain(Loss)**.

10. In cell **D19** use a function to calculate the minimum **Gain(Loss)**.

11. After completing the last three functions, you decide that calculating the average, minimum, and maximum % annual return on investment might give you a different perspective on your data. In cell **C21** enter the label: **Average % of Return on Investment**. Change its alignment to **Wrap Text** so that it fits in the cell without widening the column. Add similar labels in **C22** and **C23** for maximum and minimum % return on investment.

12. Enter the appropriate functions in cells **D21:D23**.

13. Format the worksheet and increase column widths appropriately.

14. **Save** the worksheet using the name: **investments**

15. **Print** the worksheet with a header or footer containing identifying information about you. The **Page Setup** was changed in **independent proj. 4.3** so that the worksheet will print in landscape orientation (sideways). This procedure will be explained in Lesson 5.

16. Based on the **Gain(Loss)**, which stock made the largest gain? Based on the **% Annual Return on Investment**, which stock made the largest gain?

17. **Print** the worksheet again with formulas displayed. Close and save the worksheet.

Independent Project 4.4: Analyzing Airline Flights

You work for Fly By Night Airlines. You have been asked to set up a worksheet analyzing flights that left White Plains Airport on December 15. The file **independent proj. 4.4** contains data on the Unrestricted (Full Price) fare for each flight and on the number of tickets sold at each of three rates. All flights use the same type of airplane. Maximum capacity is 150 passengers. You are to:

Fill in the columns to the right of the supplied data with:

- The total number of tickets sold for each flight

- The percent of seats sold for each flight based on the 150 passenger capacity

- The revenue generated by each flight

Fill in a summary row below the columns of data with:

- The average number of tickets sold for each of the three categories (Full Price, 20% Discount, and 50% Discount)

- The average number of tickets sold for a flight

- The average of the percent of seats sold

- The average revenue generated by a flight

- The total revenue for all of the flights.

1. Your project should include:

- A table specifying the calculations that you need to perform to obtain the results requested.

- A paper and pencil design of the worksheet showing how you will organize the calculations that you need to include, and the column labels you will add.

- A printout of the completed formatted worksheet. Include information identifying you in the header or footer.

- A printout of the worksheet displaying formulas.

2.   Save the worksheet using the name: **flights**

Lesson 5

Absolute and Relative Cell References

Objectives

In this lesson you will learn how to:

- Enter numbers as text
- Determine when to use Absolute cell references
- Determine when to use Mixed cell references
- Create a formula containing Absolute cell references

- Copy Absolute cell references
- Use a function as part of a formula
- Print a worksheet that is larger than one piece of paper
- Freeze columns and rows
- Perform simple *what-if* analysis
- Use **TOOLS/Goal Seek**

PROJECT DESCRIPTION

In this project you will complete the worksheet, **5YearProjection,** which projects ECAP Manufacturing Corporation's sales, expenses, and pretax income for the next five years. These projections are based on last year's actual sales, plus a set of assumptions about the anticipated growth rate and expenses.

In the previous lessons worksheets were used to record and analyze existing data. In this lesson you will use the worksheet to make projections. This is one type of *what-if* analysis. Since formulas automatically recalculate whenever the values in the cells they reference are changed, you can systematically change a set of values and see how these changes affect the end result. *Excel* has many advanced tools that can help you manage complex what-if analyses. However, in this project you will use a very simple what-if analysis. A set of assumptions has already been entered into **5YearProjection**. You will create formulas that project the sales, expenses, and pretax income over the next five years. Then you will change the assumptions and let *Excel* recalculate the results!

In the process of completing the project you will also expand on previously developed skills. You will learn how to incorporate a function into a formula. Since the completed worksheet does not fit on one screen, you will also learn how to freeze part of the worksheet so that designated columns and/or rows remain on the screen as you scroll the worksheet. Finally, you will learn some techniques for printing worksheets that don't naturally fit on one page.

When this project is completed, the worksheet **5Year** will resemble Figure 5 - 1.

Activity 5.1: Getting Started

1. Start *Excel*.

ECAP MANUFACTURING CORPORATION
FIVE YEAR PROJECTION

ASSUMPTIONS

Sales with Growth	104%	of previous year's sales
Returns & Allowances	2%	of sales
Materials	17%	of net sales
Labor	25%	of net sales
Overhead	150%	of labor
SGA	12%	of net sales

	CURRENT	PROJECTIONS					1996-2000
	1995	1996	1997	1998	1999	2000	Totals
Gross Sales	$1,345,560	$1,399,382	$1,455,358	$1,513,572	$1,574,115	$1,637,079	$7,579,506
R&A	26,911	27,988	29,107	30,271	31,482	32,742	151,590
Net Sales	1,318,649	1,371,395	1,426,251	1,483,301	1,542,633	1,604,338	7,427,916
Materials	224,170	233,137	242,463	252,161	262,248	272,737	1,262,746
Labor	329,662	342,849	356,563	370,825	385,658	401,084	1,856,979
Overhead	494,493	514,273	534,844	556,238	578,487	601,627	2,785,469
SGA	158,238	164,567	171,150	177,996	185,116	192,521	891,350
Income Before Taxes	$ 112,085	$ 116,569	$ 121,231	$ 126,081	$ 131,124	$ 136,369	$ 631,373

Figure 5 - 1

2. **Open** the file **5YearProjection**. Maximize *Excel* and **5YearProjection** if necessary.

    5YearProjection contains assumptions about the projected sales, the expenses for returns as a percent of gross sales, materials, and labor as a percent of net sales, and the overhead rate as a percent of labor costs (Figure 5 - 2).

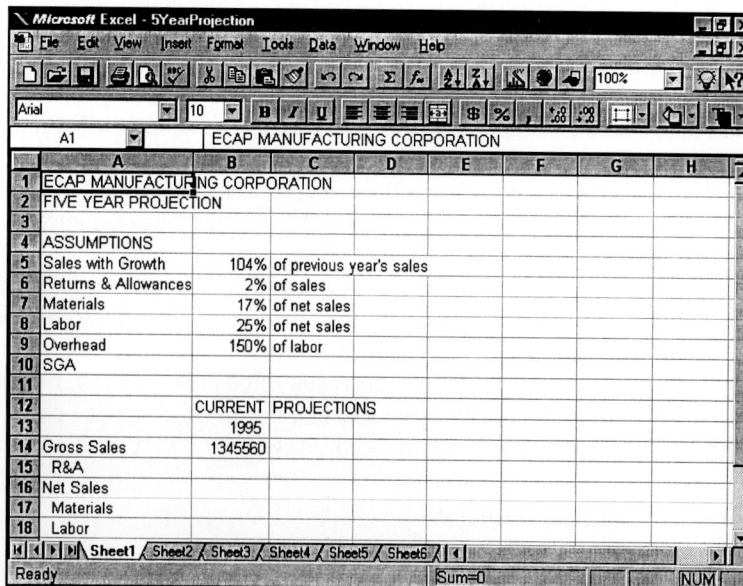

Figure 5 - 2

3. The data on **SGA** (Sales, Growth, and Administrative costs) have been omitted.

    a.   In **B10** enter: **12%**

    b.   In **C10** enter: **of net sales**

*The percentage (12%) and the text associated with it (of net sales) must be entered in separate cells. If a cell contains text in addition to values, it cannot be used in calculations. Notice that as soon as you type "of n" Excel uses AutoComplete to fill in the rest of the label based on prior labels in the same column. If you completed Independent Exercise 3.1 you already used AutoComplete. To find out more about AutoComplete, choose **What's New** from the **Contents** tab of the **Help Topics** dialog box..*

ENTERING NUMBERS AS TEXT

The first step in completing the worksheet is to enter the five years for which you want to make projections. If you just type the year names (1996, 1997, etc.), *Excel* will treat them as values since they contain only numerals. However, if you precede the number with an apostrophe ('), *Excel* will treat the number as text.

To enter a number as text:

- Type an **apostrophe** (').
- Then type the number.

Activity 5.2: Entering Numbers as Text

In this activity you will enter the labels for columns **C:G**, which will contain your projections.

1. In cell **C13**, type: **'1996** and click on the **enter box** or press **ENTER**.

   Since you preceded 1996 with an apostrophe, it is left-justified in the cell.

2. Select cell **C13**, if it is not already selected, and drag the **fill handle** to cell **G13**.

   *Just as Excel would increment the labels Division 1, Division 2, etc., it fills the remaining cells with the series, **1997, 1998...** (Figure 5 - 3).*

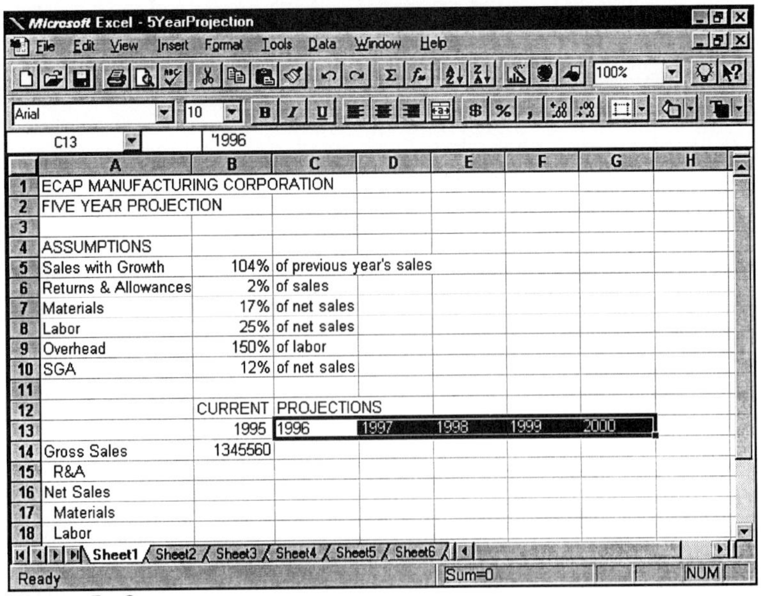

Figure 5 - 3

CELL REFERENCES

Your next step is to enter the formulas for the projected sales and expenses. However, you have a problem. To calculate the projected 1996 sales, you need to multiply last year's (1995) sales by the anticipated growth. For cell **C14** this formula would be **=B14*B5**. Then you want to copy the formula across row **14** to calculate the projected sales for 1997 to 2000.

As you saw in Lesson 3, when a formula is copied across a row, *Excel* automatically adjusts the cell references for each column. Therefore, the formula **B14*B5** will become **C14*C5**, **D14*D5**, etc. The first cell reference, **B14**, should adjust since it always refers to the previous year's sales and this changes (the previous year's sales for 1996 is in **B14**, but the previous year's sales for 1997 is in **C14**, etc.). However, the second cell reference, **B5**, refers to the projected sales and this value is always in **B5**.

Excel deals with this situation by letting you create formulas with different types of cell references. You can include *relative, absolute,* or *mixed* cell references in formulas. In Lessons 3 and 4 you only used *relative* references. This is the default and the most commonly used reference. In this lesson you will use *absolute* cell references. *Mixed* references are the most complicated to understand and the least frequently used; therefore, they will be described briefly, but not used in this book.

Relative Cell References

As we discussed in Lesson 3, if you just enter a cell reference into a formula, *Excel* automatically adjusts the column or row reference so that the same relationship is maintained between the cell containing the formula and the cells to which it refers. As indicated in Figure 5 - 4 if the formula in cell **C14** is copied one column to the right, each of the cell references adjusts so that the column reference is the letter after the one included in the original reference. Therefore, **B5** becomes **C5** and **B14** becomes **C14**.

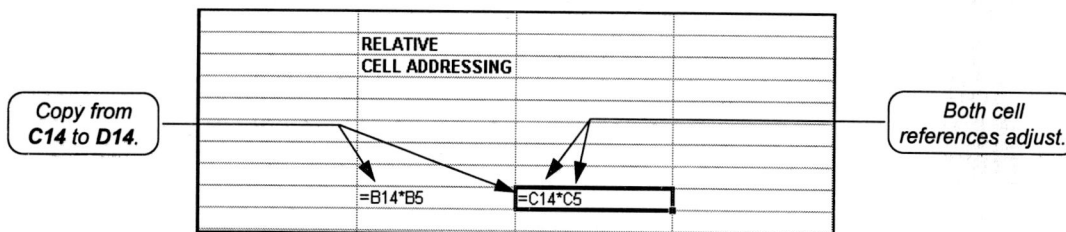

Figure 5 - 4

Absolute Cell References

To specify that a cell address should not change when it is copied, you must make the cell reference absolute when you enter it into the formula. *Absolute* cell references contain dollar signs before both the column and the row location (i.e., **$B$5**). Thus, as Figure 5 - 5 indicates, when **=B14*$B$5** is copied to **D14**, the reference to **$B$5** does not change. Since most formulas refer to more than one cell, some of the cell references in a formula may be absolute while references to other cells are relative.

While an absolute cell reference can be entered by typing a **$** before the column and row names, an easier way to make a cell reference absolute is to press the **F4** key as soon as you have pointed to the cell. **F4** is a toggle key. If it is pressed one time, dollar signs are inserted before the row and column designations (**$B$5**). If it is pressed a second time, the dollar sign is only inserted before the row number (**B$5**). A third press inserts the dollar sign only before the column name (**$B5**) and a fourth press removes all dollar signs (**B5**). Continued key presses repeat the cycle.

When the **$** precedes only part of the cell address, the reference is *mixed*. When mixed formulas are copied, the relative part adjusts while the absolute part remains the same.

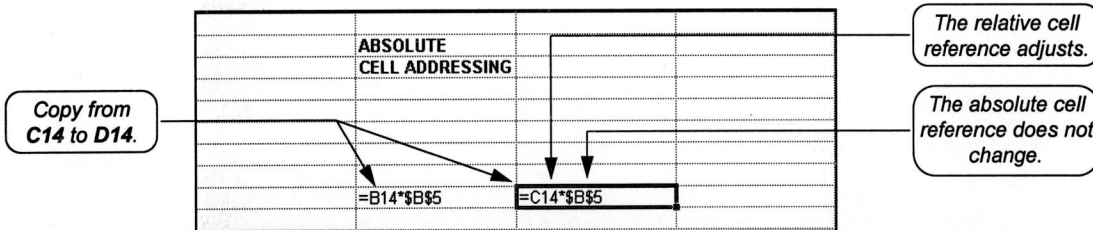

Figure 5 - 5

Mixed Cell References

Mixed cell references are references that are half relative and half absolute. If the column is relative and the row is absolute (**B$4**), then the column changes when the formula is copied but the row does not. If the column is absolute and the row is relative (**$B4**), then the row changes when the formula is copied, but the column does not. Mixed references are often used when you need to copy a formula both across and down the worksheet. This typically happens when you are trying to see the effect of changing two variables on your data. Figure 5 - 6 and Figure 5 - 7 illustrate what happens to mixed references when they are copied.

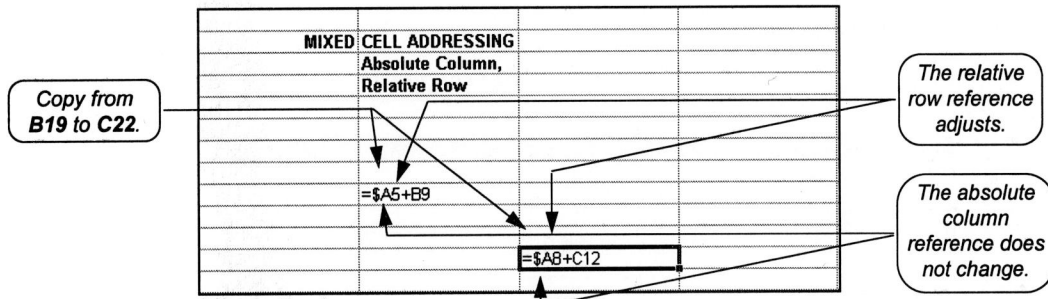

Figure 5 - 6

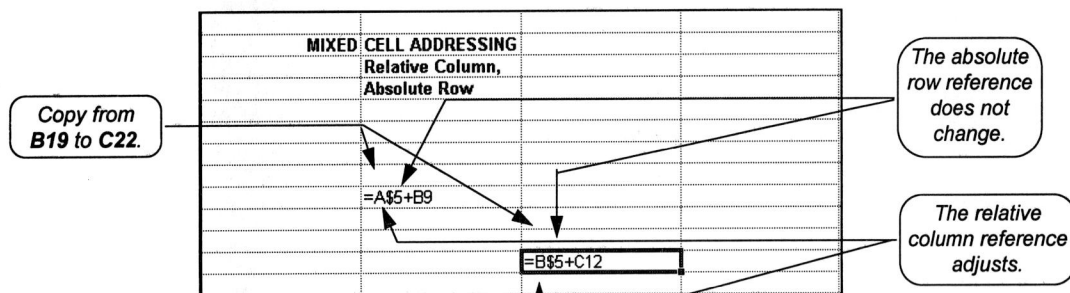

Figure 5 - 7

Creating Absolute References

To enter a formula using absolute cell references:

- Select the cell to contain the formula.
- Begin the formula by typing an equal (=) sign.
- Click on the first cell containing data that should be part of the formula. If this part of the formula should be absolute, press **F4** one time.

Dollar signs will precede both the column and row names.

- Type a mathematical operator.
- Repeat the last two steps until the formula is complete. Only use **F4** with those cell references that should not change when the formula is copied.
- Click on the **enter box** or press **ENTER**.

Activity 5.3: Entering Formulas with Absolute Cell References

In this activity, you will create formulas for the 1996–2000 sales and the 1995–2000 expense categories. Since all of these formulas will depend on the assumptions at the top of the worksheet, they will involve absolute cell references. You will also enter a formula for the net sales; this formula will use only relative cell references.

1. To create a formula to multiply the previous year's sales by the expected growth:

    a. Select cell **C14**.

    b. Type: =

    c. Click on cell **B14**.

    d. Type the mathematical operator: *

    e. Point to cell **B5**.

    f. Press the **F4** key once.

    B5 becomes the absolute cell reference, $B$5 (Figure 5 - 8).

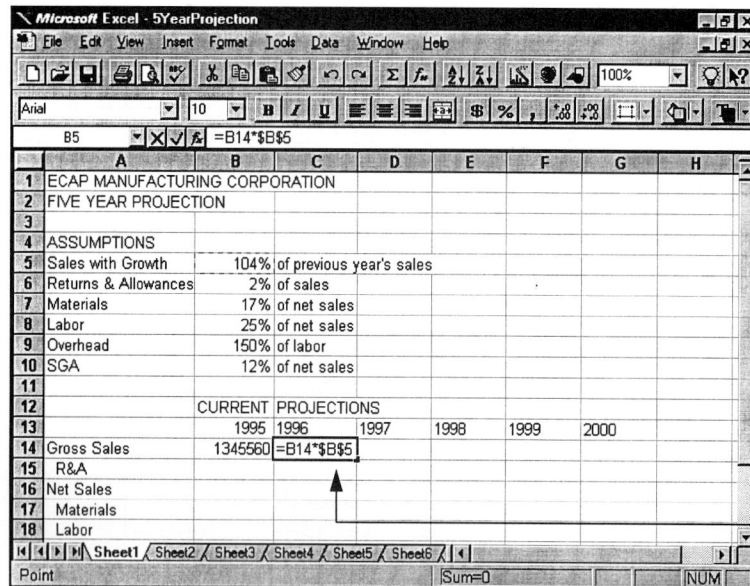

Figure 5 - 8

    g. Click on the **enter box** or press **ENTER**.

    The value in cell C14 should be 1399382.4.

    h. Make sure **C14** is still highlighted and drag the **fill handle** across row **14** to copy the formula to cells **D14:G14**.

    i. Click on **D14**.

    The relative part of the formula, B14 has adjusted to C14, while the absolute part of the formula remains $B$5 (Figure 5 - 9).

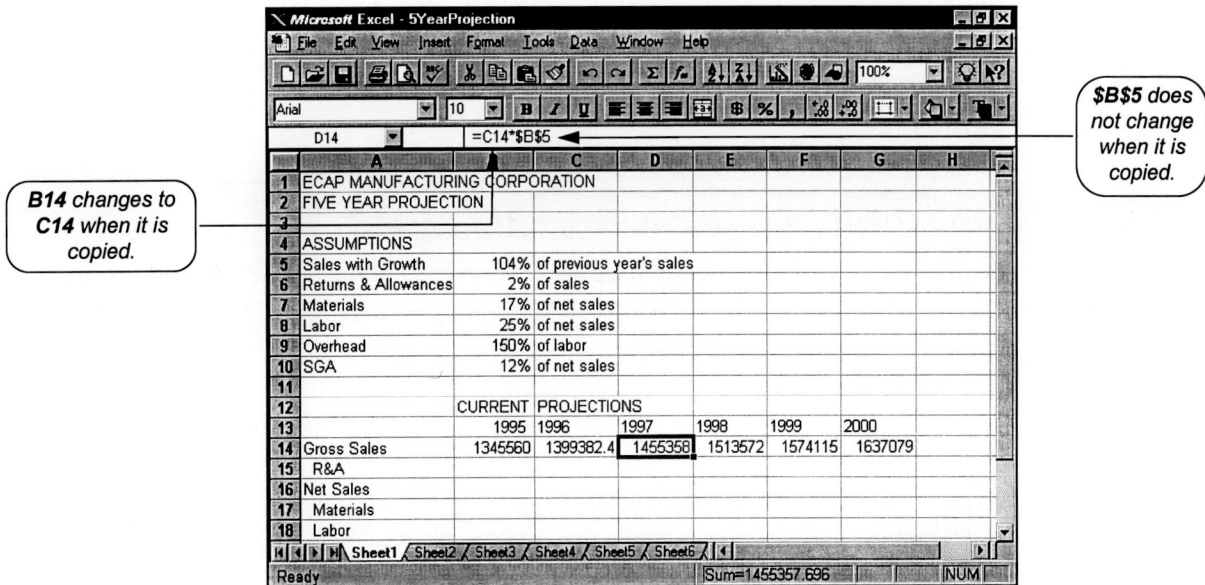

Figure 5 - 9

2. In cell **B15** use the steps above to create a formula to calculate the 1995 returns by multiplying the 1995 Gross Sales (**B14**) by the expected return rate (**B6**). Remember to make **B6** absolute so that it can be copied across the row.

   *When **B15** is highlighted the Formula Bar will display the formula =B14*$B$6 while the cell displays the result of the formula (26911.2).*

3. Use the **fill handle** to copy the formula in **B15** across the row through **G15**.

4. In cell **B16** you want to create a formula to subtract the returns and allowances from the Gross Sales. Unlike the last formula, neither of these cell references should be absolute. Therefore, use pointing to enter the formula: **=B14-B15**

   *The value in cell **B16** should be 1318648.8.*

5. Select **B16** if it is not already selected, and use the **fill handle** to copy the formula across row **16**.

6. In **B17** create a formula to calculate the 1995 Materials Expense by multiplying the 1995 Net Sales (**B16**) by the Materials rate (**B7**). Make the reference to the Materials rate absolute.

   *The value in cell **B17** should be 224170.3 and the formula should be = B16*$B$7.*

7. In cell **B18** create a formula to calculate the 1995 Labor Expense by multiplying the 1995 Net Sales (**B16**) by the Labor rate (**B8**). Make the reference to the Labor rate absolute.

   *The value in cell **B18** should be 329662.2.*

8. In cell **B19** create a formula to calculate the 1995 Overhead Expense by multiplying the 1995 Labor Expense (**B18**) by the Overhead rate (**B9**). Make cell references absolute as necessary.

   *The value in cell **B19** should be 494493.3.*

9. In cell **B20** create a formula to calculate the 1995 SGA expenses by multiplying the 1995 Net Sales (**B16**) by the SGA rate (**B10**). Make cell references absolute as necessary.

   *The value in cell **B20** should be 158237.86.*

10. Highlight **B17:B20** and use the **fill handle** to copy the formulas across the rows through column **G**.

    Your worksheet should resemble Figure 5 - 10.

✓   **PROBLEM SOLVER:** *If #VALUE! appears in any of the cells, delete the formula in the cell displaying #VALUE!, check your original formulas, make all of the references to the cells containing the assumptions absolute, and copy the formulas.*

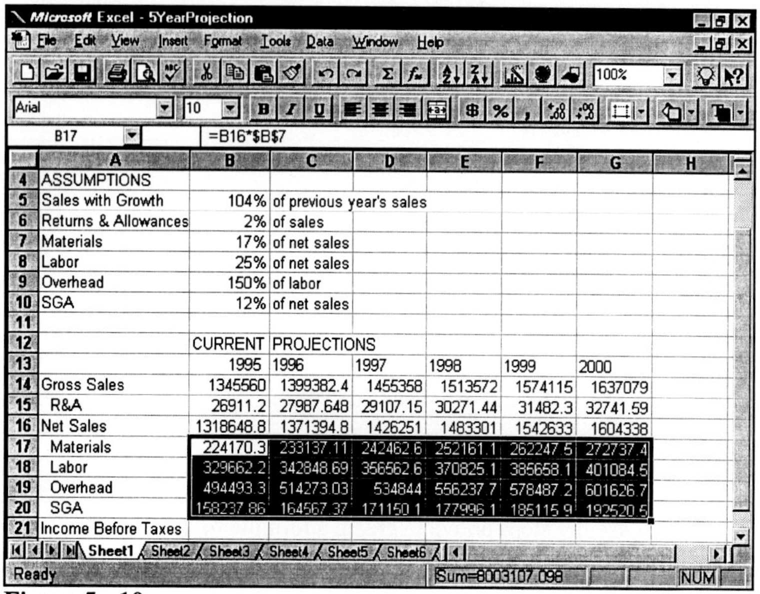

Figure 5 - 10

INCLUDING FUNCTIONS IN FORMULAS

Next, you need to calculate the pretax income. This is equal to the Net Sales minus the four expenses. You could calculate this by subtracting each of the expenses from the sales. This formula would be: Net Sales minus Materials minus Labor minus Overhead minus SGA or =**B16-B17-B18-B19-B20**. However, another, quicker way to calculate this is to subtract the sum of the expenses from the sales.

So far all of your formulas have included just cell references and operators (e.g., =**C3*C4**) or just a function (e.g., =**sum(B17:B20)**). However, it is possible for the same formula to include cell references, operators, and functions. Therefore, the following formula can be used to calculate the pretax income: =**B16-sum(B17:B20)**.

Activity 5.4: Including a Function in a Formula

In this activity you will calculate the pretax income. Then you will calculate the predicted 1996–2000 totals for the sales, each of the expense categories, and the pretax income.

1. Select cell **B21**.

2. Type: **=**

3. Point to the 1995 Net Sales, **B16**.

4. Subtract the sum of the expenses by typing: **-sum(** and then pointing to the range, **B17:B20** (Figure 5 - 11).

5. End the formula by typing: **)** and clicking on the **enter box** or pressing **ENTER**.

   The value of the formula, 112085.15, is entered in cell B21. When a function is not the only component of the formula, you must type the closing parenthesis before entering the function.

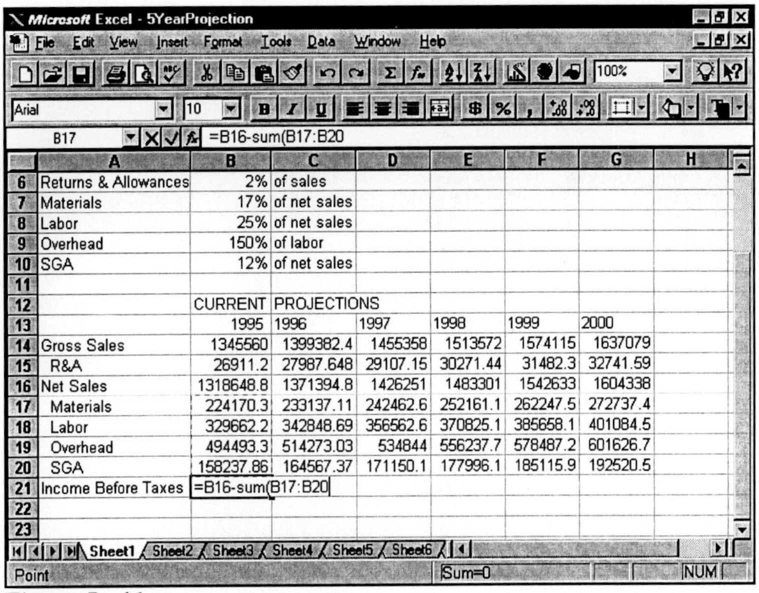

Figure 5 - 11

6. Copy the formula across row **21** (Figure 5 - 12).

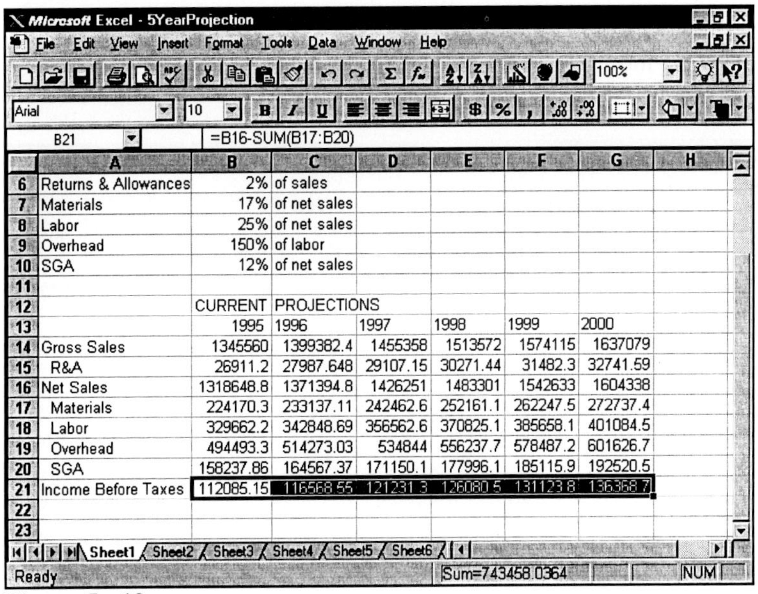

Figure 5 - 12

7. To identify the last column, enter **1996-2000** in **H12** and **Totals** in cell **H13.**

8. In **H14** enter a **sum** function to add the 1996–2000 predicted sales figures. You cannot use the range that the **AutoSum** function will enter because it will include the 1995 figure. Therefore, to create the sum for just 1996–2000:

   a. Select **H14**.

   b. Click on the **AutoSum** button.

   *The range **B14:G14** will be automatically entered into the function (Figure 5 - 13).*

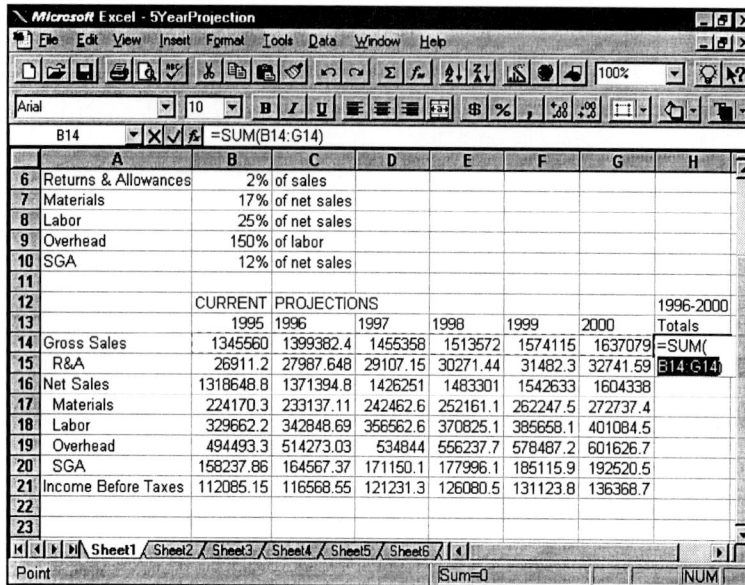

Figure 5 - 13

c. Highlight the correct range, **C14:G14**.

The range you selected will replace Excel's guessed range in the function.

d. Enter the formula by clicking on the **enter box** or pressing **ENTER**.

9. Copy the formula in cell **H14** down the column to cells **H15:H21** (Figure 5 - 14).

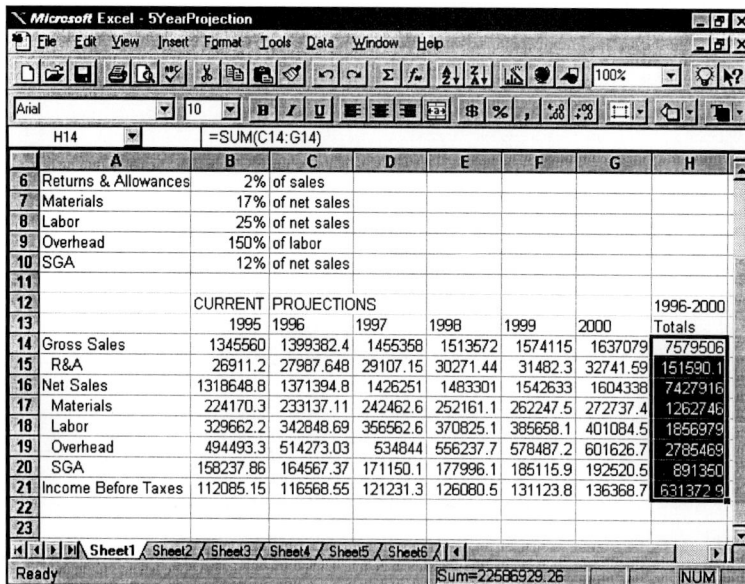

Figure 5 - 14

10. Use **FILE/Save As** to save the worksheet using the name: **5Year**

Activity 5.5: Formatting the Worksheet

1. Center the heading **PROJECTIONS** over columns **C** through **G**.

2. Center align **CURRENT** in cell **B12**, **1996-2000** in cell **H12**, and **Totals** in **H13**. Center align each of the dates (**1995**, **1996**, etc.) in their cells.

3. Format the values in **B14:H14** and **B21:H21** using the Currency Style with no decimal places.

4. Select **B14:H21** and use **FORMAT/Column,Autofit** selection to display all values.

   If you are using Arial 10 point font, the worksheet may be too big to fit on the screen.

5. Format the values in **B15:H20** for Comma Style with no decimal places.

   PROBLEM SOLVER: *If you touch the sides of the window when using the mouse to define a range, the window may start to scroll very quickly. To avoid this, gently bump the side of the window and then move the mouse slightly in the other direction. Also remember that if you define a range that is smaller or larger than the desired range, use the SHIFT+ARROW keys to shrink or expand the range.*

6. Add bottom borders under cells **A13:H13** and **A20:H20**.

   *Figure 5 - 15 shows columns **A** through **G** of your worksheet.*

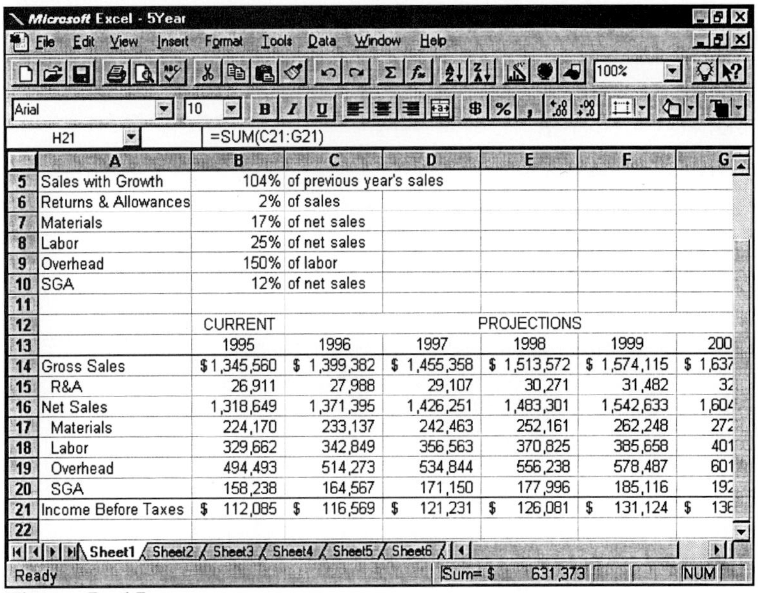

Figure 5 - 15

7. **Save** the worksheet again using the same name.

8. Click on the **Print Preview** button or select **FILE/Print Preview**.

   Only part of the worksheet is displayed as it is too wide to fit on one piece of paper.

9. Click on the **Next** button to see the rest of the worksheet.

10. Click on the **Close** button to return to the worksheet.

PRINTING A LARGER WORKSHEET

Most worksheets that you create will be too big to fit on a single sheet of paper when you print. *Excel* will automatically divide the worksheet into pages. However, you often want to modify *Excel*'s decisions. Depending on the size of the worksheet and your needs, there are several ways to print worksheets that appear to be too large to fit on a page. Some of the changes that you can make using **PRINT/Page Setup** are:

- Change the orientation of the paper from portrait (the way the pages in this book are printed) to landscape (rotating the print so that the width of the page is 11 inches and the length is 8 ½ inches).

- Decrease the margins.

- Tell *Excel* to **scale** the worksheet so that it fits on a specified number of pages (**Fit to** option on the **Page** tab of the **Page Setup** dialog box).

- Using **Print Titles** (on the **Sheet** tab of the **Page Setup** dialog box) to repeat one or more columns or rows on each page of the printout.

Since your worksheet will fit on a piece of paper if you turn it sideways, or in what is called *landscape orientation,* you will print it that way.

To print a worksheet in landscape orientation:

- Select **FILE/Page Setup**.

- Click on the **Page** tab if it is not already selected.

- Click on the **Landscape** option button.

- Make any other desired changes to the page setup, click on **OK** and print the document.

Activity 5.6: Printing in Landscape Orientation

1. Select **FILE/Page Setup**.

2. Click on the **Page** tab.

3. Click on the **Landscape** option button (Figure 5 - 16).

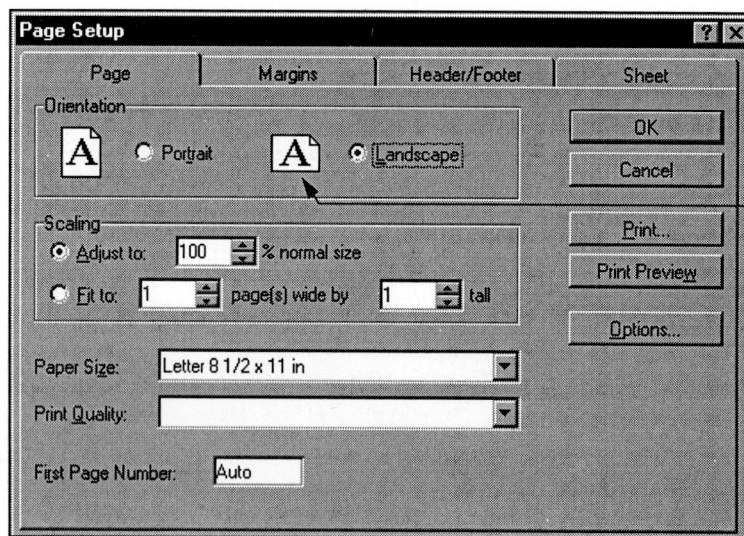

Figure 5 - 16

4. Click on the **Header/Footer** tab. Create a **Custom Header** that says: **Created by (your name)** in the left section. Delete **&[Tab]** from the center section.

5. Click on **OK**.

6. **Print** the document.

7. Press **CTRL+`** to display formulas.

8. **Print** the document.

9. Press **CTRL+`** to redisplay values.

10. **Save** the file again using the same name.

FREEZING COLUMNS AND ROWS ON THE SCREEN

If you have changed the column widths to fit the formatted values, you probably cannot see the whole worksheet. Therefore, *Excel* lets you freeze one or more columns and/or rows on the screen so that they remain visible as you scroll the rest of the screen.

To freeze columns or rows:

- Click on the cell immediately to the right of any columns that you want to remain visible and immediately below any rows that should remain visible.

- Choose **WINDOW/Freeze Panes**.

To reset the screen so that all columns/rows scroll:

- Choose **WINDOW/Unfreeze Panes**.

CHANGING ASSUMPTIONS

We now want to see how your projections change if you change assumptions. What effect will the changed projections have on your projected 1996–2000 totals? When your worksheet was created, assumptions were placed on the worksheet. You could have instead created a formula for the next year's sales by multiplying the previous year's sales by 104%. However, that would not be good worksheet design. The assumptions were included on the worksheet so that it would be easy for anyone looking at the worksheet to see what the assumptions were, and so that if you change the assumptions, all of the formulas that depend on them will automatically change. This lets us use the worksheet for simple ***what-if*** analysis.

Activity 5.7: Viewing the Effects of Changed Assumptions

After the 5-Year Projection worksheet was created, it was shared with company officials. Some of them suggested that the assumptions weren't accurate. What would be the effect on the five-year totals if the projected sales including growth was 106% instead of 104%? What if material costs could be held to 15% of net sales instead of 17%? In this activity you will see what the effects of these changes would be.

1. Scroll the screen so that row **4** is the top row on the screen.

2. To keep the assumptions, the row labels in column **A**, and the column labels in rows **12** and **13** on the screen at all times, click in cell **B14**.

3. Choose **WINDOW/Freeze Panes** (Figure 5-17).

4. In cell **B5** enter: **106%**.

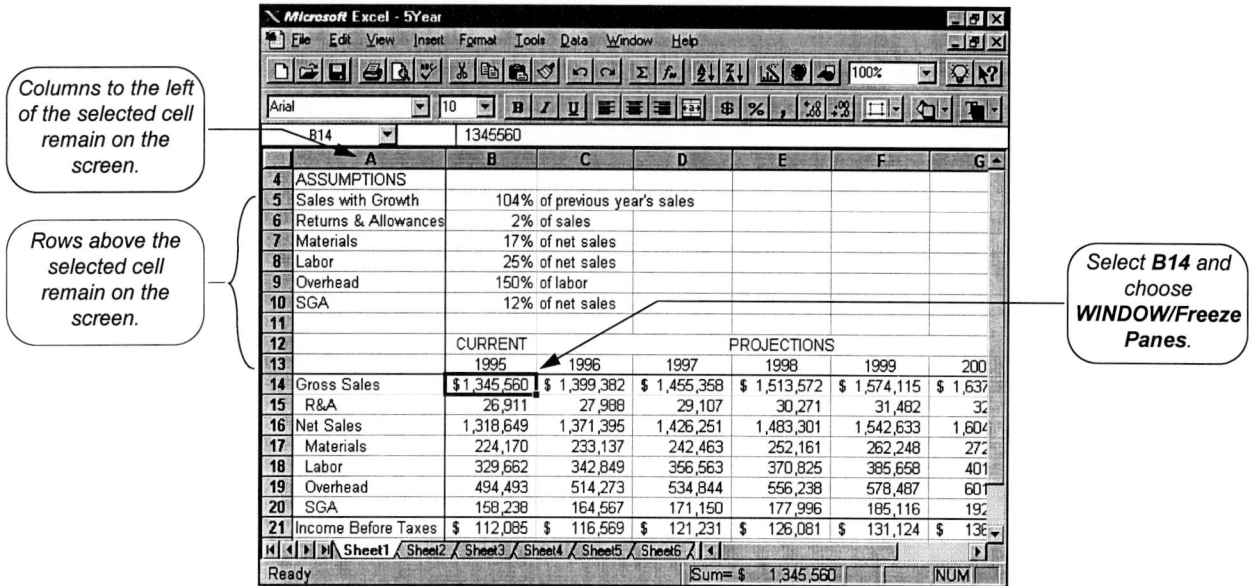

Columns to the left of the selected cell remain on the screen.

Rows above the selected cell remain on the screen.

Select **B14** and choose **WINDOW/Freeze Panes.**

	A	B	C	D	E	F	G
4	ASSUMPTIONS						
5	Sales with Growth	104%	of previous year's sales				
6	Returns & Allowances	2%	of sales				
7	Materials	17%	of net sales				
8	Labor	25%	of net sales				
9	Overhead	150%	of labor				
10	SGA	12%	of net sales				
11							
12		CURRENT			PROJECTIONS		
13		1995	1996	1997	1998	1999	200
14	Gross Sales	$1,345,560	$ 1,399,382	$ 1,455,358	$ 1,513,572	$ 1,574,115	$ 1,637
15	R&A	26,911	27,988	29,107	30,271	31,482	32
16	Net Sales	1,318,649	1,371,395	1,426,251	1,483,301	1,542,633	1,604
17	Materials	224,170	233,137	242,463	252,161	262,248	272
18	Labor	329,662	342,849	356,563	370,825	385,658	401
19	Overhead	494,493	514,273	534,844	556,238	578,487	601
20	SGA	158,238	164,567	171,150	177,996	185,116	192
21	Income Before Taxes	$ 112,085	$ 116,569	$ 121,231	$ 126,081	$ 131,124	$ 136

Figure 5 - 17

5. Compare your worksheet with your printout of the original worksheet. How many cells change? Scroll the screen so that you can see the values in all of the columns.

6. Change the materials percent in **B7** to **15%**.

7. Scroll the screen to see which values changed.

8. Choose **WINDOW/Unfreeze Panes** to remove the panes.

9. Use **FILE/Save As** to save the worksheet using the name: **New5Year**

10. Print the worksheet. Close the file.

SUMMARY

In the lesson you increased your ability to create useful formulas by learning to control whether or not a formula adjusts when it is copied. You also learned new skills for viewing and printing larger worksheets. The problem you solved in this lesson involved using worksheets to make projections rather than analyzing existing data. Independent Project 4.4 introduces another technique used in making projections.

KEY TERMS

Absolute cell reference	Freezing panes	Mixed cell reference
F4	Landscape orientation	Portrait orientation

INDEPENDENT PROJECTS

The four independent projects in Lesson 5 provide practice entering complex formulas that use relative and absolute cell referencing. Some projects also give you practice using and printing larger worksheets. In addition Independent Project 5.1 expands on your ability to create series and Independent Project 5.4 introduces Goal Seeking in *what-if* analyses.

Independent Project 5.1: Completing a Sales Worksheet

You work for a company that sells T-shirts. You are told to create a worksheet that compares the sales of each of three salespersons in the month of March. You are given a worksheet which contains all the raw data. You need to compute the percent of sales for each salesperson for each week of the month, and each salesperson's total sales and total commission.

When you finish this project, your worksheet should resemble Figure 5 - 18.

T-Shirt Sales						
March						
Week of:	*Blasek*	*% of Sales*	*Pierce*	*% of Sales*	*Selwyn*	*% of Sales*
3/4/96	$ 300	23%	$ 645	34%	$ 724	43%
3/11/96	435	33%	267	14%	341	20%
3/18/96	234	18%	546	29%	234	14%
3/25/96	346	26%	432	23%	402	24%
Total	$ 1,315		$ 1,890		$ 1,701	
Comm%	25%		27%		29%	
Comm$	$ 328.75		$ 510.30		$ 493.29	

Figure 5 - 18

Use Figure 5 - 18 and the following instructions to help you complete the project:

1. Open **independent proj. 5.1**.

2. In **A6** enter: **Week of:**

3. In **A7** enter: **3/4/96**

4. You want to create a series, but instead of including every day you only want to include every seventh day (the beginning of each week). Therefore, when you point to the **fill handle**, press the **right** mouse button as you drag down to **A10**.

5. A shortcut menu will appear. Choose **Series**. The **Series** dialog box appears, containing many options for creating a series. The pointer is in the **Step Value** text box. Type: **7** and then click on **OK**. A series of dates, 7 days apart, will be entered.

6. **Left-align** the dates that you just entered and format **Week of:** to match the other column labels.

7. In cell **B11** calculate the total sales for Blasek.

8. Copy the function to cells **D11** and **F11**. Remember, if you use **EDIT/Copy** and **EDIT/Paste** you can copy to more than one cell. To copy to the last cell either press **ENTER** instead of using **EDIT/Paste** or press the **ESC** key after pasting to the last cell, so that the copy command is ended and the moving border is removed from the cell(s) that were copied.

9. Enter the formula for the amount of commission for Blasek in cell **B16**. The commission is equal to the total sales multiplied by the commission percentage.

10. Copy the formula to cells **D16** and **F16**.

11. Format all three cells for either **Currency Style** or **Currency Format** with 2 decimal places. (Figure 5 - 18 uses **Currency Style**.)

12. In cell **C7** calculate the percent of the month's sales that Blasek made in the first week of the month. The percent is equal to the Blasek's first week's sales divided by Blasek's total sales for the month. Make cells absolute as necessary so that the formula will adjust correctly when copied to the other weeks in the month.

13. Copy the formula to cells **C8:C10**.

14. Format the column using **Percent Style** with no decimal places.

15. Create similar formulas for the other two salespersons. Format the results to match those in column **C.**

16. Since the **EDIT/Copy** and **EDIT/Fill** commands (or dragging the **fill handle**) copy cell formats as well as contents, part of the bottom border in row **10** is missing. Replace the bottom border under row **10**.

17. **Save** your worksheet using the name: **tshirt**

18. **Print** the worksheet with appropriate changes to the page setup.

19. **Print** the worksheet again displaying formulas.

20. Close and save the worksheet.

Independent Project 5.2: Completing a Sales Worksheet

Nationwide Sporting Goods wants to project 1996 sales based on 1995 sales. The calculated projections will be based on an assumed growth rate and an assumed inflation rate, both of which have been entered into your worksheet. You will use the cells containing these assumptions in your formulas so that you can easily recalculate sales projections if the assumptions change. To complete the worksheet you will create some complex formulas using absolute cell addressing.

When you finish **Projection**, your worksheet should resemble Figure 5 - 19.

Nationwide Sporting Goods			
Projected 1996 National Sales			
ASSUMPTIONS			
Growth Rate =	8.0%		
% Inflation =	3.6%		
	DOLLAR VOLUME SOLD		
		1996	1996
PRODUCT	1995	(in 1996 $)	(in 1995 $)
Baseball Bats	$ 16,928	$ 18,282	$ 17,647
Olympic Frisbees	21,064	22,749	21,959
Golf Club Sets	29,374	31,724	30,622
Athletic Wear	23,618	25,507	24,621
Kayaks	13,833	14,940	14,421
Tennis Raquets	19,818	21,403	20,660
Camping Equipment	23,332	25,199	24,323
Football Pads	30,251	32,671	31,536
Boxing Gloves	9,370	10,120	9,768
Totals	$ 187,588	$ 202,595	$ 195,555

Figure 5 - 19

Use Figure 5 - 19 and the following instructions to help you complete the project:

1. Open the file **independent proj. 5.2**. Cell **B6** contains the assumed growth rate and cell **B7** contains the assumed inflation rate. Sales data for 1995 has been included.

2. In cell **C12** enter a formula for the projected 1996 baseball bat sales in 1996 dollars. The projected sales are equal to the 1995 sales multiplied by the sum of 1 plus the projected growth rate. Remember to use absolute cell references for any cells that should not change when the formula is copied down the column. Use parentheses when necessary for correct calculation.

3. Copy the formula from **C12** to the other cells in column **C**.

4. In **D12** enter a formula to calculate projected 1996 baseball bat sales in 1995 dollars, which is equal to the 1996 projected baseball bat sales divided by the sum of 1 plus the assumed inflation rate.

5. Copy the formula in **D12** down the column through **D20**.

6. Format **C13:D20** for Comma Style with no decimal places. Replace the bottom border under the cells in row **20**. Format **C12:D12** for **Currency Style** or **Currency Format** with no decimal places. (Figure 5 - 19 displays **Currency Style**.)

7. In **B21** enter a function to sum the 1995 product sales.

8. Copy the function from **B21** to **C21:D21** and format to match row 12.

9. **Save** the worksheet using the name: **Projection**

10. Change the page setup to insert appropriate headers and footers. Print the worksheet.

11. **Print** the worksheet again, displaying formulas.

12. Change the assumed **Growth Rate** to **6.5%** and the assumed **% Inflation** to **4.5%**.

13. **Print** the changed worksheet.

14. **Save** the worksheet as: **Projection 2** and close.

Independent Project 5.3: Completing a Grading Worksheet

You are a teacher. The file, **independent proj. 5.3**, contains the raw data on your students' test and project scores. You need to calculate a grade for each test and the average of the projects. The final grade is a weighted combination of the test average, final, and average project scores. The data for each test is the number wrong. You need to calculate the score for each test, the average score for the midterm tests, the weighted scores for the three grade components, and the final grade. The total number of points possible on each test and the weights for each of the three grade components are shown at the top of the worksheet.

When you finish this project, the first 29 rows of your worksheet should resemble Figure 5 - 20 although the formatting may be different.

CS202 Fall Semester Grades											
Total points											
Test 1	44										
Test 2	40										
Final	36										
Grade weights											
Tests	30%										
Final	35%										
Projects	35%										
	Test 1		**Test 2**		**Test Average**		**Final**			**Projects**		
Student	Points		Points		Average	Weighted	Points		Weighted	Average	Weighted	Final
Initials	Missed	Grade	Missed	Grade	Grade	Grade	Missed	Grade	Grade	Grade	Grade	Grade
ab	2.50	94	2.00	95	95	28	6.25	83	29	9.40	33	90
cc	10.00	77	16.50	59	68	20	18.00	50	18	8.38	29	67
bg	16.30	63	14.25	64	64	19	15.00	58	20	7.40	26	65
sg	2.00	95	1.00	98	96	29	5.00	86	30	10.00	35	94
mh	1.25	97	1.00	98	97	29	4.00	89	31	9.20	32	93
mj	6.75	85	5.00	88	86	26	2.25	94	33	8.50	30	88
gl	2.50	94	2.00	95	95	28	7.75	78	27	9.50	33	89
rj	21.00	52	11.50	71	62	19	13.75	62	22	8.95	31	71
kl	4.00	91	1.50	96	94	28	3.00	92	32	9.70	34	94
cm	1.00	98	2.50	94	96	29	2.00	94	33	9.60	34	95
um	4.25	90	4.50	89	90	27	14.25	60	21	9.00	32	80
fm	3.00	93	1.00	98	95	29	2.75	92	32	8.30	29	90
wp	4.50	90	3.00	93	91	27	2.00	94	33	10.00	35	95
ap	3.50	92	2.00	95	94	28	5.50	85	30	9.80	34	92
br	7.50	83	2.00	95	89	27	5.75	84	29	9.80	34	90
jr	1.00	98	-	100	99	30	-	100	35	9.70	34	99

Figure 5 - 20

Use Figure 5 - 20 and the following instructions to help you complete the project:

1. Open the file **independent proj. 5.3**. Cells **B4:B6** contain the total possible points for each test. Cells **B8:B10** contain the weights that you give each of the three components of the final grade.

2. Scroll to the right so that you can see all the columns in the worksheet.

3. Make **A1** the active cell again.

4. Since the worksheet is so wide, the first thing that you should do is freeze panes so that you can see the student initials, the total points per test, and the grade weights at all times. Scroll the screen so that row **3** is the first row visible. Click on **C14** and **freeze panes**.

5. The formula for the Test 1 Grade (**C14**) should divide the difference between the total points possible (**B4**) and the points missed (**B14**) by the total points possible (**B4**) and then multiply by **100**. Remember to make absolute any cell references that should *not* change when the formula is copied. Also use parentheses where necessary. You may want to write down the formula before you enter it.

6. Copy the formula down column **C**. Use Figure 5 - 20 to check results.

7. Create a formula for Test 2 in cell **E14** similar to the formula for Test 1 and copy it down the column.

8. In **F14** create a formula for the average test grade. Since the two test grades are not next to each other, it is probably easier to enter a formula that adds the two test grades and then divides the sum by 2, than it is to use the average function. Copy the formula down the column.

9. In **G14** enter a formula that calculates the weighted test grade. The weighted test grade is equal to the average test grade multiplied by the weight for test grades (cell **B8**). Copy the formula down the columns.

10. In **I14** create a formula for the final grade. This should be similar to the formulas for the grades on tests 1 and 2. Copy this formula down the column.

11. In **J14** calculate the weighted final grade and copy it down the column.

12. In **L14** create a formula for the weighted project grade. Since the projects were graded on a scale from 1 to 10 instead of 1 to 100, the weighted project grade equals the average project grade multiplied by the weight multiplied by 10. Copy the formula down the column.

13. In **M14** create a formula for the final grade. The final grade is equal to the total of the weighted test average grade, the weighted final grade, and the weighted projects grade. Copy the formula down the column.

14. Unfreeze panes.

15. Format all the grades and weighted grades that you calculated using Comma Style with no decimal places.

16. Format the three columns that are labeled **Points Missed** and the **Average Grade** for **Projects** for Comma Style with 2 decimal places.

17. Save the worksheet as: **grades**

18. Print the worksheet with appropriate headers and footers. Use Landscape orientation.

19. Print the worksheet again displaying formulas. Make sure the header or footer contains a page number.

20. Close and save the worksheet.

Independent Project 5.4: Completing a Common Size Income Statement

You are an employee of ECAP Corporation. You have been asked to create a "Common Size Income Statement" for 1994 and 1995. Common Size Income Statements show the costs and expenses for a period in relation to the sales for that period. The purpose of common size statements is to emphasize relationships rather than numbers. These statements are important when performing financial statement analysis. The file, **independent proj. 5.4**, contains the data that you need for your analysis. You need to add the formulas and format the results of the formulas.

1. When finished, your worksheet should contain:

   * The following formulas:

Result	Calculation
Gross Profit for 1994 and for 1995	Net Sales minus Cost of Goods Sold
Operating Income for 1994 and for 1995	Gross Profit for the year minus General & Administration and Selling Expenses
Income before Taxes for 1994 and for 1995	Operating Income for the year minus Interest Expense
%1994 and %1995	For each item, its percent of the Net Sales

Table 5 - 1

   * In all cases, create formulas that use appropriate cell referencing so that they can be copied down columns or across rows.

   * Appropriate formatting.

2. Save the file as: **income**

3. Print the worksheet using appropriate page setup and identifying headers or footers.

4. Print the worksheet showing formulas.

5. Use your worksheet to answer the following question: Was before-tax income in 1995 lower than in 1994 simply because sales were lower, or were there other reasons?

6. In the chapter you performed *what-if* analysis by changing assumptions. There are no explicitly stated assumptions in this worksheet, but you can still perform *what-if* analysis. Change the value for Cost of Goods Sold in 1995 until it is the same percent of Net Sales as it was in 1994. **HINT**: You can arrive at the appropriate value for Cost of Goods Sold by trying various numbers until the percent is the same as it was for 1994, or you can use the **TOOLS/Goal Seek** command to let *Excel* calculate the value for you. Use the **Index** tab of the **Help Topics: Microsoft Excel** dialog box to find help on **goal seeking**. When given a list of topics found, display **Seek a specific solution to a formula**. Be sure to read the definition of **Goal Seek** in the **Help** window that appears.

7. After you make that change, what is the income before taxes? Is it a higher or lower percent of net sales than the 1994 income before taxes?

8. **Save** your worksheet as **income**. **Print** the worksheet. Use a header or footer that indicates that the value of the cost of goods sold is a goal and not the actual figure.

Lesson
6 Charts

Objectives

In this lesson you will learn how to:

- Differentiate between the types of charts
- Define the parts of a chart
- Use the **ChartWizard** to create charts
- Embed a chart in the worksheet
- Format the text in a chart
- Create a three-dimensional chart
- Create a chart on its own sheet

- Change the type and AutoFormat of the chart
- Format Y-axis values
- Edit data used in a chart
- Print charts
- Switch between sheets in a workbook
- Rename sheets in a workbook
- Print multiple sheets in a workbook

CHARTING

Often the best way to get an understanding of the patterns in worksheet data is by creating a picture — or chart of the data. *Excel* makes this task easy by providing the **ChartWizard** to help you create the chart. Once the chart is created, you can easily enhance or edit it. More importantly, since the chart is linked to the worksheet, changes made to the worksheet are instantly reflected in the chart.

Excel has 14 different types of charts: area, bar, column, line, pie, doughnut, radar, XY scatter, 3-D area, 3-D bar, 3-D column, 3-D line, 3-D pie, and 3-D surface. Each type has at least one *subtype* or variation that can also be created. In addition, combination charts mixing column and line charts or column and area charts can be created. The most common types of charts are described in Table 6 - 1.

PROJECT 1 DESCRIPTION

In this lesson you will add charts to the worksheets created in Lessons 1 and 3. In the project in Lesson 1 you created a worksheet that calculated the hours worked by three consultants as well as their salaries, billing amount, and profit generated. Now you are going to enhance that worksheet by adding a chart. You have been told to create a chart that shows the proportion, or percent, of the profit contributed by each employee. The most common chart used to illustrate how a total is divided into parts is a *pie* chart. You will *embed*, or place, the pie chart immediately below the worksheet data on the same sheet as the data. When finished your worksheet will resemble Figure 6 - 1.

Type of Chart	Example	Use
Pie, 3-D Pie	Figure 6 - 1	Compares the percent of the total contributed by each part; can be used to compare only one series of data
Column, 3-D Column	Figure 6 - 22	Compares noncontinuous items; the value of each item is displayed as a vertical column
Bar, 3-D Bar	Figure 6 - 32	The same as a column chart except that each item is displayed horizontally
Line, 3-D Line	Figure 6 - 33	Compares items, usually over time; used to show trends in data
Area, 3-D Area	Figure 6 - 34	Shows the continuous change in volume of multiple data series; usually shows changes over time
Stacked Column	Figure 6 - 36	A subtype of the column chart, the columns are stacked for all series being compared on top of each other so that the totals can also be compared
100% Column	Figure 6 - 35 Nos. 5, 10	A subtype of the column chart, 100% columns compare each data series as a percent of the whole
Combination	Figure 6 - 42	Uses two different formats, usually bar and line or bar and area, to compare data of different types or to make one series of data stand out from the rest

Table 6 - 1: Types of Charts

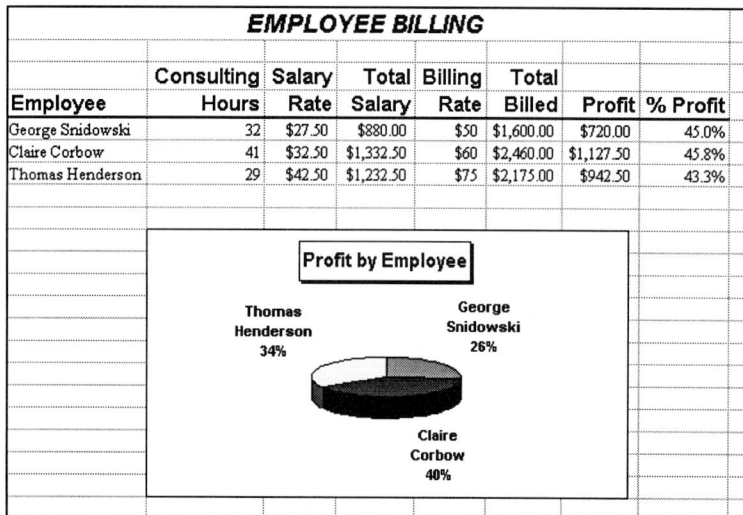

Figure 6 - 1

A PIE CHART

Pie charts are often the easiest to understand. Pie charts contain only one *data series*. A *data series* is a series of related data such as the hours worked by the employees or the profit generated by each employee. In *Excel* the data for each series is from a single worksheet row or column. Each value (or cell) in the series is called a *data point*. In our pie chart the data series is the profit resulting from the three employees' consulting. It is located in cells **G5:G7** . The profit generated by each employee is a data point and will be represented by a wedge of the pie. A pie chart must include information that identifies each wedge or slice of the pie.

In your pie chart the employee names are the identifying information. In a pie chart this information can be included right next to each wedge or in a *legend* that lists each employee's name and the color or pattern used in the wedge for that person. *Excel* also allows you to add a title for the chart while you are creating it.

USING THE CHARTWIZARD

The **ChartWizard** works just like the **FunctionWizard**. Just as the **FunctionWizard** provides a series of steps that help you enter a function, the **ChartWizard** guides you through the creation of a chart.

To use the ChartWizard to create a new chart embedded on the worksheet:

- Select a worksheet range. The range should include the data series to be charted. It often also includes the information for the legend and for some of the titles used on the chart.

- Click on the **ChartWizard** button 📊 or select **INSERT/Chart, On This Sheet**. *The mouse pointer will change to a* 📊 .

- To let the **ChartWizard** size the chart for you, position the mouse pointer where you want the upper left corner of the chart to be and click the mouse button. To position the chart yourself, place the mouse pointer at the point where you want the upper left corner of the chart to be. Click and drag until the rectangle formed is the size and shape that you want the chart to be. Release the mouse button.

- In the **ChartWizard - Step 1 of 5** dialog box, confirm that the correct range has been entered and click on the **Next** button.

- In the **ChartWizard - Step 2 of 5** dialog box, click on the chart type of your choice and click on the **Next** button.

- The **ChartWizard - Step 3 of 5** dialog box displays the *AutoFormats* (predefined formats) available for the chart type you selected. Click on your preferred format for the chart and click on the **Next** button.

- The **ChartWizard - Step 4 of 5** dialog box displays a sample chart of your data using the chart type and format you have selected. *Excel* has guessed that each data series is in either a row or a column. If this guess is incorrect, click on the other option. If you have included any text that can be used for labels on the chart, tell *Excel* how many rows and/or columns are to be used for each kind of label. When the Sample Chart is correct, click on the **Next** button.

- The **ChartWizard - Step 5 of 5** dialog box also includes a Sample Chart. Indicate whether or not you want a legend. Type a **Chart Title**, if desired. If you are creating a chart that has X and Y axes (we will discuss these later), type titles for these axes. Click on **Finish**.

If you notice a mistake in your chart when you are in any of the **ChartWizard** dialog boxes, use the **Back** button to return to previous dialog boxes.

Activity 6.1: Creating a Pie Chart

In this activity you will create a pie chart that shows the percent of the total profit contributed by each employee.

1. Start *Excel* and open **employee billing, rev. 1**. (If you have not completed Lesson 2, you can use **employee billing**.)

2. The data for the chart is the nonadjacent range **A5:A7** and **G5:G7**. Select the range **A5:A7**. Press the **CTRL** key and, while keeping it depressed, select the range **G5:G7** (Figure 6 - 2).

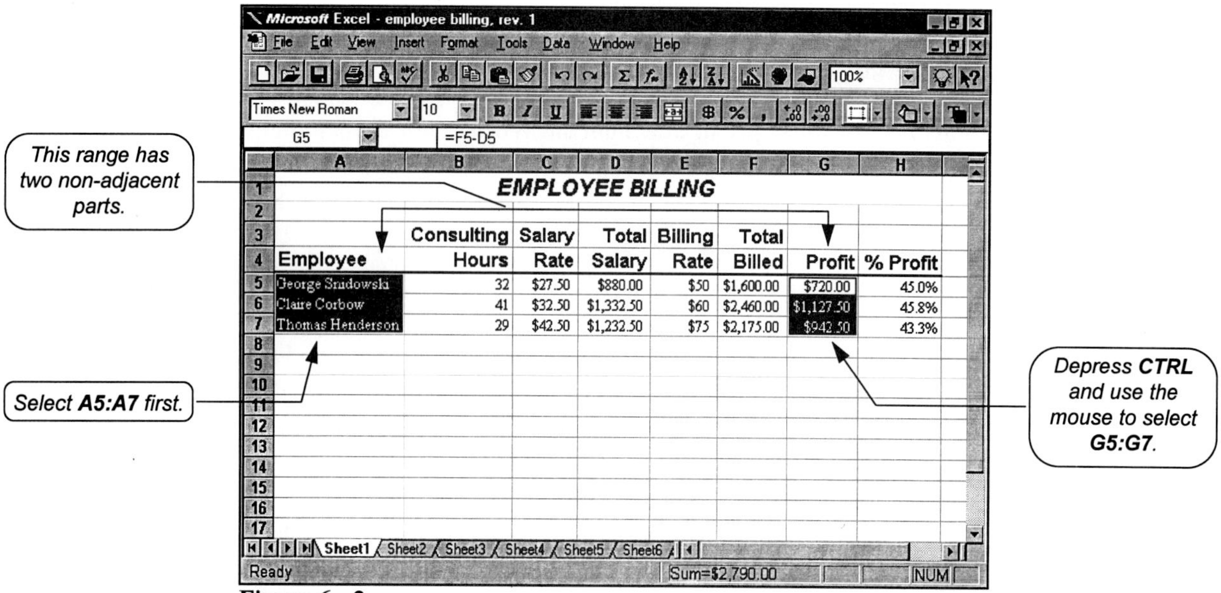

This range has two non-adjacent parts.

Select **A5:A7** first.

Depress **CTRL** and use the mouse to select **G5:G7**.

Figure 6 - 2

3. Choose **INSERT/Chart,On This Sheet** or click on the **ChartWizard** button.

    The mouse pointer changes to a ⁺ₗₗₗ *when you move the pointer onto the worksheet grid.*

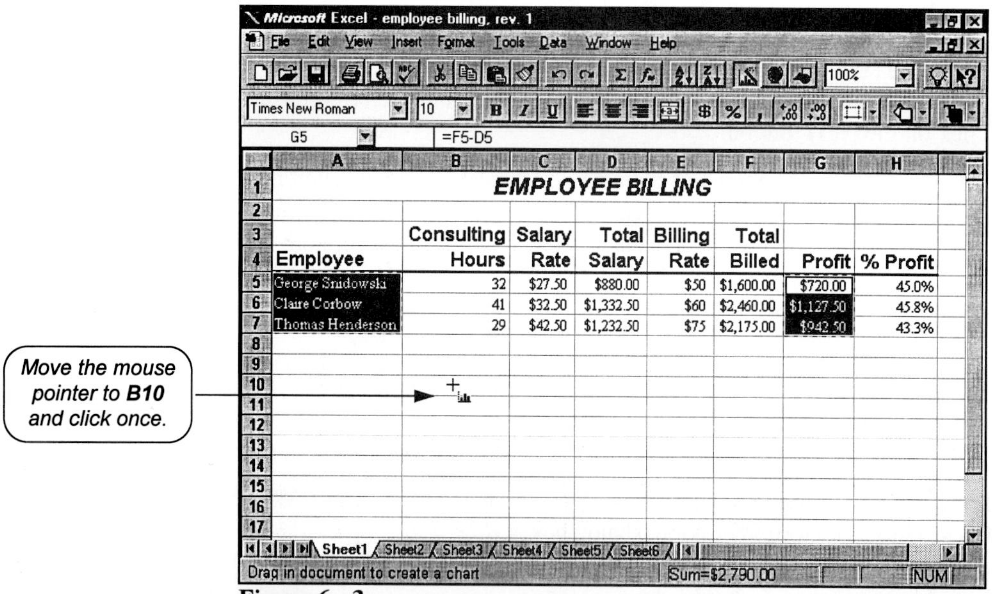

Move the mouse pointer to **B10** and click once.

Figure 6 - 3

4. Point anywhere in cell **B10** (Figure 6 - 3) and click the left mouse button once to let *Excel* automatically place the chart.

    *The first **ChartWizard** dialog box (Figure 6 - 4) appears. The range you selected is entered in the **Range** text box.*

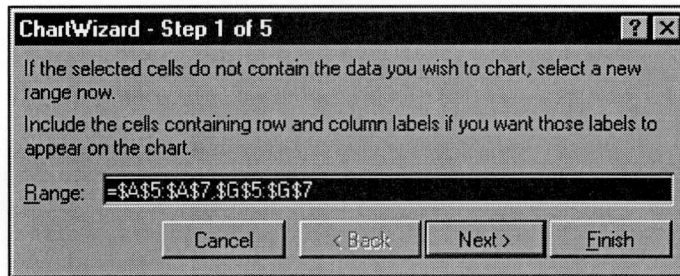

Figure 6 - 4

5.   In the **ChartWizard - Step 1 of 5** dialog box, click on **Next**.

6.   In the **ChartWizard - Step 2 of 5** dialog box, click on the **Pie** (Figure 6 - 5) and then click on **Next**.

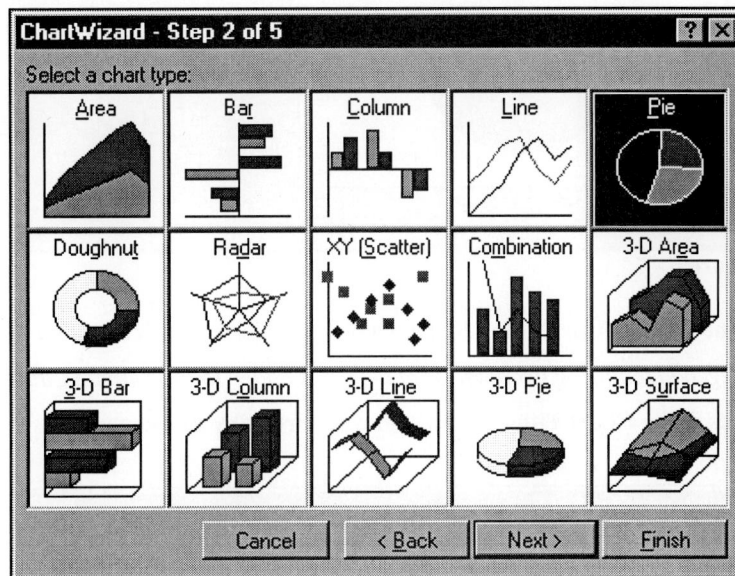

Figure 6 - 5

7.   In the **ChartWizard - Step 3 of 5** dialog box, click on the format number **6** (Figure 6 - 6) to display the percent represented by each employee's part of the profit. Click on **Next**.

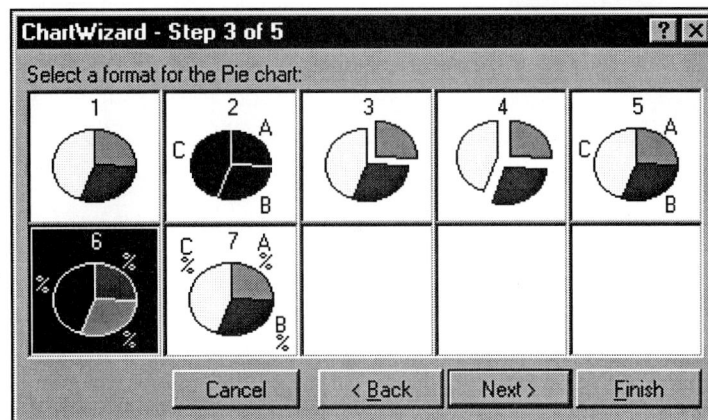

Figure 6 - 6

8. To make the **ChartWizard - Step 4 of 5** dialog box resemble Figure 6 - 7:

    a. The data series is in a **Column (G**—the profits generated by each employee), not a row. If the Rows option button is selected, click on **Columns.**

    b. The **First 1 Column (A**—the names of the employees) will be used as the pie slice labels and the **First 0 Rows** are used for the chart title. If you need to change either of these numbers, click on the ▲ to increase the number in the spin box or the ▼ to decrease the number.

    c. When your dialog box matches Figure 6 - 7 click on **Next.**

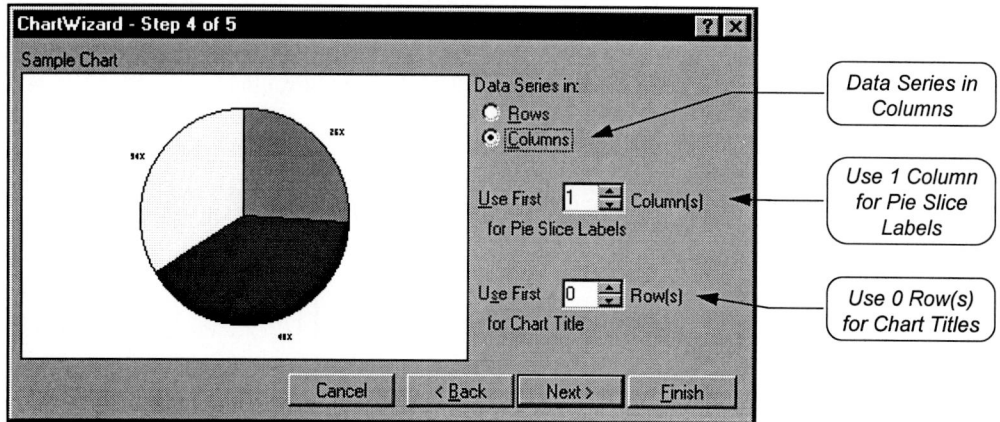

Figure 6 - 7

9. In the **ChartWizard - Step 5 of 5** dialog box, click on the **Yes** option button to add a legend.

    *A legend identifying each wedge of the pie is added to the **Sample Chart** (Figure 6 - 8).*

10. Click in the **Chart Title** text box and type: **Profit by Employee**

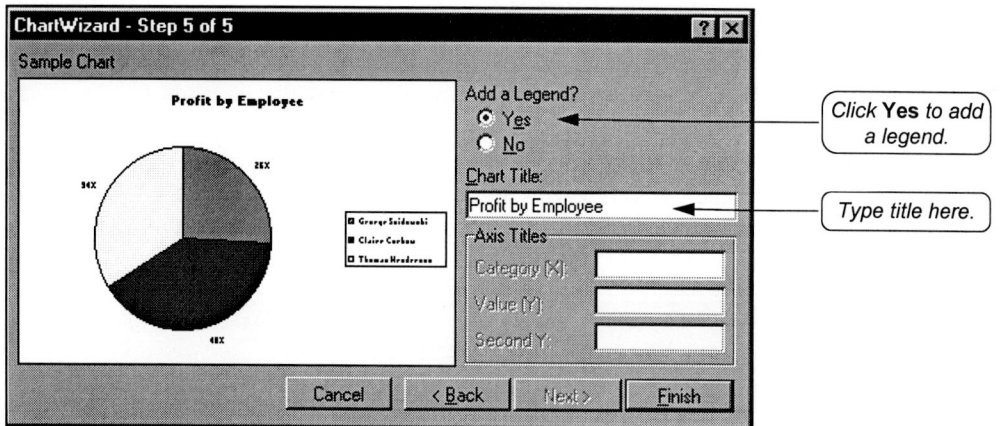

Figure 6 - 8

*The **Axis Titles** are all in light print, and therefore unusable, because **Pie** charts do not have X and Y axes.*

11. The dialog box should resemble Figure 6 - 8. Click on **Finish**.

    *Excel centers the chart under the data on the worksheet beginning in the cell you clicked in. The **Chart** toolbar is also displayed. It may be displayed as a rectangle on the screen as in Figure 6 - 9 or it may be along one of the borders of the worksheet. The chart is selected (as indicated by the selection squares on the corners and sides of the chart).*

12. Point to each of the buttons on the **Chart** toolbar. Look at the name of the button and read the description of the button that appears on the **Status Bar**.

13. Click anywhere on the worksheet outside of the chart.

    *The chart is no longer selected. The selection squares and the **Chart** toolbar no longer appear on the screen.*

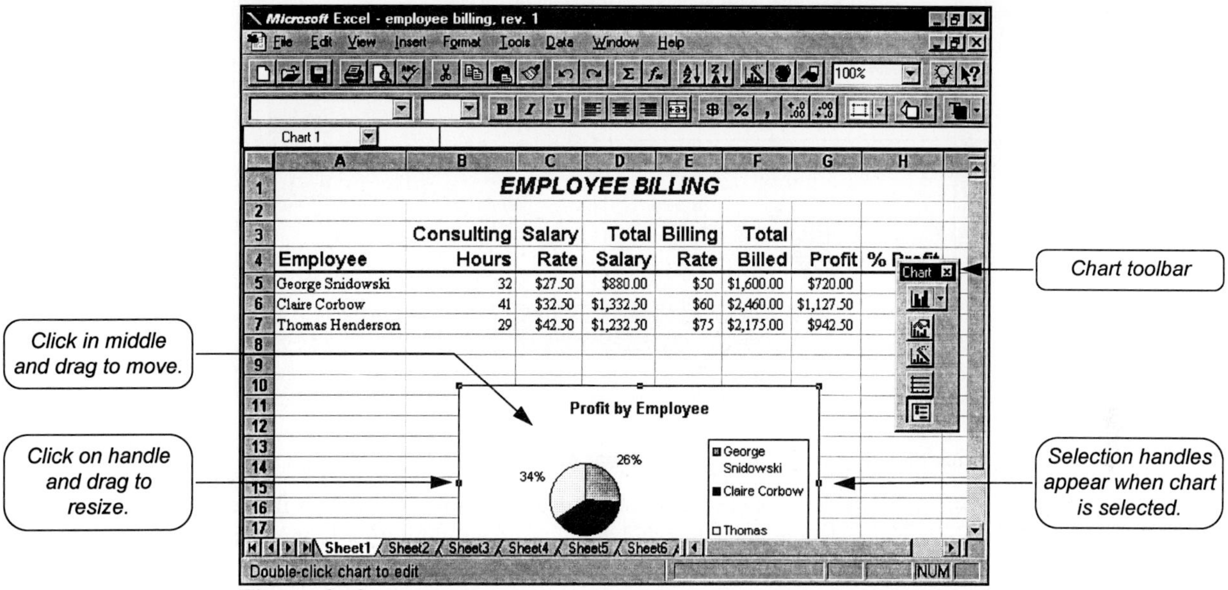

Figure 6 - 9

14. Use **FILE/Save As** to save the worksheet with the file name: **employee billing with pie chart**

MOVING AND SIZING EMBEDDED CHARTS

Embedded charts can be moved and sized on the worksheet.

To move an embedded chart:

- Click on the chart once to select it, if it is not already selected.
- Point with the mouse anywhere in the chart. Click and drag the chart to the new location.

To resize an embedded chart:

- Click on the chart once to select it, if it is not already selected.
- Point with the mouse to any of the selection squares on the chart borders.
- When the mouse pointer changes to a ↔ , drag until the chart is the size and shape you want.

Activity 6.2: Moving and Resizing an Embedded Chart

1. Click anywhere on the chart to select it.

2. Point to the middle of the chart and drag it so that its left border is touching the left border of the worksheet and the top border is along the gridline between rows **9** and **10** (Figure 6 - 10).

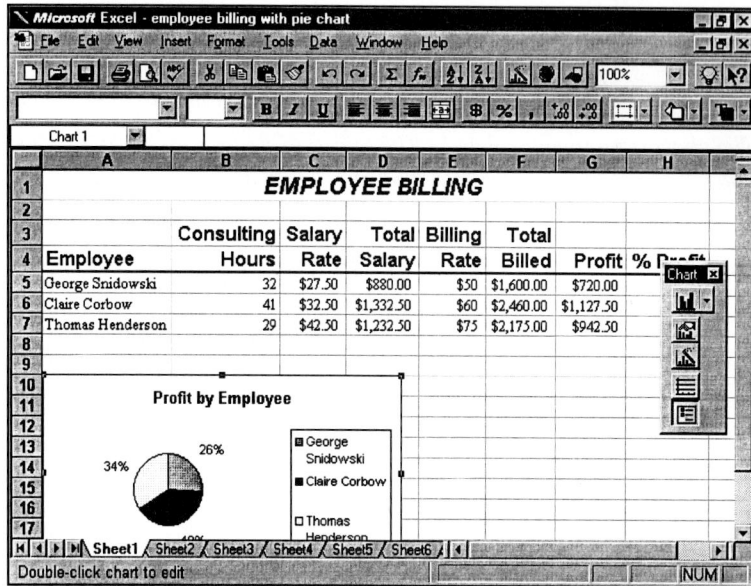

Figure 6 - 10

3. Click the [▼] on the vertical scroll bar to scroll the worksheet until row **22** is visible.

4. Point to the selection square in the bottom right corner of the chart frame. When the mouse pointer changes to a ↔, click and drag until the right border is approximately on the line between column **E** and **F** and the bottom border is on the gridline between row **21** and **22**. Release the mouse button.

5. Point to the middle of the chart, make sure the pointer is a ⤢ and drag it again so that the left frame border is on the gridline between columns **A** and **B** (or wherever the chart is approximately horizontally centered on your worksheet) as in Figure 6 - 11.

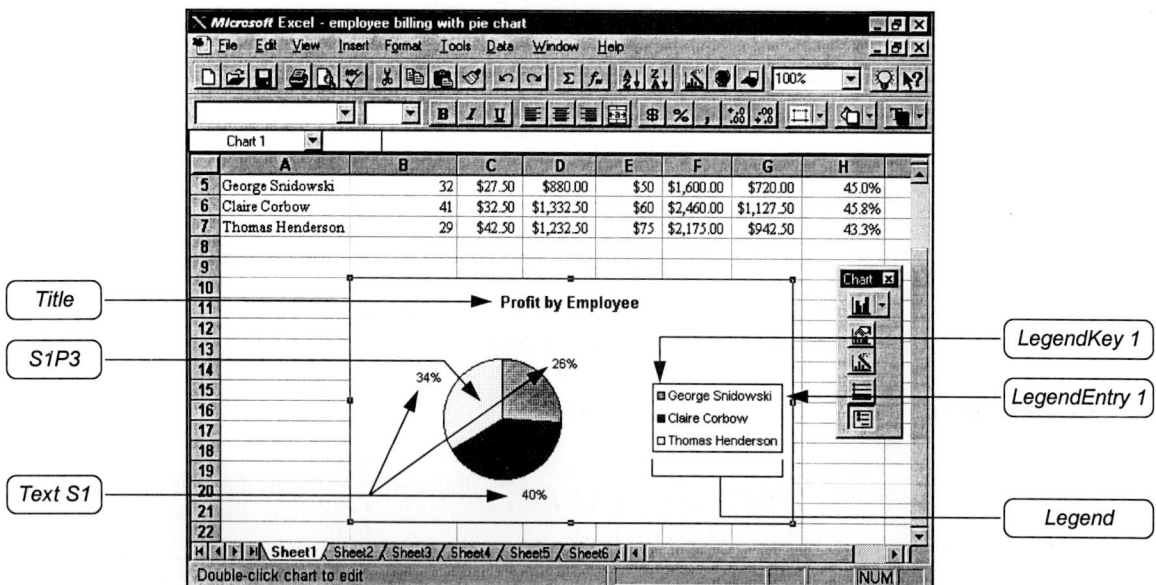

Figure 6 - 11

6. Click outside of the chart to deselect it.

MODIFYING AN EMBEDDED CHART

Once created, an *Excel* chart can be modified in many ways. The chart type can be changed. You can insert, delete, or change titles, legends, data points, and gridlines. Fonts and colors can be changed, and borders, arrows, and other graphic objects can be added. You will have an opportunity to use a few of these options in this project and the next one. Once you learn the procedures, however, you can experiment with other changes using **Help** when you run into problems. Figure 6 - 11 indicates *Excel's* names for the different parts of the chart that can be modified. *Excel* calls each of these parts of the chart *items*.

To select an embedded chart so that it can be modified:

- Double-click on the chart.

  The chart is surrounded by a different frame and the names and contents of the menus change to the chart menus.

To select a new AutoFormat for the chart:

- Choose **FORMAT/AutoFormat**.

- Choose a new chart type from the **Galleries** list box if desired.

- Choose the **AutoFormat** of your choice and click on **OK**.

To format a part of the chart:

- Click on the part of the chart that you want to format. *Excel* indicates the selected part by surrounding it with small squares and displaying its name in the **name box** (left end) of the Formula Bar. To select one entry in a legend, data series, etc., click once to select the entire group and then click a second time on the specific item that you want to select.

- Click on the selected item with the **right** mouse button to display a shortcut menu. (You may click on the object with the **right** mouse button without first clicking with the **left** mouse button. However, when you are first using charts it is easier to first select the part of the chart with the **left** mouse button, make sure you have made the correct selection, and then click on that same selection with the **right** mouse button.)

- Choose the formatting command from the shortcut menu and make the desired changes to the dialog box.

CAUTION: *If you click outside of the chart frame during editing, the chart will no longer be in edit mode. Double click on the chart again to select it so that you can modify it.*

ALTERNATE METHODS: *You can also change the format of a chart item by (a) double-clicking on the item and then making changes to the dialog box that appears; or (b) clicking on the item and then using the Formatting toolbar to make the changes; or (c) clicking on the item and then using the* **Format** *menu commands.*

Activity 6.3: Changing the Format of Parts of the Chart

After looking at the chart you decide that you would rather have a three-dimensional pie instead of the current two-dimensional pie. Also, you would prefer the pie section labels to appear next to the wedges instead of in a separate legend. You also decide to format the title of the chart so that it stands out more.

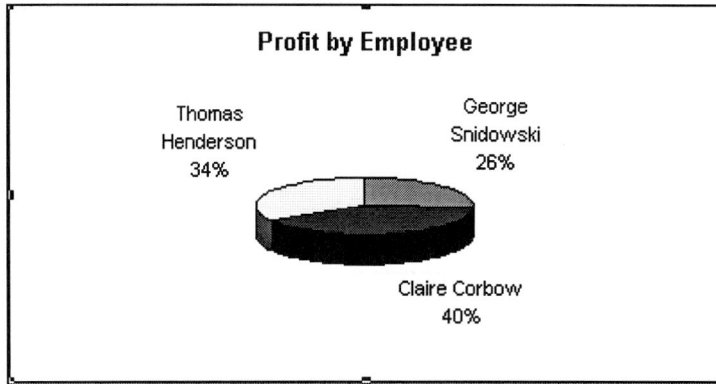

Figure 6 - 16

To enhance the chart title:

10. Click anywhere on the chart title.

11. While still pointing to the chart title, click the **right** mouse button (Figure 6 - 17).

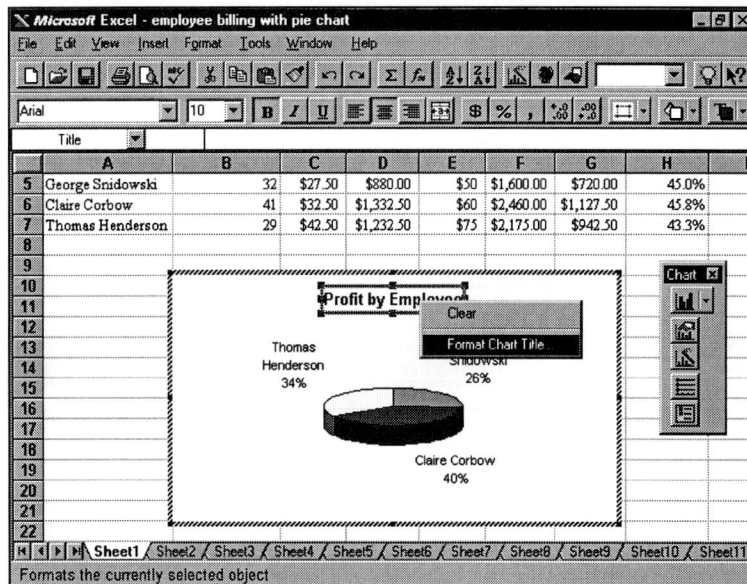

Figure 6 - 17

12. Select **Format Chart Title** from the shortcut menu.

13. Click on the **Font** tab if it is not already selected.

    The Font tab displays the same choices you used in the worksheet when formatting cells (Figure 6 - 18).

14. Choose a **Size** of **11**.

15. Click on the **Patterns** tab.

16. Click on the **Shadow** check box to mark the box.

    As soon as you mark Shadow, the Border changes from None to Automatic, because a border must be inserted before it can have a shadow (Figure 6 - 19).

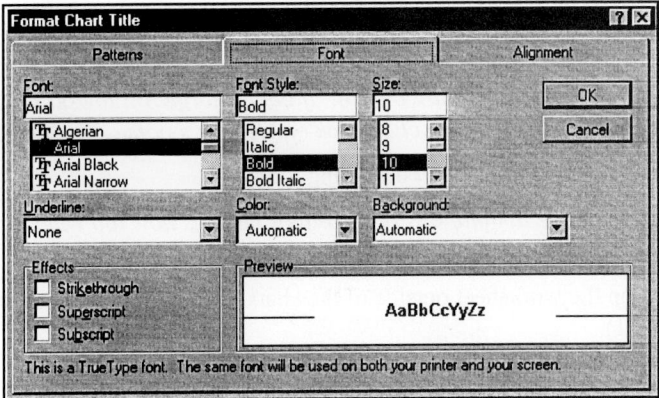

Figure 6 - 18

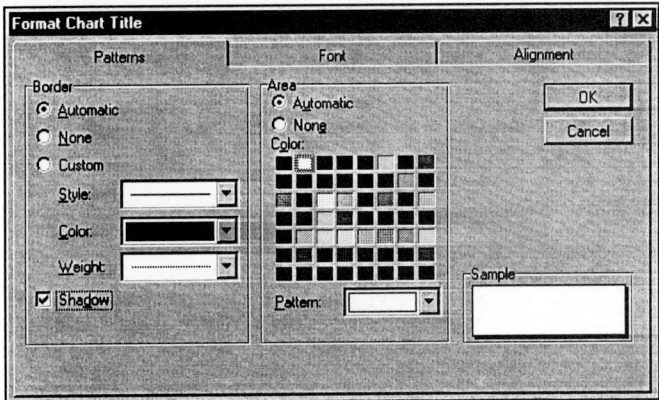

Figure 6 - 19

17. Click on **OK**.

The title, Profit by Employee, is larger and is enclosed in a border with a shadow (Figure 6 - 20).

Figure 6 - 20

18. With the left mouse button, click on **George Snidowski** or any of the other labels.

   Text S1 *(Text, Series 1) appears in the **name box** on the Formula Bar. All three of the wedge labels should be selected (Figure 6 - 20). If only **George Snidowski** is selected, click on a blank part of the chart and then click back on George's name.*

19. Click on the **Bold** button on the Formatting toolbar.

   The wedge labels are in bold. Claire Corbow's name is now too wide to fit on one line and will be split between two lines.

20. Click twice on the worksheet outside of the chart frame to exit from editing the chart (Figure 6 - 21).

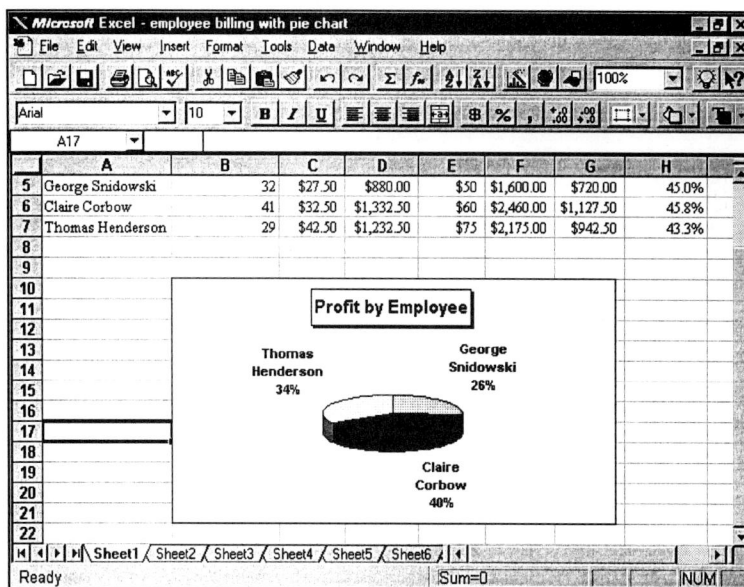

Figure 6 - 21

21. **Save** the worksheet again.

PRINTING AN EMBEDDED CHART

Now you're ready to print the worksheet and the chart. Printing a worksheet with an embedded chart is exactly the same as printing a worksheet that doesn't contain a chart.

Activity 6.4: Printing a Worksheet with a Chart

1. Click on the **Print Preview** button to see what your worksheet and chart will look like when printed.

2. **Print** the worksheet.

3. **Close** the file. **Exit** from *Excel* or continue with the next project.

PROJECT 2 DESCRIPTION

In the second project in this lesson, you will add a chart to the **nationwide sales, rev. 1** worksheet that you created in Lesson 3. The **nationwide sales, rev. 1** worksheet summarizes the 1995 sales by product and region. Column, bar, or line charts are usually used to show trends or compare data. You will create a column chart (Figure 6-22) to visually compare the sales of the products in the different regions. Unlike pie charts, column charts can contain data from more than one series and data are plotted on a grid with two axes; therefore, you will learn some additional terms before creating the chart.

Since the **nationwide sales, rev. 1** worksheet has more than one section, it would be easier to create the chart on a separate sheet in the workbook. In the Introduction to *Excel* you learned that a workbook can contain more than one sheet. However, up to now you have used only one sheet in each of your projects. Therefore, while working on this project, you will learn how to move between different sheets and how to rename the sheets so that you can identify the content of each easily.

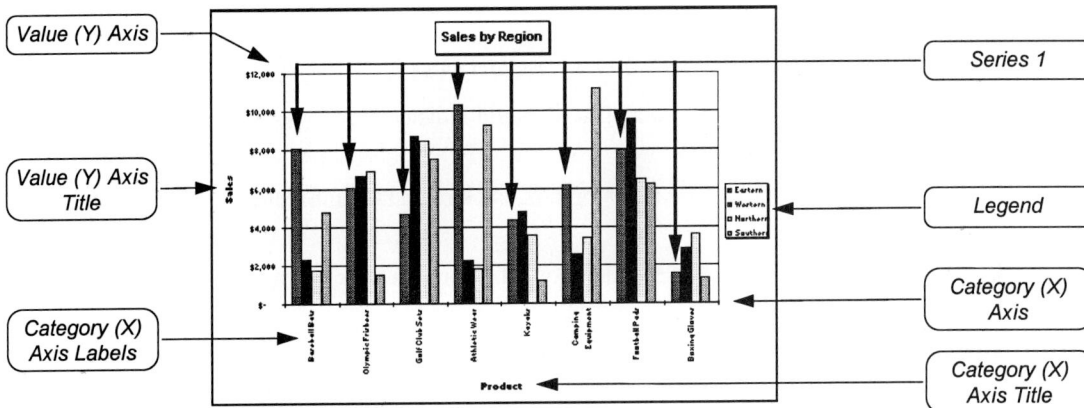

Figure 6 - 22

CREATING A COLUMN CHART

Excel refers to charts containing vertical bars as *column charts* and charts containing horizontal bars as *bar charts*. Some other programs refer to both types as bar charts. As Figure 6 - 22 indicates your column chart will contain four data series (one for each region of the country). Each data series has a value or bar for each of the products being compared. You will need to understand the following terms to understand the options in the **ChartWizard** dialog boxes.

- **X-axis** — Usually the horizontal axis, this is also called the *category* axis because it indicates the way in which you have classified the data being charted. Frequently the categories on the X-axis represent periods of time (days, months, quarters, etc.) because column, bar, and line charts are often used to see how data change over time. In your chart the categories on the X-axis are the different products. *Excel* refers to the category names as the *Category (X) Axis Labels*. In the chart you will create, the product categories are in column **A** of the worksheet.

- **Y-axis** — Usually the vertical axis, this is also called the *value* axis because it is used to measure each of the items being charted. When you create a chart, *Excel* automatically enters a scale of numbers along the Y-axis.

- **Data series** — This is a series of related data points contained in a single row or column. The pie chart that you created in Project 1 contained one data series. The column chart you will create in this project contains four data series — one for each region of the country. They are contained in columns **B, C, D,** and **E** of the worksheet. Each of the products represented on the X-axis will have one bar for each data series. Each data series is represented in a different color or pattern.

- **Legend** — As we saw in Project 1, the legend is a box containing the names of each data series (which *Excel* calls the *legend text*) and the pattern or color by which they are represented.

- **Titles** — The chart and the X- and Y-axes may have labels, or *titles* that help the viewer understand what the chart is illustrating.

Activity 6.5: Creating a Column Chart

1. Start *Excel* if necessary and open the file **nationwide sales, rev. 1.**

2. Select the cells representing the column labels for the four regions, the product names, and all the associated values. If you completed Lesson 3, this range will be **A6:E14.**

3. Choose **INSERT/Chart, As New Sheet.**

    You cannot use the ChartWizard button to create a chart as a new sheet.

4. The **ChartWizard - Step 1 of 5** dialog box should indicate the range **=$A$6:$E$14.** Click on **Next** to accept this range.

5. In the **ChartWizard - Step 2 or 5** dialog box, click on the **Column** chart if it is not already selected. Click on **Next.**

6. In the **ChartWizard - Step 3 of 5** dialog box, click on column chart number **1.** Click on **Next.**

7. The **ChartWizard - Step 4 of 5** dialog box displays a sample chart (Figure 6 - 23). All of the default settings should be correct. Each of your data series is a **column.** The **First 1 Column** in the range **(A)** contains the **Category (X) Axis Labels** (the names of the products) and the **First 1 Row** contains the **Legend Text** (the names of the four regions). Click on **Next.**

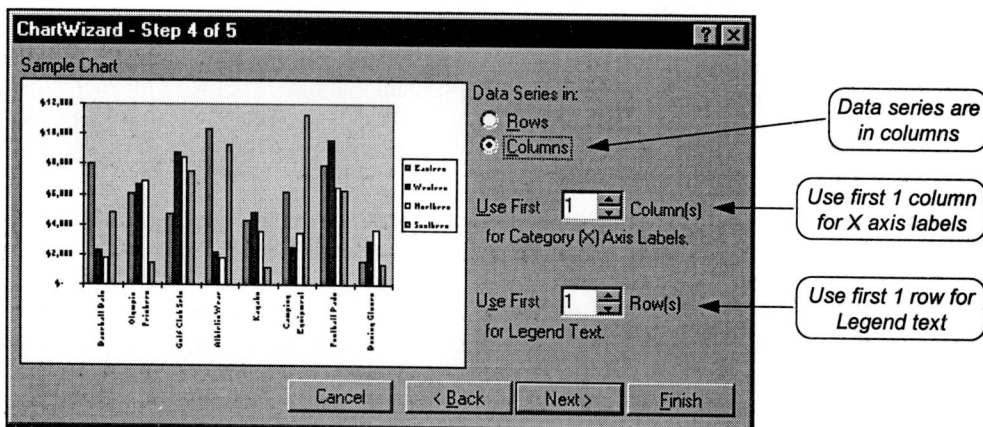

Figure 6 - 23

8. In the **ChartWizard - Step 5 of 5** dialog box, press the **TAB** key or click in the **Chart Title** box. Type: **Sales by Region**

9. Select the **Category (X)** text box and type: **Product**

10. Select the **Value (Y)** box, type: **Sales** (Figure 6 - 24*),* and then click on **Finish.**

    Your chart is displayed on its own Chart sheet (Figure 6 - 25). Notice that Excel has added a Chart tab to the tabs at the bottom of the workbook. You will learn how to go back to the worksheet after we have worked with the chart.

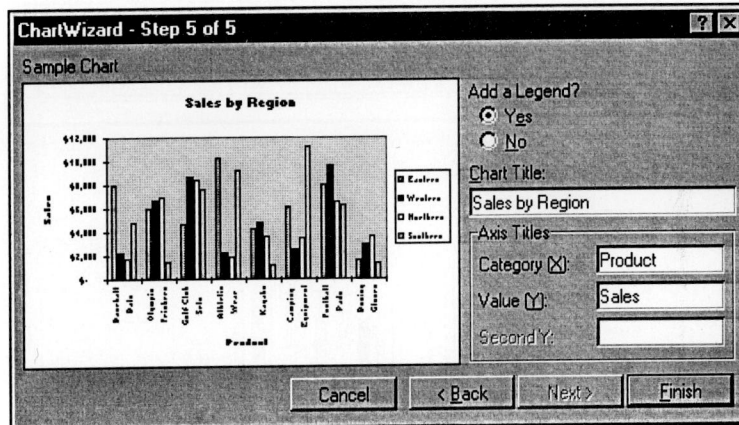

Figure 6 - 24

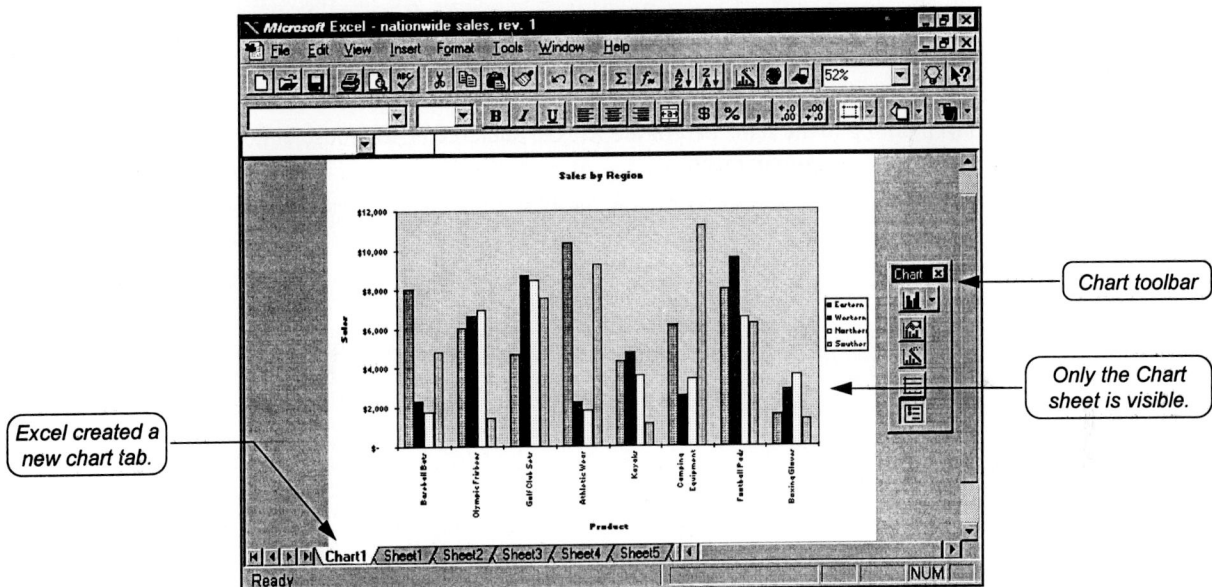

Figure 6 - 25

11. **Save** the file with the new name: **Nationwide Sporting Goods with Chart**

Activity 6.6: Formatting the Chart

In this activity you will change the alignment of the X-axis labels so that the **Category (X) axis** labels are horizontal. You will also format the **title**, **legend**, and **Value (Y) axis** text. In the process you will use some of the alternate methods listed in the first project in this lesson for formatting parts of the chart.

1. Point to a part of the X-axis that is in between bars (Figure 6 - 26) and click the mouse button.

PROBLEM SOLVER: *Small squares should appear only at the two ends of the X-axis, and the **name box** of the Formula Bar should say **Axis 2**. If a different part of the chart is indicated in the **name box**, you have clicked in the wrong place. Repeat step 1.*

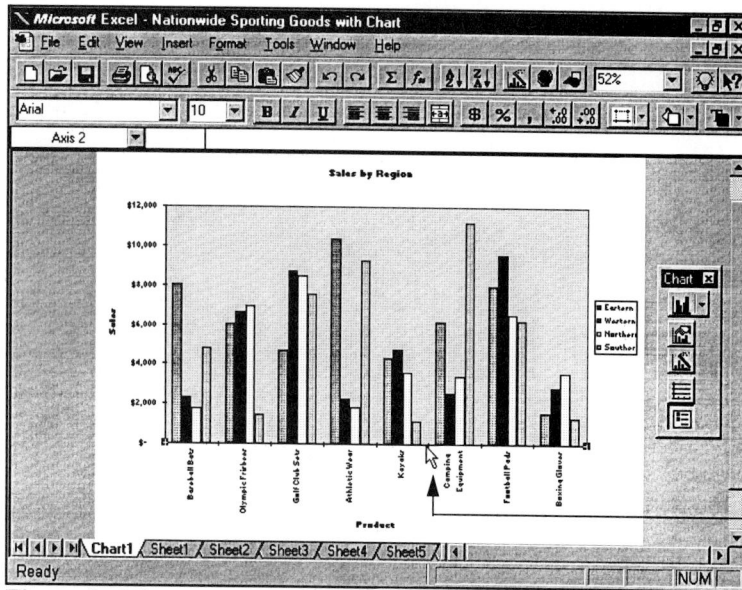

Point to X-axis between bars.

Figure 6 - 26

2. Still pointing to the same part of the X-axis, click the **right** mouse button. Choose **Format Axis** from the shortcut menu.

3. Click on the **Alignment** tab of the **Format Axis** dialog box (Figure 6 - 27).

4. Click on the horizontal alignment box (Figure 6 - 27). Click on **OK**.

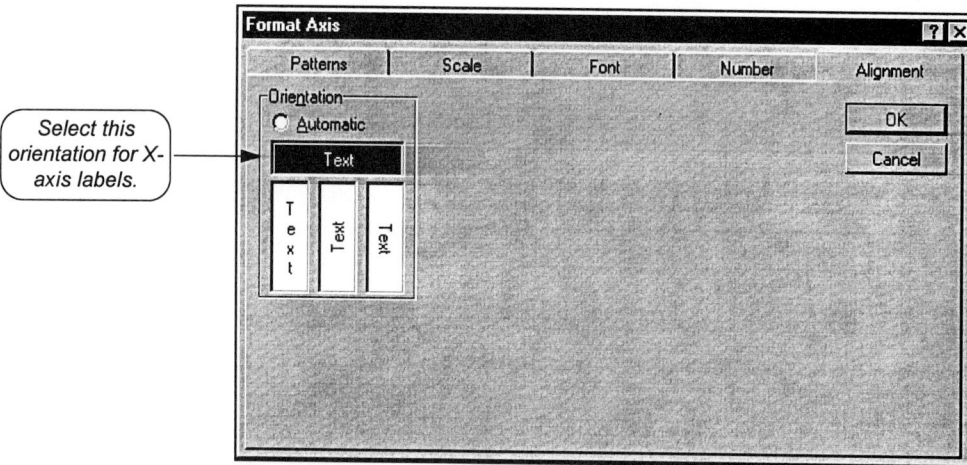

Select this orientation for X-axis labels.

Figure 6 - 27

5. Point to a part of the chart area that does not contain bars and click with the **left** mouse button. If the **name box** says **Plot** (Figure 6 - 28), you have selected the correct area. Click in the same place with the **right** mouse button.

6. Choose **Format Plot Area** from the shortcut menu.

7. Click on the solid white box in the **Color** part of the **Area** section (Figure 6 - 29). Click on **OK**.

8. Click anywhere in the **Legend** with the **right** mouse button. Choose **Format Legend** from the shortcut menu. Choose the **Patterns** tab, mark **Shadow**, and click on **OK**.

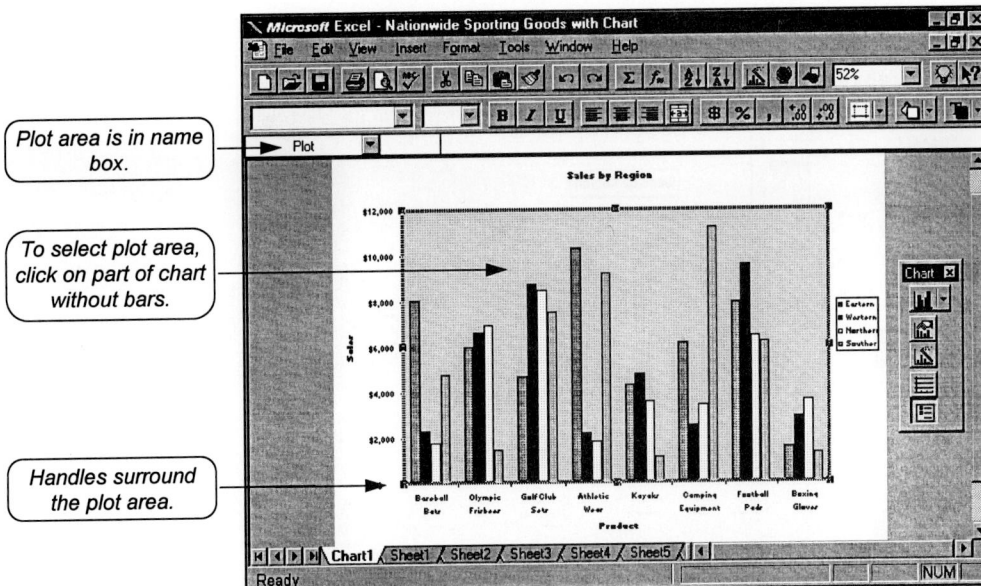

Figure 6 - 28

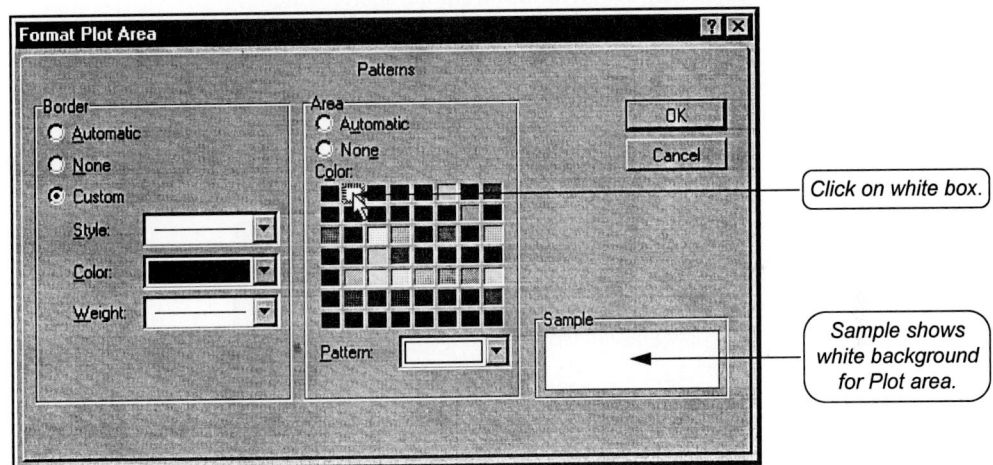

Figure 6 - 29

9. Point slightly below the worksheet title, **Sales by Region,** and double-click.

   *The **Format Chart Title** dialog box is displayed.*

10. Use the **Font** tab to change the Font size to **16.** Use the **Patterns** tab to add a **Shadow.** Click on **OK.**

11. Click once on the **Y-axis** title, **Sales.** Use the **Font Size** drop-down box on the Formatting toolbar (Figure 6 - 30) to change the size to **12.**

12. If you cannot see the **X-axis** label (**Product**), click on the [image] on the vertical scroll bar until it is displayed. Click once on the **X-axis** label.

13. Use the **Font Size** button to change the font size of the **X-axis** title, **Product,** to **12** points.

14. Click on the **Y-axis** with the **right** mouse button.

    *The name box should say **Axis 1.** If not, try selecting the **Y-axis** again.*

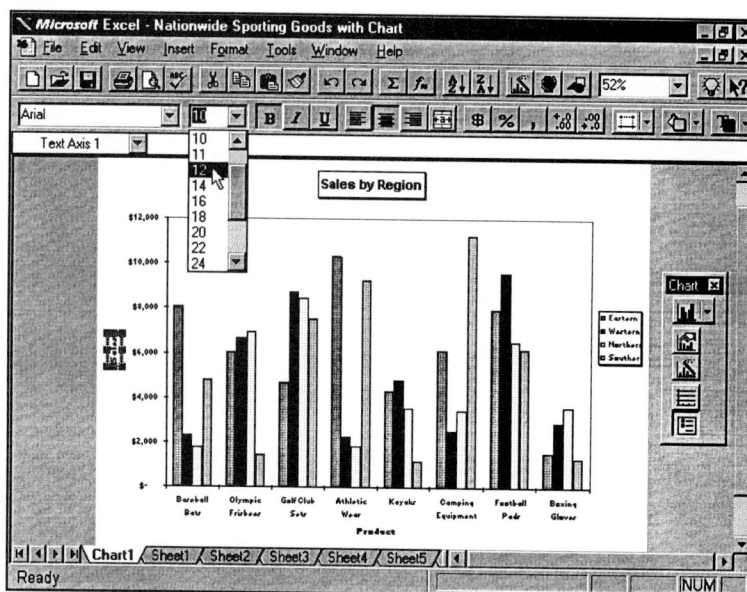

Figure 6 - 30

15. Choose **Insert Gridlines** from the shortcut menu.

   *Gridlines are lines that go across the width or height of the chart. Major **Y-axis** gridlines go across the chart at the point of each value marked on the **Y-axis**. They help you read the value of the bars on the chart.*

16. Choose **Major Gridlines** on the **Value (Y) Axis** (Figure 6 - 31) and click on **OK**.

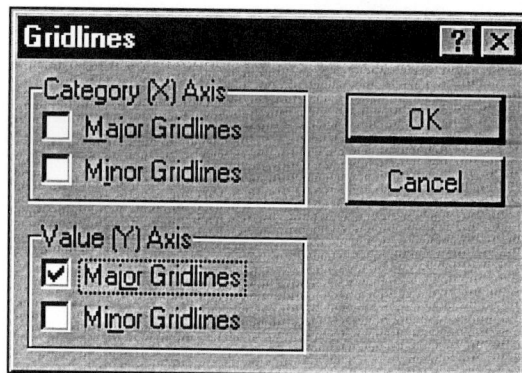

Figure 6 - 31

17. **Save** the workbook again using the current name.

PRINTING A CHART FROM A SEPARATE SHEET

Printing a chart from a chart sheet is performed in the same way as printing a worksheet or printing a chart that is embedded on a worksheet. The difference is that the default paper orientation is landscape.

Activity 6.7: Printing the Column Chart

1. Choose **FILE/Print Preview** or click on the **Print Preview** toolbar button.

The chart is displayed in landscape orientation (the page is wider than it is long). If you do not have a color printer, the colors in the bars and the legend are automatically changed to shades of gray.

2. Click on the **Print** button.

3. **Selected Sheets** should be marked in the **Print What** section of the **Print** dialog box. If it isn't, choose it. Click on **OK**.

CHANGING THE TYPE OF CHART

Different types of charts are better for different data. To help you understand the differences between charts, you will display the **Nationwide Sporting Goods with Chart** data using different chart types and subtypes.

To change the chart type, use one of these three methods:

- Click on the triangle to the right of the **Chart Type** tool ⬛ on the Chart toolbar and then click on the chart type of your choice; *or*

- Choose **FORMAT/Chart Type**. The **Chart Type** dialog box lets you select a **2-D** or **3-D** chart and then select from the available chart types. The **Options** button in the dialog box also lets you select **Subtypes** of the chart and change other display options; *or*

- Choose **FORMAT/AutoFormat** and select a different chart type from the **Galleries** list box. This method also lets you select one of the **AutoFormats** for the chart type that you choose. The **AutoFormats** include all of the subtypes included in the **Chart Type** options, plus several formatting options such as the inclusion of gridlines.

Activity 6.8: Changing the Chart Type and Subtype

In this activity you will have the opportunity to see how changing the chart type affects your chart.

1. Choose **FORMAT/Chart Type**. Choose **Bar** and click on **OK**.

*Your chart is rotated so that the columns are now horizontal bars. The **Category (X) Axis** is now the vertical axis and the **Value (Y) Axis** is now the horizontal axis (Figure 6 - 32).*

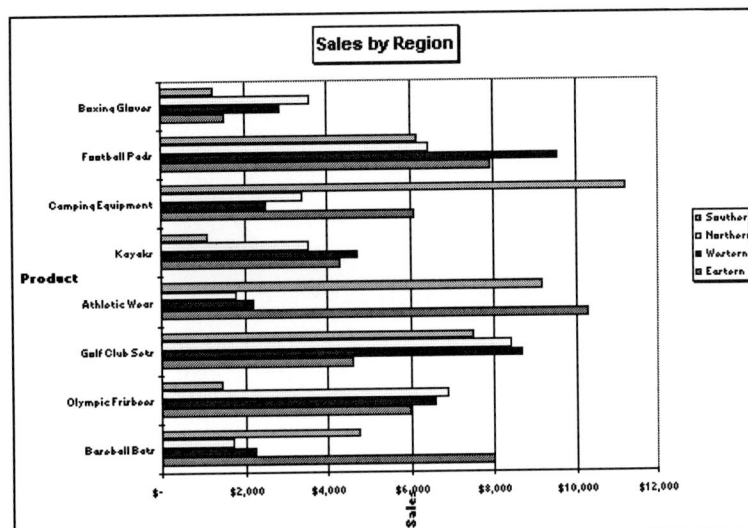

Figure 6 - 32

2. Click on the triangle to the right of the **Chart Type** tool on the Chart toolbar. Click on the picture of a line chart.

   The line chart (Figure 6 - 33) can be used to compare the sales for the products in the different regions. However, line charts are more appropriate for showing trends over time than for comparing unrelated items such as baseball bats and golf clubs.

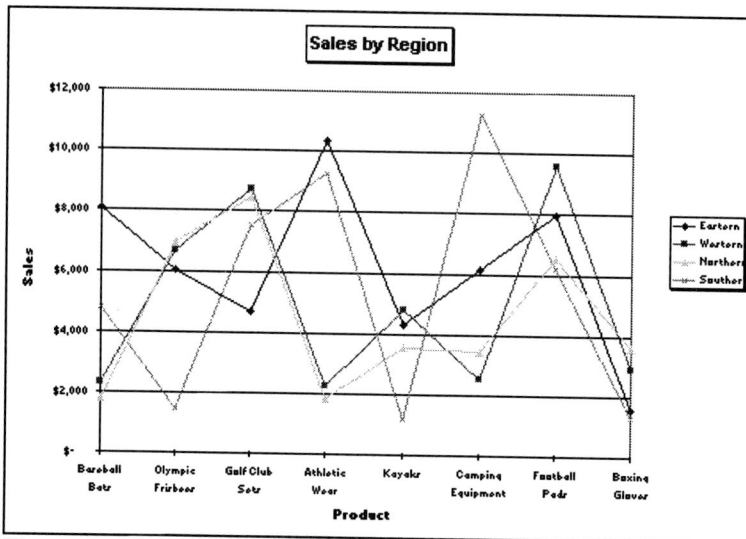

Figure 6 - 33

3. Use **FORMAT/Chart Type** or the **Chart Type** button to change the chart to an area chart.

   In an area chart (Figure 6 - 34) the areas for each of the data series at a given point are charted on top of each other. Thus each section of your area chart shows the volume of sales for one region and the top line of your area chart indicates the total sales for all four regions. Like line charts, area charts are usually used to show changes over time rather than to compare different items.

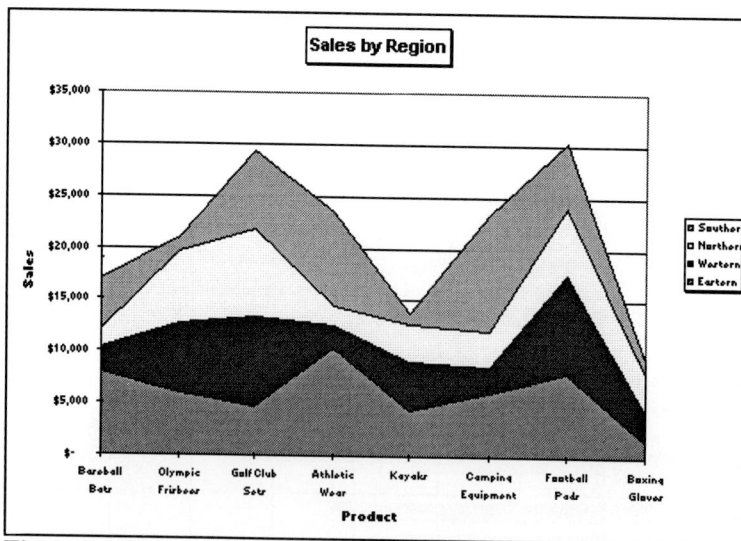

Figure 6 - 34

4. Choose **FORMAT/AutoFormat.** Choose **Column** from the **Galleries** list box (Figure 6 - 35).

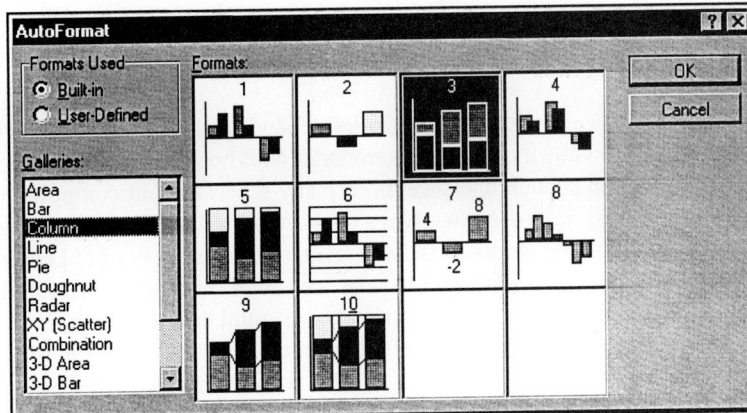

Figure 6 - 35

*Formats **3, 5, 9,** and **10** are different from the others in that the columns are stacked on top of each other rather than next to each other. Formats **3** and **9** represent **stacked column** charts. The column for each series in each category is stacked to create one column. This allows you to compare the totals more easily than a regular column chart does.*

*Formats **5** and **10** represent **100% column** charts. A **100% column** chart is a cross between a bar and a pie chart. It is made up of stacked columns as in the stacked column chart. However, each column is the same height. Each segment shows the percentage to the whole contributed by that segment, just as each wedge in the pie chart represents the percentage of the whole contributed by that segment.*

5. Choose format number **3**, a stacked column chart, and click on **OK**.

6. Click on the **Horizontal Gridlines** button on the Chart toolbar.

   In the stacked column chart it now becomes clear that the total sales for football pads was the highest, with golf club sales running a close second (Figure 6 - 36).

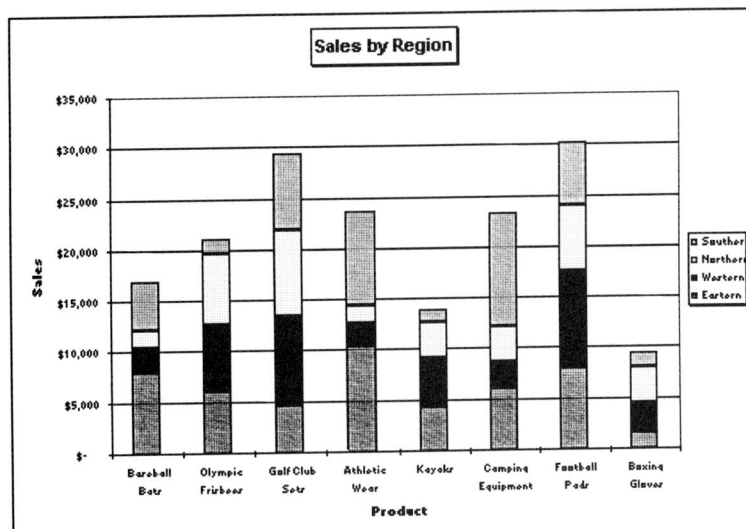

Figure 6 - 36

7. **Save** the file again using the existing name.

   *Your saved file will now contain the **stacked column** chart rather than the **column** chart that was included the last time you saved the file.*

WORKBOOK SHEETS

Next you will change some data in the worksheet and see how it affects the chart. Before you can do that, you need to know how to move around a workbook with more than one sheet.

A workbook can contain one sheet or as many sheets as your computer's memory will hold. In this workbook you have used two types of sheets — a worksheet and a chart sheet. Some workbooks have multiple worksheets. Multiple worksheets are used to keep related data together in one file. For example, in **nationwide sales** instead of placing the Projected vs. Actual part of the worksheet on the bottom of the first sheet, you could have placed it on a sheet of its own. In the future you might want to add another sheet containing sales data for 1996.

Similarly, it is often easier to manage your data if a chart is placed on a chart sheet within the workbook rather than embedded on the worksheet.

The sheets in a workbook are listed on tabs at the bottom of the workbook. The active sheet is always displayed on top, and the associated tab looks different from the other tabs. Sometimes, you may want to select more than one tab at a time so that multiple sheets can be printed or edited as a group. When you create a new workbook, a group of tabs is present even if the sheets they are associated with are empty. Therefore, it is a good idea to name the sheets that you are using.

To move between sheets:

- Click on the tab of the sheet that you want to select; *or*

- Press **CTRL+PAGE UP** to move to the previous tab and **CTRL+PAGE DOWN** to move to the next tab.

To rename a sheet:

- Point to the sheet tab and click the **right** mouse button to display the shortcut menu.

- Choose **Rename** from the shortcut menu.

- Type the new name in the **Rename Sheet** dialog box and click on **OK**. The name can have up to 31 characters. It can contain letters, numbers, and spaces but cannot be enclosed in square brackets or contain the following characters: : / \ * ?. It is preferable to keep the names short because long names cause the size of the tab to increase.

Activity 6.9: Using Multiple Sheets in a Workbook

1. Point to the **Chart 1** tab and click the **right** mouse button (Figure 6 - 37).

2. Choose **Rename** from the shortcut menu.

3. In the **Name** text box in the **Rename Sheet** dialog box, type: **Sales Chart** and click on **OK**.

4. Point to the **Sheet 1** tab and click with the **left** mouse button.

   The worksheet should be displayed.

5. Click on **Sheet 1** with the **right** mouse button.

6. Choose **Rename** from the shortcut menu and name the sheet: **1995 Sales** (Figure 6 - 38).

7. **Save** the workbook again using the existing name.

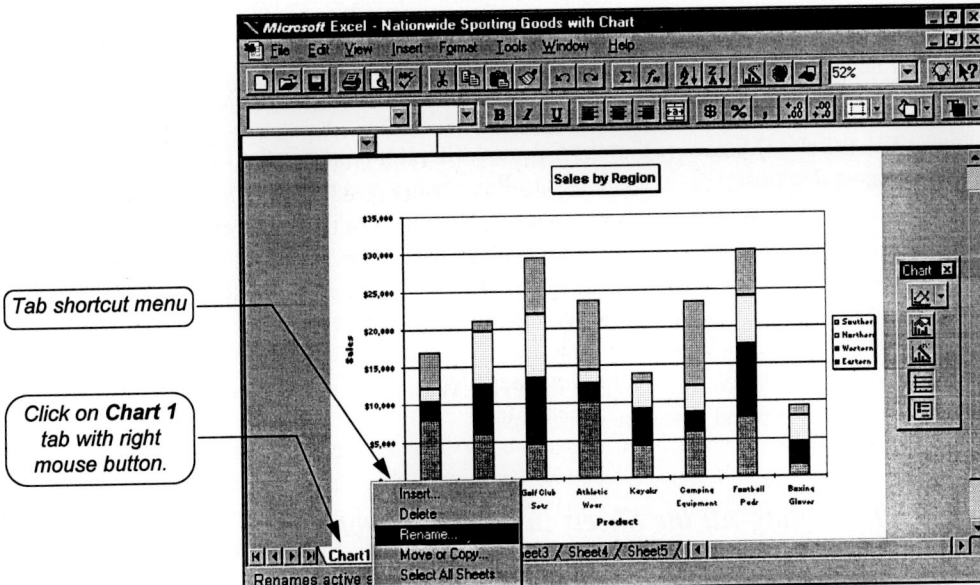

Tab shortcut menu

Click on **Chart 1** tab with right mouse button.

Figure 6 - 37

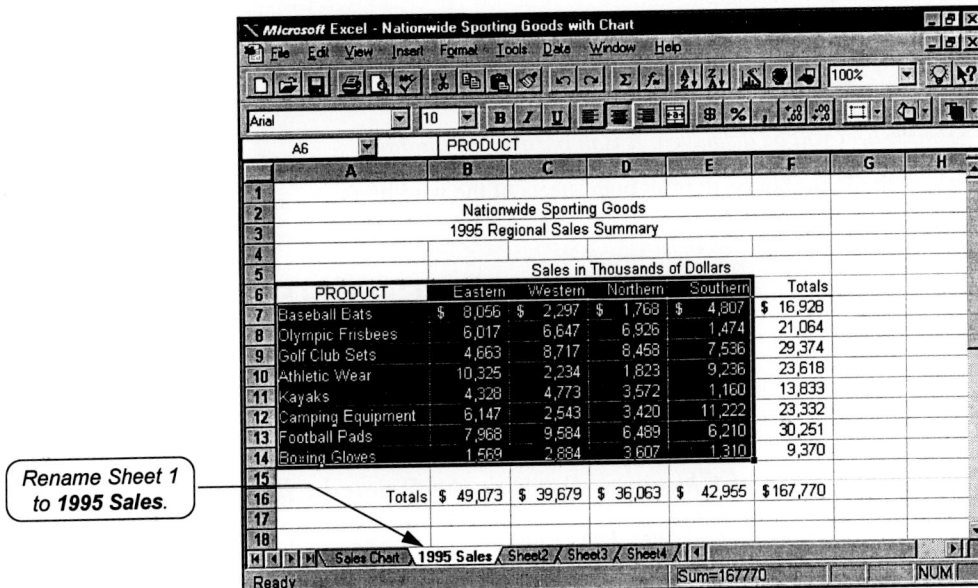

Rename Sheet 1 to **1995 Sales**.

Figure 6 - 38

PRINTING MULTIPLE SHEETS IN A WORKBOOK

Now you're ready to print your new chart, only this time you want to print the related worksheet data as well. Since the chart and the worksheet that you want to print are the only sheets in the workbook that are not empty, you can either tell *Excel* to print the entire workbook or you can select the sheets that you want to print.

To print selected sheets in a workbook:

• Select the first sheet by clicking on it.

- Select additional nonadjacent sheets by pressing and holding down the **CTRL** key while you click on additional tabs.

- Select a range of sheets by selecting the first sheet and then holding down the **SHIFT** key before clicking on the last sheet tab.

- Choose **FILE/Print**. Make sure that the **Selected Sheet(s)** option in the **Print What** option box is selected. Make any desired changes to **Page Setup** and **print** the worksheets.

To print all sheets in a workbook:

- Choose **FILE/Print**.

- Choose the **Entire Workbook** option in the **Print What** option box. Make any desired changes to Page Setup and **print** the workbook.

Activity 6.10: Printing All the Sheets in the Workbook

1. Choose **FILE/Print**.

2. Choose the **Entire Workbook** option in the **Print What** option box.

3. Click on the **Preview** button.

   The chart will be displayed since it is the first tab. It is displayed in landscape orientation.

4. Click on the **Next** button.

   The worksheet will be displayed. It is in portrait orientation.

5. Click on the **Print** button to print both sheets of the workbook.

EFFECTS OF CHANGING DATA ON RELATED CHARTS

One of the advantages of creating a chart in *Excel* is that the charts are updated automatically when the data are changed.

Activity 6.11: Effects of Changing Data on the Related Chart

You receive the following revised sales data: sales of golf club sets in the northern region was really **8,958** and sales of football pads in the southern region was really **5,000**.

1. Change the value of the sales for golf club sets in the northern region (cell **D9**) to **8958** and the value for football pads in the southern region (cell **E13**) to **5000**.

   Compare your screen with the printout that you just made to see which values changed.

2. Click on the **Sales Chart** tab to display the revised chart. Compare your screen with the printout that you just made of the sales chart. Notice that the total sales represented by the golf club sales is now larger than that represented by the football pads (Figure 6 - 39).

3. **Save** your file **as: Nationwide Sporting Goods with Chart, ver. 2**

4. **Print** the revised worksheet and chart.

5. **Close** the worksheet.

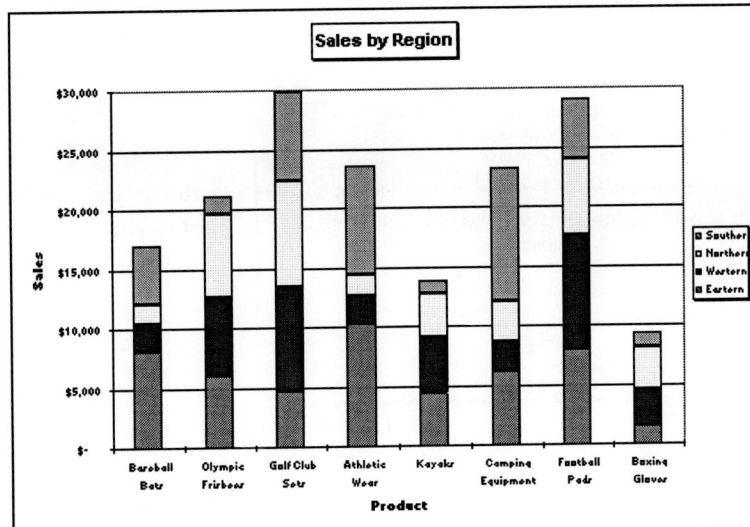

Figure 6 - 39

SUMMARY

In this lesson you learned to create charts on the worksheet and on separate sheets. You also saw how easy it is to modify and format charts. More importantly you saw some of the different kinds of charts *Excel* can create and how they aid in data analysis. In the independent projects you will get additional practice in seeing the different purposes of different charts and in using multiple sheets in a workbook.

KEY TERMS

100% column chart	Combination chart	Pie chart
Area chart	Data point	Stacked column chart
AutoFormat	Data series	Titles
Bar chart	Embed	Value (Y) axis labels
Category (X) axis labels	Gridlines	Workbook sheets
Chart galleries	Legend	X-axis
ChartWizard	Legend text	Y-axis
Column chart	Line chart	

INDEPENDENT PROJECTS

The four independent projects in Lesson 6 will give you practice creating and formatting pie, column, line, and mixed charts. You will also use workbooks that contain multiple worksheets or multiple chart sheets.

Independent Project 6.1: Charting a Sales Worksheet

You work for a clothing store. You are given a worksheet that shows the first quarter sales divided by department (men's, women's, and children's). You have been asked to create a chart to compare total first quarter sales for the three departments. You decide that a pie chart will show the percent of sales accounted for by each department best.

When you finish the first chart, your worksheet should resemble Figure 6 - 40.

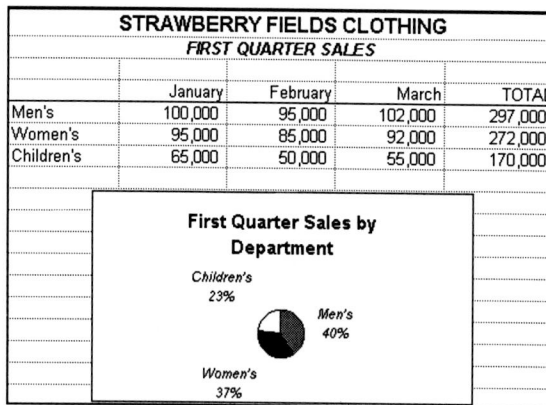

STRAWBERRY FIELDS CLOTHING
FIRST QUARTER SALES

	January	February	March	TOTAL
Men's	100,000	95,000	102,000	297,000
Women's	95,000	85,000	92,000	272,000
Children's	65,000	50,000	55,000	170,000

First Quarter Sales by Department

Children's 23%
Men's 40%
Women's 37%

Figure 6 - 40

Use Figure 6 - 40 and the following instructions to help you complete the project:

1. Open the file **independent proj. 6.1**.

2. Use the **ChartWizard** to create a **pie** chart on the worksheet. Your range should include the labels in **A5:A7** and the totals in **E5:E7**.

3. Click in **B9** to let *Excel* automatically place your chart, beginning at that point.

4. Use **Format 7** for the pie chart.

5. The **ChartWizard - Step 4 of 5** dialog box should indicate that the data series are in columns, the first **1** column is used as slice labels, and the first **0** rows are used as the chart title.

6. Do not add a legend. Give the chart the title: **First Quarter Sales by Department**.

7. Move the chart so that it is visible on the screen and approximately centered under the worksheet.

8. Double-click on the chart to edit it.

9. Make the slice labels (**Text S1**) **italic**.

10. Change the font size of the title to **11** point.

11. **Save** the file **as: Department Pie Chart**

12. **Print** the worksheet (including the chart); use appropriate headers and footers.

13. The worksheet is reviewed and it is discovered that part of the women's department sales is missing. Change **February Women's** sales to **95,000** and **March Women's** sales to **104,000**.

14. Select the data labels (**Text S1**) and use the **Increase Decimal** button to add one decimal place to the percentages.

15. **Save** the worksheet **as: Department Pie Chart, ver. 2**

16. **Print** the worksheet with the new data, totals, and chart. Close the file.

Independent Project 6.2: Charting a Sales Worksheet

In Independent Project 5.1 you added formulas to a worksheet to help analyze March sales' patterns for T-shirt company salespersons. In this project you will chart each of the three salesperson's sales to see if there are any trends indicating that some weeks have stronger sales than others. You will create your chart on a separate sheet.

Figure 6 - 41 shows the first chart that you will create. (If you use **independent proj. 5.1** instead of **tshirt**, the **X-axis** labels and some of the formatting of the labels will be different.)

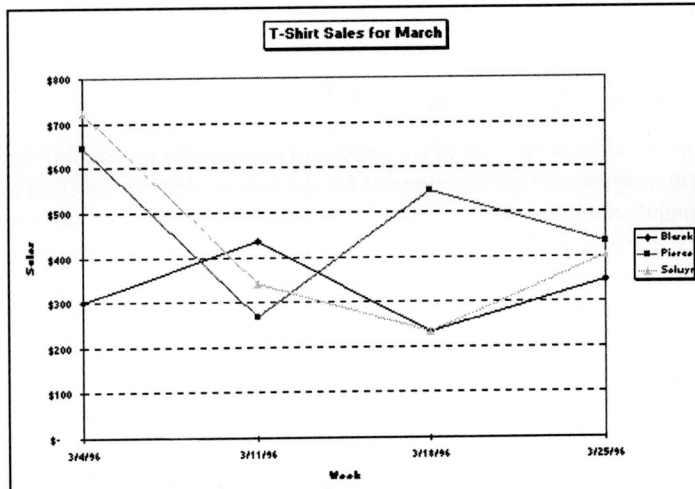

Figure 6 - 41

Use Figure 6 - 41 and the following instructions to help you complete the project:

1. If you completed Independent Project 5.1, open **tshirt**. If you did not complete Independent Project 5.1, open **independent proj. 5.1**. The data that we are going to chart is on the original worksheet.

2. Select the range **A6:B10**. While it is still selected, add the ranges **D6:D10** and **F6:F10**.

3. Insert a chart as a new sheet.

4. Make your chart a line chart. Use the format that includes lines, markers, and horizontal gridlines.

5. Data series are in columns, the first **1** column is used for **X-Axis** labels and the first **1** row is used for legend text.

6. Use the following titles:

   Chart Title: **T-Shirt Sales for March**
   Category (X): **Week**
   Value (Y): **Sales**

7. Format the **plot area** so that the **Area** color is white.

8. Format the **chart title** so that its **font size** is **14**, and it has a border with a **shadow**.

9. Format the **legend** so that it has a border with a shadow.

10. **Save** the file **as: T-Shirt Chart**

11. Make **Sheet1** the active sheet. Change its name to **March Sales**.

12. **Save** the worksheet again using the current name.

13. **Print** the worksheet and the chart.

14. Do all of salespersons show the same pattern (i.e., are the same weeks best for each)?

15. Change the chart type to a **column** chart.

16. **Print** just the chart.

17. Change the chart to a **stacked column** chart.

18. **Print** just the chart.

19. Which of the three charts shows the total sales per week best? Which shows the trends for each salesperson best?

20. **Close** and **save** the worksheet.

Independent Project 6.3: Creating a Mixed Chart

In this project you will create a chart to compare automobile sales for each of three different manufacturers in nine states. To make it easier for the person viewing the chart to compare sales of individual manufacturers within and across states and to compare total sales for individual cars, you will create a mixed chart. The sales of each of the three automobile makers, Ford, GM, and Chrysler, will be represented by bars, and the total sales will be shown as a line. The worksheet that you will chart is similar to the first part of the worksheet that you rearranged in Independent Project 3.2. In Independent Project 3.2 you rearranged the worksheet so that sales of cars from each country were shown on a different part of the worksheet. In **independent proj. 6.3** each country's cars are located on a different sheet of the workbook. Therefore, you will also practice selecting and printing different sheets in the workbook.

When finished your chart should resemble Figure 6 - 42, although the formatting may be different.

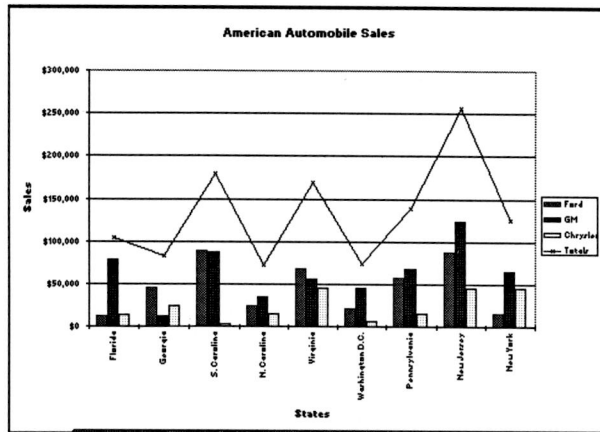

Figure 6 - 42

Use Figure 6 - 42 and the following instructions to help you complete the project:

1. Open **independent proj. 6.3**. Notice that the tabs at the bottom of the worksheet are labeled with the names of different countries.

2. Create a column chart of all the data on American car sales on a new sheet. The range should include the names of the states, the names of the automobile manufacturers, and for each state, the sales for each manufacturer and the total sales for the state. Do *not* include the total sales for each manufacturer (row **14**).

3. In the **ChartWizard** dialog boxes choose a column style that includes horizontal gridlines, but does *not* stack the columns on top of each other. On the **ChartWizard - Step 4 of 5** box make sure that the selections are correct to produce the chart shown in Figure 6 - 42 except that the **Totals** will be represented as a tall bar, not a line. Use the following labels:

Chart Title:	**American Automobile Sales**
Category (X) Axis Title:	**States**
Category (Y) Axis Title:	**Sales**

4. Select the **Plot** area, and format it so that the **Area** color is white.

5. Select one of the bars in the Totals series (**S4**). Display the shortcut menu and change the **Chart Type** of just the **Selected Series** to **Line**.

6. If the line color is light, select the line, choose **Format Data Series** from the shortcut menu and use the **Patterns** tab to choose darker line and marker colors.

7. Increase the sizes of the **Chart title**, and **X-** and **Y-Axis** labels.

8. **Save** the file **as: Auto Chart**

9. Rename the **Chart1** tab to **American chart**.

10. Select the **American chart** and **American** tabs.

11. Choose **FILE/Print**. Make sure the **Selected Sheets** option is selected.

12. Choose the **Preview** button from the **Print** dialog box. On the Print Preview screen, use the **Next** or **Previous** button to preview both the chart and the related worksheet. Use the **Page Setup** button to make any desired changes to the headers and footers. **Print** the chart and worksheet.

13. **Save** the file again using the existing name.

14. Switch to the sheet that shows **UK** sales.

15. **Print** just that worksheet.

16. Create a chart of **UK** car sales that matches the one that you created for American automobile sales. Format it similarly, change the name of its sheet tab and **print** the chart.

17. **Save** the file again using the current name and **close** the file.

Independent Project 6.4: Creating Two Charts

You are in charge of analyzing complaints received by the nine divisions of your company during the first quarter. To do this, you are going to create two charts, one to compare the total complaints received each month, and a second to compare the complaints per division per month. The data are in the file **independent proj 6.4**.

When completed your project should include two charts:

A **pie chart** comparing the percent of the total 1st Quarter complaints occurring in each month.

1. **Create** the chart on a separate sheet.

2. Use the months as part of the **wedge labels** or in the **legend**. Create a **title** for the chart.

3. **Format** the chart as you wish.

4. Give the **chart tab** an appropriate name.

5. **Print** the complete worksheet and the chart.

A **column chart** comparing the complaints for each of the divisions in each month.

1. **Create** the chart on a separate sheet.

2. Choose any type of **column chart** that you want except for 100% column.

3. Provide appropriate **titles** and **labels** for the chart.

4. **Format** the chart as you wish.

5. Give the **chart tab** an appropriate name.

6. **Print** the chart.

7. **Save** the worksheet **as: complaint chart**

Appendix:
Features Reference

The following table contains a summary of the main features presented in the lessons. As you know, most features in *Excel* can be performed in a variety of ways. Many of the menu bar commands can also be selected from the shortcut menus. Listed mouse shortcuts involve the use of the buttons on the Standard and Formatting toolbars and other mouse techniques. Shortcut keys are keystrokes or function keys. Many features require that the text be selected prior to executing the command. If you need more detail on using these features, the table contains a reference to the lesson describing its use.

Features	Menu Bar Commands	Mouse Shortcut	Shortcut Keys	
Alignment	FORMAT/Cells, Alignment	Align Left button Center button Align Right button Center Across Columns button	CTRL + 1 (Format Cells dialog box)	2
Bold	FORMAT/Cells, Font	Bold button	CTRL + B	2
Borders, add, change or remove	FORMAT/Cells, Borders	Border button	CTRL + 1 CTRL + SHIFT + _ (removes borders)	2
Center across Columns	FORMAT/Cells, Alignment	Center Across Columns button	CTRL + 1	2
Charts, changing type	FORMAT/Chart Type (or AutoFormat)	Chart Type button		6
Charts, creating	INSERT/Chart	ChartWizard button (on same sheet)	F11 (default type on new sheet)	6
Clear cell contents	EDIT/Clear, Contents	Drag fill handle up until selection is gray	DELETE	1
Clear contents and format	EDIT/Clear,All			
Column Width	FORMAT/Column	Drag right column header border (or double click border to AutoFit)		1
Column, select		Click on column header	CTRL+SPACEBAR	1
Comma Format	FORMAT/Cells, Number	Comma Style button	CTRL + SHIFT + !	2
Copy cell contents to adjacent cells	EDIT/Fill	Drag fill handle	CTRL + R (fill right) CTRL + D (down)	3
Copy cell contents to nonadjacent cells	EDIT/Copy EDIT/Paste	Copy button Paste button; or Point to selection, press **CTRL** and drag to new location	CTRL + C CTRL + V	3
Currency Format ($ is next to number)	FORMAT/Cells, Number (Choose Currency format to put $ next to number)		CTRL + SHIFT + $	2
Currency Style ($ is on left side of cell)	FORMAT/Cells, Number (Choose Accounting to put $ on left side of cell)	Currency Style button		
Delete Rows/Columns	EDIT/Delete			3

Features	Menu Bar Commands	Mouse Shortcut	Shortcut Keys	
Edit cell contents		Double-click on cell	F2	1
Exit Excel	FILE/Exit	Click on *Excel* Close button	ALT + F4	I
Font	FORMAT/Cells, Font	Font button	CTRL + 1	2
Font Size	FORMAT/Cells, Font	Font Size button	CTRL + 1	2
Footers	FILE/Page Setup, Header/Footer			
Formulas, displaying on worksheet	TOOLS/Options, View (Mark Formulas)		CTRL + `	1
Font Style	FORMAT/Cells,Font	Bold, Italic, Underline buttons	CTRL + B CTRL + I CTRL + U	2
Freeze (row/columns)	WINDOW/Freeze panes			5
Functions, Insert	INSERT/Function	Function Wizard button	SHIFT + F3	4
Headers	FILE/Page Setup, Headers/Footers			2
Help	HELP/Microsoft Excel Help Topics			I
Help on a specific question	HELP/Answer Wizard	F1		1
Help, context sensitive		Help button		I
Insert Rows (Columns)	INSERT/Rows (Columns)			3
Italics	FORMAT/Cells, Font	Italic button	CTRL + I	2
Move cell contents	EDIT/Cut EDIT/Paste	Cut button Paste button; or Point to selection and drag	CTRL + X CTRL + V	3
New File, create	FILE/New	New Workbook button	CTRL + N	1
Open a file	FILE/Open	Open button	CTRL + O	1
Page Setup for printout	FILE/Page Setup			2
Percent Format	FORMAT/Cells, Number	Percent Style button	CTRL + SHIFT + %	2
Preview printout	FILE/Print Preview	Print Preview button		2
Print	FILE/Print	Print button	CTRL + P	1,2, 5
Row, Select		Click on row header	SHIFT+SPACEBAR	3
Save a file, using a different name	FILE/Save As		F12	2
Save a file, using same name	FILE/Save	Save button	CTRL + S	1
Series, create	EDIT/Fill, Series	Drag fill handle		5
Sort data	DATA/Sort	Sort Ascending/ Descending buttons		3
Spelling, Check	TOOLS/Spelling	Spelling button	F7	2
SUM function	INSERT/Function	AutoSum button	ALT + =	3
Underline	FORMAT/Cells, Font	Underline button	CTRL + U	2
Undo	EDIT/Undo	Undo button	CTRL + Z	1
Workbook, change tab		Click on new tab	CTRL + PAGE DOWN/PAGE UP	6
Workbook, rename sheets	FORMAT/Sheet, Rename	Double-click sheet tab		6

Index